MEAN STREETS

A Journal of American Crime and Detective Fiction

Volume 1
Spring 2020

Copyright © 2020 by
Pace University Press
41 Park Row, 15th Floor
New York, NY 10038

All rights reserved
Printed in the United States of America

ISSN 2691-6487
ISBN 978-1-935625-49-0

Member

Council of Editors of Learned Journals

Paper used in this publication meets the minimum
requirements of the
American National Standard for Information
Sciences–Permanence of Paper Printed ♾rary Materials,
ANSI Z39.48–1984

MEAN STREETS

EDITED BY
Rebecca Martin
Walter Raubicheck

Pace University
Pace University

MEAN STREETS

Editors

Rebecca Martin
Pace University

Walter Raubicheck
Pace University

Editorial Board

Malcah Effron
Massachusetts Institute of Technology

Tonia Payne
Nassau Community College

Mary Rawlinson
SUNY Stony Brook

Roger Salerno
Pace University

Susan Elizabeth Sweeney
College of the Holy Cross

Samantha Walton
Bath Spa University, UK

MEAN STREETS

Volume 1, Spring 2020

Table of Contents

Editors' Introduction 1
    Rebecca Martin and Walter Raubicheck

ESSAYS

A Feminist Detective Revealed: Textual Gest in
Sue Grafton's Early Hard-boiled Detective Fiction 7
    Cathrine Avery

Temporality and Contemporary Crime in
Sue Grafton's Later Alphabet Series 35
    Nicole Kenley

Peanut Butter and Pickle Sandwiches:
Sue Grafton's Alphabet Series and Everyday Life 61
    Eric Sandberg

Christianity in Sue Grafton's Alphabet Mysteries 85
    Peter Bush

Narrative Technique in Sue Grafton's Kinsey Millhone
Short Stories 111
    Ramie Tateishi

The Street Was Hers: Deconstructing the Hard–boiled
in Megan Abbott's Noir Fiction 137
    Nathan Ashman

Janet Evanovich and the Rise of the Chick Detective 163
   Andrea Braithwaite

Cruel and Usual: The Criminal Quotidian
of Shirley Jackson 189
   Het Phillips

APPRECIATIONS

Violent Justice: The Real Hero in
C. S. Harris's St. Cyr Series 215
   Mary C. Rawlinson

Neuro-Noir, Bipolar Detectives, and
Abigail Padgett's Bo Bradley 223
   Susan Elizabeth Sweeney

REVIEWS

*Female Corpses in Crime Fiction: A Transatlantic
Perspective*, Glen S. Close 229
   Linda Ledford-Miller

*Domestic Noir: The New Face of 21st Century Crime
Fiction*, Laura Joyce and Henry Sutton (eds.) 233
   Linda Ledford-Miller

*The Detective and the Artist: Painters, Poets and
Writers in Crime Fiction, 1840s-1970s*, J. K. Van Dover 237
   Monica Lott

Contributors 241

Call For Papers 247

The first issue of *Mean Streets*
is dedicated to Sue Grafton

1940–2017

Editors' Introduction

Rebecca Martin and Walter Raubicheck

Mean Streets: A Journal of American Crime and Detective Fiction is the first scholarly journal to specialize in a significant and expanding category of American literature: crime fiction. It has had a significant influence and continues to have meaningful impacts on other literatures and media, as shown by its global contributions to television and cinema, but it remains a quintessential expression and exploration of American life and values. The perennial popularity of this genre has been complemented in the past 25 years by a steadily increasing scholarly interest from a variety of perspectives: historical, aesthetic, feminist, psychoanalytical, sociological, racial/ethnic studies, and more. *Mean Streets* hopes to encourage this ongoing, dynamic discussion and will provide an appropriate venue for scholars who are interested in the American practitioners of the genre such as Edgar Allan Poe, Dashiell Hammett, Raymond Chandler (whose essay "The Simple Art of Murder" is the source for the famous phrase that is our title), Rex Stout, Sue Grafton, Ross Macdonald, Amanda Cross, Sarah Paretsky, James Ellroy, Michael Connelly, Walter Mosley, and so many others.

American detective stories have been associated since 1920 with the "hard-boiled/private eye" tradition established by Chandler and Hammett and still vital today. However, many American mystery writers have excelled in the so-called British "whodunit" tradition as well, such as S.S. Van Dine, Ellery Queen, John Dickson Carr, Martha Grimes, and many others. Our journal will be open to a literary discussion of both types of mysteries, as well as the hybrids (Rex Stout, Patricia Highsmith, Erle Stanley Gardner).

The hard-boiled tradition began in the pages of *Black Mask* and, permanently established by Hammett and Chandler between 1920 and 1950, has maintained its popularity and vitality ever since in both literature and film, due not in small part to the entrance in the field of women authors who created female hard-boiled detectives. Arguably the most influential of these writers was the late Sue Grafton (1940-2017), whose "alphabet series" featuring Kinsey Millhone, ran from 1982 (*A is for Alibi*) until 2017 (*Y is for Yesterday*). In honor of her literary achievement, we are dedicating our first issue to Grafton, featuring a number of critical articles about what makes her work so distinctive and powerful. We also want to highlight several other women who have written crime fiction and share Grafton's feminist sensibilities: Shirley Jackson, Megan Abbott, and Janet Evanovich. All these authors are primary evidence of how central to the history of crime fiction women writers have always been. It is difficult to think of another literary genre during the past hundred years that has included so many female authors among its brightest luminaries. Any survey of the acknowledged masterpieces in crime fiction must include works by Agatha Christie, Dorothy Sayers, Margery Allingham, Ngaio Marsh, P.D. James, and Ruth Rendell, among many others.

The first crime novel to foreground feminist issues, to make them thematic, was *Gaudy Night* (1935) by Dorothy Sayers. Set in the first women's college at Oxford, Shrewsbury, the protagonist is Harriet Vane, a graduate of the college and a successful author of detective fiction. She is torn between her powerful desire to support herself by her writing and the ongoing offer of marriage from the enormously wealthy Lord Peter Wimsey, the detective who has been center stage in all of Sayers's previous novels. Wimsey also challenges Harriet to add depth to her puzzle-plots by stressing character in action, not just action. In the current action Harriet has been asked by her college to solve a poison-pen mystery that is undermining the morale of the female dons, and she does so with only a little assistance from Wimsey, the professional. By the end of the novel Harriet comes to see that marrying Wimsey need not threaten her own independence and career.

Unlike Sayers, Sue Grafton examines the obstacles facing women created by American society in the 1980s, one which is still puzzled and challenged by a female sleuth. Also, unlike her British forebears who set their work in the professional British classes typical of the "Golden Age" of detective fiction, Grafton explicitly places her work within the hard-boiled genre: in this sense her immediate predecessor was Ross MacDonald, creator of the Lew Archer series, who also uses Southern California (of the 1960s and 1970s) as his preferred world. Indeed Kinsey resembles Archer more than she does Sam Spade or Phillip Marlow in her keen awareness of the psychological causes of the crimes she investigates.

Grafton was not the first of the women authors who turned the tide of detective fiction toward investigators with a difference: female, unsentimental and unapologetic, pragmatic and acutely aware of the groundbreaking nature of their role and, at least superficially, feminist. In Britain, P.D. James launched Cordelia Gray with *An Unsuitable Job for a Woman* in 1972. American Maxine O'Callaghan began her series featuring Delilah West with a short story in 1974. Marcia Muller published her first novel, *Edwin of the Iron Shoes*, featuring investigator Sharon McCone, in 1977. In 1982, both Sarah Paretsky's V.I. Warshawski and Grafton's Kinsey Millhone appeared in *Indemnity Only* and *A is for Alibi*, respectively. McCone and Warshawski are still fighting crime, while Kinsey Millhone has been permanently laid to rest by Grafton's 2017 death, but there is no doubt that Grafton's work has been the most successful. Without analyzing all three series, each of which has its merits, how do we account for Grafton's success?

The essays in this issue of *Mean Streets* give some indications of the answer but perhaps the most important one is this: Kinsey Millhone is a capacious character, one who is very much an individual but who is also very open to interpretation. It is possible for readers to see in her what they want to see. The essays here demonstrate how successful Grafton was in creating a character who could be all things, if not to all people, then to most. Kinsey Millhone does not go out of her way to insist on her feminist principles, but her independent thinking, comfort being alone with herself, and her lack of reliance on men to rescue her, either from violence or from her loneliness, speak volumes. She has no stated politics and is unsympathetic with those who will not take responsibility for themselves, but she is also sensitive to circumstances that can create obstacles to success and growth, particularly in the case of women. It is easier for some people to save themselves and thrive than for others to do so, and she knows this from her own life. What Kinsey Millhone does is look at life through the eyes of a woman, a woman who is aware that women's lives have particular constraints and challenges. She does not see women as natural victims—that is made very clear—but she sees them operating within a social structure that limits their choices and throws up obstacles to their ability to succeed, whether that takes the form of financial success, personal happiness, or just getting out from under a bad situation life has handed them.

Perhaps in some ways, Kinsey is a wish-fulfillment character. She is skeptical about institutions, but believes that the law and its practitioners make correct decisions more times than not. While she is alert to dishonesty and self-deception, she also experiences instances in which people prove they can change. In looking at choices made and talents leveraged by Grafton the writer, we see other reasons for her success. In confining her stories to the 1980s, Grafton keeps Kinsey in a now safely-distant past, but for readers who may wish to see in the violence of life and the failures of institutions that Grafton highlights in her work a commentary on life several decades later, they are quite able to do so. Grafton's easy, free-flowing and conversational style is inviting, but she is also capable of introducing more nuance stylistically, as she does when she consciously mines *noir* tropes in *K is for Killer* (1994) and *V is for Vengeance* (2011).

Finally, Grafton can be very funny. It is not possible to quantify the effect of this quality on the success of the series, but a little not-too-mean-spirited sarcasm, tongue-in-cheek skepticism, and humorous self-denigration can go a long way toward mitigating the darkness.

Essays

A Feminist Detective Revealed: Textual Gest in Sue Grafton's Early Hard-boiled Detective Fiction

Cathrine Avery

Abstract

This essay examines textual gest in Sue Grafton's early hard-boiled detective novels to uncover the possibilities available within this literary form to articulate women-oriented political agendas. Textual gest is derived from Bertolt Brecht's concept of "gestus" or gest, in which the details of everyday life are given attention in order to reveal a character's socio-political positioning. In relation to Grafton's hard-boiled novels, textual gest reveals the attitudes and responses of the detective or what Brecht terms her "social impulses." For the purposes of this essay textual gest is a method of revelation, of exposure, a methodology to counter the critical antagonism towards the concept of a feminist detective that stems from the masculinist tenor of the original hard-boiled novels. Critics have argued that traditionally this literature is one where male behavior is the norm and that the conservative formula reinforces a masculinist hegemony and as such a female detective is an anomaly. However, the textual gest in Grafton's novels offers the means to reveal the habitual, private and domestic lives of women. Thus, by rejecting the norm of masculine behavior, Grafton's work opens up an alternative set of narrative structures, one in which the victim is no longer the obstacle that needs to be broken down as a means to solving the central investigative conundrum and where the violence of the criminal act is no longer framed by a masculinist prerogative.

Criticism directed at the concept of a feminist hard-boiled detective is typically grounded in the literature's hetero-patriarchal origins, which form the basis of its characterization and narrative structure. The hard-boiled male detective embodies a "tough" masculine mythology expressed through a violent rejection of those likely to undermine his dominant status. He is positioned at the center of the quest narrative, through which he works to reinstate the ruling conservative ideology. The concept of a woman detective, who can effectively challenge the genre's heritage, is perceived as an anathema. Kathleen Gregory Klein has argued that the structure of the hard-boiled novel will inevitably take pre-eminence over the expression of political values: "The predictable formula of detective fiction is based on a world whose sex/gender valuations reinforce male hegemony. Taking male behavior as the norm...a detective novel with a professional woman detective is, then, a contradiction in terms" (223). This failure to change the restrictive construction of the formula is seen as an immovable stumbling block for feminist writers, which is then exacerbated by the naturalized violence within the form. Liahna Babener has defined the "female sleuth as the deputy henchmen for patriarchy" because of the violence and misogyny expressed by the early hard-boiled detective writers such as Raymond Chandler, whose work functions as a generic template (146). This essay, through an examination of the textual gest or detail in Sue Grafton's early work, will offer the means to counter the limitations identified by this critical approach and present an alternative to this character/narrative dichotomy. The concept of "gestus" and what Bertolt Brecht calls the "realm of gest" identifies the minutiae of everyday life which make visible a character's social positioning and the causality of their behavior (198). For Brecht, whose work has as its focus the theatre, this allows an actor to pay critical attention to a character's "manifold utterances" including "physical attitude, tone of voice and facial expression [which] are all determined by social gest" (198). Elizabeth Wright observes that "gest manifests itself as a set of social relations" (27). In the context of the hard-boiled novel, the concept of gest can reveal the historically specific "social impulses" of the detective (Brecht 190). Thus, gest is a method of revelation; it can also produce what Brecht calls an "alienation effect," one that allows the familiar to be turned into the "uncertain and the contradictory" (192). In turn, this can give meaning to the detective's individuality outside the traditional structure of this literature. The concept of textual gest can be aligned to what Teresa De Lauretis calls the "micro-political practices of daily life," that is the minutiae of the private, domestic and habitual lives of women as a form of political investment (25). De Lauretis argues that these micro-political practices can make known "both agency and sources of power or empowering investments" and, in doing so, "a different construction of gender can be posed" (25). In effect, it is through the detail of daily life that a feminist detective is found.

Grafton was first published in 1982 when she started the "alphabet series" starting with *A is for Alibi* and ending with *Y is for Yesterday*, published in 2017. My examination here is her work published in the 1980s and 1990s, in part to maintain a workable focus within this essay and because of the significance of this timeframe to both the burgeoning of women's detective fiction and much of the critical antagonism directed at the concept of a feminist detective. Grafton's work sits squarely in the hard-boiled format with private investigator Kinsey Millhone as her central character. She reproduces the original hard-boiled structuring with its investigative narrative, which starts with a criminal event and concludes with a solution. This conformity to the formulaic foundation of the genre has been at the center of much of the criticism directed at Grafton. However, as this essay will show, she also works to create plausible and realistic representations of women's lives and, in particular, her writing is marked out by an emphasis on detail, specifically the minutiae of daily living and the behavior of her detective. Questions about female representation are central to Millhone's self-introduction, which takes place in each novel and are indicative of the structure of her life. The following comes from *D is for Deadbeat*: "I'm female, self-supporting, single now, having been married and divorced twice. I confess I'm sometimes testy, but for the most part, I credit myself with an easygoing disposition, tempered perhaps by an exaggerated desire for independence" (1). Part of Millhone's self-introduction also includes a reference to her appearance. In *F is for Fugitive* she comments on her hair, which is a regular topic: "My hair is dark and I cut it myself with a pair of nail scissors every six weeks. The effect is just about what you would expect - ragged, inexpert" (12). These quotes present a woman whose personal circumstances are central to her characterization. Millhone's "exaggerated desire for independence" combined with the visual imagery of "ragged, inexpert" establishes her social positioning, offering a textual gest of femininity that does not create a substitute mythology but does counter expectations of women as dependent on men and vain about their appearance. By undercutting the depiction of the male detective through an emphasis on the quotidian patterns of women's experiences, Grafton's work reconfigures the detective, locating her outside the norms of male behavior instituted within the original male authored novels. Once the masculine mythology has been debunked, the conventional narrative, by extension, is diminished in importance. The textual gest that gives value to the private life of Millhone can also offer the means to recognize the effect of the criminal event. Thus, the crime is no longer simply a puzzle that needs to be solved; rather, it can be understood as a set of social relations between the perpetrator and the victim. As a consequence, there is less emphasis on a comforting, seamless movement from crime to solution and closure; instead the victim of crime and the impact of violence becomes the central consideration.

Grafton's alphabet novels give rise to an interesting dichotomy, one that exemplifies the ideological tensions of a feminist detective. On the one hand, academics such as Walton and Jones have applauded the achievement of women writers within the genre:

> By 1990 the female 'tough gal' outgrowth of the male hard-boiled novel was making waves in the mainstream of American popular culture. The sub-genre of the professional woman investigator had become well established and was being publicly celebrated through unprecedented sales and economic rewards. (11-12)

Other critics such as Munt have questioned the representation of liberal socialism within the feminist detective novel because it attempts to assimilate progressive feminist ideas into a conservative ideological framework: "Implicit within liberal theory is an optimistic belief in reform, a strategy seen as extendable to all areas of social life, including cultural forms such as crime fiction, commonsensically held to be a masculine genre" (30). Munt adds, "these texts strain between ideological allegiances" and further that they occupy an "unstable positioning between dominant and subordinate cultural locations" (30). Plain aligns herself with Munt when she discusses women crime writers of the1980s producing "a fairytale of feminist agency" which fails to dismantle the existing conservative structures of the hard-boiled format or to propose strategies to counter patriarchy (92-93). A persistent critical theme directed at Grafton is that her work does not go far enough in her rejection of the male detective of the original texts. Coward and Semple comment that it is "highly problematic to replace the tough gun-toting man with a female equivalent with little or no criticism" (46). This censure, directed at Grafton and others who have produced a feminist reworking of the hard-boiled school, would appear to be uncompromising. However, academics who have responded positively to this reworking refer to the opportunities available in a genre that scrutinizes gender relations and uses a first-person narrative to explore questions about femininity. Walton and Jones define feminist detective fiction as "exploring positions of resistance and agency," suggesting that the hard-boiled detective novel gives women writers a form to investigate, question and revise naturalized gender definitions (93). In keeping with the perspective of Walton and Jones and as a counter to the extended criticism of the feminist detective, this essay will show that by focusing on the textual gest in Grafton's work it is possible to discard the "gun toting" original and open up to examination the gender scripts within her work. Thus, the feminist detective that textual gest reveals does not dismantle patriarchy but she can disrupt the conservative narrative structure typical of the masculinist text.

Minutiae as a feminist strategy: the textual gest of femininity

Textual gest opens up to us the particularized female detective, producing a level of narrative comfort but simultaneously turning the familiar into the "uncertain and the contradictory" (Brecht 192). Millhone's self-introduction is a point in case: the wording may vary a little but the mantra of name, employment, age, sex, and marital status leaves little room for doubt that this is a woman who is not just known to us, but very familiar. Millhone's habits, her friends, her home, her car, are elements of Grafton's creation that are as much a part of the investigation as the crime and its solution. For instance, in almost every novel the reader is reassured by the reappearance of Millhone's indestructible all-purpose black dress. Like a symbol of comfortable longevity, the dress operates to challenge the construction of socially acceptable femininity that the "little black dress" creates, suggesting a counter to the physical objectification of women. In doing so, the familiar, the textual gest of the little black dress, is turned into the contradictory—forcing the reader to reappraise this conventional symbol of femininity. The humor that Grafton imbues this dress with does not reduce its basic semiotic necessity as a textual gest and motif, giving to the reader a point of habitual recognition. In *G is for Gumshoe* Millhone is forced off the road during an investigation. Although she suffers numerous bruises and her car is broken beyond repair, her black dress survives. Along with a number of other items, the dress is sent to Millhone's home after the car is towed to a garage:

> The articles were packed as I remembered them, my all-purpose dress close to the surface. I pulled it out and inspected it, relieved to find it in better shape than I'd hoped. It was only moderately encrusted with mold, though it did smell of swamp gas, a scent that hovered somewhere between spoiled eggs and old toilet bowls. (180)

The survival of the dress reassures us; the comedy attached to its survival does not diminish the threat of personalized damage inherent in this close proximity to the criminal event. In this way, the dress operates to re-establish a code, a formula to regain access to a predictable ordered world of known and knowable objects. The fact that in *H is for Homicide*, the dress is first mentioned at the beginning of the novel before Millhone becomes embroiled in the chaos of a violent relationship, and then resurfaces at the close of the novel, reinforces this sense of an ordered world. It re-appears as the novel closes at a wedding, a familiar, familial social event which furthers this function. While these elements are a mixture of the banal, the comic and, at times, the painful detritus of human relationships, they are fundamentally the means by which we can gain subjective access to the text through an intimate engagement with the personal life of the female detective as well as the more public element of her investigative employment. The textual gest that defines Millhone's social positioning reveals a femininity that is not fantasy mythologized; rather, it exposes a domestic realism that alters the centrality of the criminal event. The end result is a woman whose familiarity is a primary element of her make-up.

Unlike the original male detective, whose characterization of the tough hero feeds into his mythical portrayal, Millhone's familiarity needs to counter the fantasy-of-agency that is all too possible within the genre. In *J is for Judgement* Millhone is employed to go to a holiday resort in Mexico to locate Wendell Jaffe, a man who has faked his own death to avoid criminal charges for a Ponzi scheme. By day three, having failed to find him, she retires to the pool where she sunbathes:

> I had donned a faded black bikini, boldly exposing a body riddled with old bullet holes and crisscrossed with pale scars from assorted injuries that had been inflicted on me over the years. Many people seem to worry about my health. At the moment I was faintly orange having recently applied a primer coat of Tan in a Can to disguise my winter pallor. Of course, I'd missed in places and my ankles were oddly splotched with what looked like tawny hepatitis. (15-16)

The textual gest of a "faded black bikini," "bullet holes," and "Tan in a Can" produces an uncertain amalgam of femininity. The bikini and bullet holes would seem to suggest a fantasy woman who is part object of stereotypical beauty and part "tough guy" substitute. "Tan in a Can" followed by "tawny hepatitis" undercuts this fantasy with self-deprecating humor negating the objectification of a sunbathing woman in a bikini. Thus, juxtaposed to this supposed fantasy woman is another kind of woman altogether, one whose personalized individuality works to undermine the mythical qualities she can gain access to as a female detective. Nicci Gerard considers the pleasure and the value of reading such thrillers, commenting that it "is not so much the competent plot but the excavation of an independent woman's domestic life, which is both mundane and in crisis. . . .We recognize and identify with her; not superhuman or stunning, but a bungling, touchy, anxious, ageing, not-so-modern modern woman" (62). The fact that the detectives created by writers such as Grafton are individual women with individual lives and agendas means that the reader is given an interpretative process that is bound up in their messy, open-ended private selves which is revealed through the textual gest. By writing to make her central character real Grafton undermines any notion of a universal "tough" woman, thereby creating in these texts a distinctive sense of identity and subjectivity, such that the problems and solutions within the formulaic center of the narrative can be read in conjunction with a lifestyle that is anything but fantasy. Grafton's rejection of the fantasy-of-agency creates a detective whose ordinariness readers can identify with, and the textual gest turns the personal into a micro-political investment.

Rejecting narrative norms, rejecting male hegemony

Grafton's rejection of the hard-boiled detective's "tough" mythology revises the expectations of the form. Klein has reasoned that this is a literature that is governed by "male behavior as the norm," which in turn determines the "predictable formula" of a quest narrative and the reinstatement of a dominant conservative ideology (223). However, Grafton's emphasis on "the excavation of an independent woman's domestic life" not only rejects the norm of male behavior but in doing so opens up to question the conformist narrative closure and the restoration of the status quo (Gerard 62). Grafton's emphasis on the personal extends beyond the private life of Millhone to recognize the impact of the criminal event. As a consequence, there is no simplistic movement from crime to resolution; rather, it is the victim and the effects of violence that take precedence. The need to arrive at a conclusion is a narrative imperative for the genre, without which the novels would fail to function at a satisfactory level. Thus, the increased recognition that the victim is more than a starting point of a satisfying puzzle, but rather an individual, is an element of the hard-boiled novel that Grafton has developed, and in doing so she fractures the male hegemony of narrative logic. In *E is for Evidence* the death of Olive, a character the reader has come to know, is more than simply the next stage in the criminal's progress. Grafton does not reject the formulaic process towards closure but she does produce opportunities to engage with the textual gest of the criminal event that do not negate the victim as generic convention requires. Many of Millhone's responses center on the investigation, the who and the why; however, the fact that we are given the life of Olive with its preoccupations and indulgences, along with Millhone's references to her living body—"all curves and flawless skin ... bare shoulders"—allows us to understand the impact of her death (109). Millhone is caught in the bomb blast that kills Olive, and it is through her physical and emotional response to the effect of the explosion that we gain insight into the destructive effects of violence: "I was bleeding from the nose, bleeding from both ears, where the pain was now excruciating" (129). Once Millhone has assessed her own physical state, she attempts to work out what has happened to Olive. The process is protracted because of Millhone's own injuries: "And then, of course, I understood what I was looking at. The blast had opened her body, exposing tangles of flesh, yellow fat, and jagged bone along her backside. I closed my eyes" (129). The horror of Olive's death clearly exacts a price, and not just in terms of the physical battering of Millhone's own body. The "yellow fat and jagged bone" cannot be seen as part of the investigative process but has to be recognized as a personal loss. The language of "along her backside" is not a forensic detail, or a term that involves sexualizing the female body; it is a commonplace word attached to a set of starkly blunt images that outline the effects of a bomb. Grafton's description of the evisceration of Olive combines the ordinary with the brutal; the word "backside" makes the violence real, its textual gest positioning Millhone as part of the experience of violence as much as her own physical damage. In this way, the death of Olive is not lost within the narrative abstraction but instead becomes a focal point that the reader must engage with. Thus, textual gest revises the traditional positioning of the victim, establishing a loss rather than an objective cataloguing of injuries. The damaged bodies of women in Grafton's novels are not a conduit to understanding the mystery at the center of the text, but they are a painful reading in loss and suffering.

The textual gest within Grafton's work makes visible Millhone's social positioning and her rejection of a conservative narrative resolution. In *A is for Alibi* Millhone shoots and kills a murderer. Grafton opens the novel with her mantra of name, employment, age, and marital status; however, it is the commentary that follows this mantra that signals Millhone's positioning: "My name is Kinsey Millhone. I'm a private investigator, licensed by the State of California. I'm thirty-two years old, twice divorced, no kids. The day before yesterday I killed someone and the fact weighs heavily on my mind. I'm a nice person" (7). Initially the language is blunt and direct; we are not being asked to dwell on her marital status, and she is not bemoaning the lack of children. These are statements of fact, delivered in uncomplicated colloquial language. The final two sentences operate differently: Millhone is revealing that she has caused the death of a man and it "weighs heavily." The violence conforms to generic expectation but the burden of this violence is in opposition to the bravado of the male gumshoe. The gest of "weighs heavily" is confessional; it rejects the casual referencing of death that is typically part of the traditional hard-boiled text. William F. Nolan, discussing *Black Mask* writer Carroll John Daly, comments that Daly's detective Race Williams "loved sending bullets into bad guys" (38). Nolan then goes on to quote seven examples of Williams' shooting prowess, finishing with: "Both my guns had spoken...and, so help me God, but a single hole appeared in Lutz's forehead. I've done a deal of shooting in my day—mighty fine shooting—but never anything like this" (39). In contrast to this Grafton starts her first novel with Millhone making her ethical position clear, that killing a murderer is unacceptable and leaves an indelible mark. Millhone continues, "I am a nice person," as if to reassure the reader that this is not normal behavior on her part. The combined effect of these two sentences challenges the formulaic patterning of the male detective and the narrative trajectory. Millhone identifies her distaste for violence despite the fact that it brings the plot to its conclusion. There is no sense here that she feels that the death is justified because the man was about to kill her. Instead, it is her discomfort that is predominant. She goes on to say: "Killing someone feels odd to me and I haven't quite sorted it through" (7). At the close of the novel Millhone's sense of unease is again forcibly expressed: "The shooting disturbs me still. It has moved me into the same camp as soldiers and maniacs....I'll be ready for business in a week or two, but I'll never be the same" (253). Such an acknowledgment that violence has a permanent, damaging effect contrasts dramatically with the self-glorification of Daly. Millhone's unease bookends the novel, reinforcing Grafton's disruption of the narrative norm.

While the death of the murderer brings about the expected closure of the text and complies with the generic format, thereby confirming Klein's criticism, this residual feeling of discomfort at killing a man is further extended to become a focal point in *B is for Burglar*. This failure to limit the narrative thread offers the means to consider the politics of femininity outside of the traditional "whodunnit" resolution. Grafton's writing establishes her interest in examining the way the form allows private perceptions to influence public expectations, particularly through the process of understanding the impact, rather than the delivery, of the formulaic violence (Warner and Jones 175). By undermining key elements within the narrative norm, Grafton opens up a space for feminist expression. Importantly, through Millhone, Grafton explores both the vulnerability of her female detective and the place that vulnerability comes from. When Henry Pitts, Millhone's landlord and friend, advises her to get protection, Millhone acknowledges her weakness but then questions where such perceptions of female defenseless originate:

> God, even my recent brush with death had taken place in a garbage bin...someplace small and cozy with me sobbing like a kid.

> 'I was thinking about that stuff today and you want to know the truth? All this talk about women being nurturing is crap. We're being sold a bill of goods so we can be kept in line by the men. If someone came after me today, I'd do it again, only this time I don't think I'd hesitate.'
> (*B is for Burglar* 83)

Millhone admits to "sobbing like a kid" in response to the threat of death, identifying her vulnerability and the physical effect of tension and danger. She is not, however, prepared to accept that her behavior is unacceptable because of her gender. She rejects the idea of "'women being nurturing'" and identifies it as a means to control women, in effect to "'be kept in line by the men.'" While the political observations might appear understated, if not crude, the use of the vernacular, what we might see as the textual gest of Millhone's "manifold utterances," adds realism to the exchange (Brecht 197). Grafton's inclusion of such commentary establishes a femininity at odds with expectations about female behavior. Later Millhone says to Pitts, "'Look, maybe I haven't dealt with that. I just don't want to be a victim anymore. I'm sick of it,'" reinforcing the way private perceptions, that is, the vernacular gest, can influence public expectations (83). Thus, "'I haven't dealt with that'" counters the heroic "tough guy," and "'I just don't want to be a victim'" revises the way women are typically portrayed in the hard-boiled novel. Together these expressions of femininity question the norm of male behavior and along with it the narrative axis and gender division on which this genre has been critically based.

Returning status to the victim of crime

The repositioning of the victim of crime is perhaps one of the most fundamental ways in which the feminist potential of Grafton's work can be defined. The difficulty inherent in changing this foundational element of the genre is made clear by De Lauretis in her analysis of gender specific violence and its portrayal in literature. De Lauretis argues that "the representation of violence is inseparable from the notion of gender" and that the act of violence is gendered masculine (33). "The hero must be male regardless of the gender of the character, because the obstacle, whatever its personification. . . is morphologically female. . . . The mythical subject is constructed as human being and male" (43). The logic here, if applied to the hard-boiled detective novel, proclaims the detective as male regardless of gender. The obstacle, or the victim of crime, is female, a puzzle to be solved. Typically, early hard-boiled detective writers such as Dashiell Hammett did not accord value to the victims of crime beyond the clues they generated. In *The Maltese Falcon* Sam Spade does not even acknowledge the loss of his business partner Miles Archer when he views his body: "Archer lay on his back. Two men stood over him. One of them held an electric torch on the dead man" (11). Hammett's language is minimalistic, almost dismissive, and Spade does not dwell on the man's death but focuses on the crime, asking the police about witnesses. For the female detective the need to change this logic is an imperative. In *K is for Killer*, despite the title of the novel, the focus is on the victim, Lorna Kepler. In the process of uncovering the killer, Millhone offers the means to recover the victim's subjectivity and deny the negation of Kepler as victim through the impact of the criminal event and the burden of narrative resolution. We are given the textual gest of Kepler's life so that we are unable to package her into a simple narrative continuum. We are introduced to her family, her friends, her colleagues, her habits and her contradictions. In particular, Kepler's friend Danielle presents a view of Kepler that rejects any notion of her as an obstacle to be studied and solved. Danielle talks of Kepler as someone who "'straightened me out'" (109). Danielle praises Kepler repeatedly, identifying life skills that Kepler taught her, including investing her money so that she could have independence. Danielle speaks of Kepler as a strong, clever woman, one who "'[k]new what she wanted and went after it'" and who was going to earn "'[a] million bucks, for starters'" (108). Millhone's language changes in response to Danielle's admiration for her friend. When Millhone discovers Kepler has nearly five thousand dollars saved from her work as an administrative assistant and prostitute, she comments: "Not bad for a part-time clerk/harlot" (196). The term "harlot" is dismissive—the language of opprobrium—a textual gest that socially positions Millhone. It fails to take on board how the negation of women through language was increasingly addressed during the 1990s both as a way of reclaiming negative terms and commenting on the sex industry's manipulation of women's bodies. However, this tone of disapproval changes after talking to Danielle, and Millhone's language changes: "'I'm sorry I never got to meet her. She sounds nice'" reinforcing Kepler as an individual, not a "'harlot'" and not a victim (216).

Kepler was a night-owl, and in the process of interviewing friends and colleagues, Millhone becomes orientated to a night-time schedule that replicates Kepler's lifestyle: "By some curious metamorphosis, I was being drawn into the shadowy after-hours world Lorna Kepler had inhabited. Night turf, the darkness, seemed both exotic and familiar" (234-35). By immersing herself in Kepler's behaviors, Millhone recreates her life rather than her death. At the start of the investigation, Millhone is given access to the police's photographic evidence but it is not the corpse and the damage to the body that she focusses on; rather, it is the violation of Kepler's privacy. Millhone describes the cabin Kepler lived in, using language to create the textual gest of a home rather than a crime scene: "the crowded countertops in use, the soft pillows" (96). This, coupled with a reference to the public act involved in photographing her private space, recognizes Kepler's right to privacy, irrespective of the fact that she is not there to demand this right: "There was something distasteful about the unexpected glimpses of her living space. Like a houseguest who arrives early" (96). Thus, Grafton does not give emphasis to Kepler the victim but the textual gest of Kepler the woman, and in doing so challenges the genre's narrative trajectory that posits Kepler as the obstacle.

In *G is for Gumshoe*, the victim of crime is Agnes Grey, an elderly woman who has gone missing. Millhone finds Grey in a convalescence hospital and is disturbed by a disjointed story that Grey tells her. The story is one of danger and secrets complicated by mental ill-health. The textual gest ascribed to Grey does not discriminate against her because of age and dementia. When Millhone meets Grey in hospital for the first time, she admires Grey's attitude: "She was stark naked, dancing a dirty boogie on the bed. . . . Her behavior seemed far healthier than the passivity of her wardmates. . . . Agnes had probably been a hell-raiser all her life, and her style, in old age, hadn't changed a whit" (47-48). When Grey dies Millhone attempts to sort through the story that Grey has told her, to understand what is real and what has become distorted through time and mental deterioration. Millhone does not question the veracity of Grey's narrative, despite the odd mix of irrelevant detail and gaps. Millhone eventually discovers the complicated truth about the killer: he is Grey's brother and he has murdered four people, two of whom were Grey's sisters. The fact that Grey has lived in virtual isolation and anonymity to protect her daughter from the reach of her brother is, for Millhone, a testimony of Grey's strength of character. As with Kepler, it is the life of Grey that is given priority; the resolution of the narrative is not about unravelling the mystery of Grey, the obstacle, but proving Grey rational despite her largely unintelligible account.

In the original hard-boiled format, the male detective acts as a buffer between the violence engendered by the crime and the order that society requires. David Glover perceives this as part of the conservative nature of these texts, identifying this as a literature whose "role is to reconcile, consolidate, obtain consent" which it gains from its capacity to provide reassurance through closure and an affirmation of the dominant value system (68). The aim of the traditional male detective is one of exposure but not at the expense of the social order he is part of. The feminist detective does not further the oppressive nature of the dominant morality but rather sets out to know the source of the violence and its impact. Ultimately, she too acts as a buffer between the crime and its victims but her purposes are different, in that she attempts to protect and give value to the victim. *In H is for Homicide*, Millhone participates in car insurance fraud after she is kidnapped by the violently abusive Raymond Maldonado. Her initial objective is to uncover the insurance crime but much of the novel deals with Maldonado's manipulative violence towards his unwilling girlfriend Bibianna Diaz. Millhone challenges Maldonado despite the threat to herself:

> He caught my look. 'What are you looking at?' His words were belligerent, but the tone was mild.
>
> 'I was just trying to figure out why you're so obsessed with Bibianna. Why insist on marriage when she's clearly not that hot for it?' I held my breath, but he didn't seem to take offence.
>
> 'She can't mess with me. No way. People who screw with my head have to learn they can't. She hasn't got the word yet.' (230-231)

Even though at one stage Millhone has the opportunity to escape, she is unwilling to leave Diaz to the mercy of Maldonado's violence, and by remaining she acts as a physical buffer between Maldonado's fists and Diaz. This emphasis on the personal allows an additional level of narrative tension, binding as it does the private concerns with the more public, legal aspects of the investigation. Danae Clark, in her essay on the television police series *Cagney and Lacey*, discusses the positioning of the viewer/reader within this structure: "The investigative structure can translate personal conflict into public concern and anchor identification to a specific political stance especially when the plot and the drama of the characters' lives are integrally connected" (172). This process of translating "personal conflict into public concern" through the plot has been noted by Phyllis Betz. She observes: "as the detective searches for the answers to the crime and her own mystery, the reader is encouraged by her success in both of her endeavors," establishing the way the female detective can assign value to the marginalized in society (175).

The judgment that the female detective makes is specific in terms of its allocation. At the close of the novel Maldonado is punished for the abuses he has inflicted on Diaz and not those perpetrated against a legal system. Millhone operates here as a judge, deciding which crime is the one for which Maldonado must pay. This is very much in keeping with the traditional format where, as Grimes comments, in relation to the archetypal hard-boiled detective, Sam Spade, "he is forced to be judge and jury" (537). Women have so often been lauded as the savior of men, the good angel ministering to their needs; here the female detective acts as the avenging angel. Maldonado tells Millhone that Diaz deserves to be hurt for failing to be a good and obedient woman. By identifying Diaz as the cause of his behavior, she becomes the means of "removing the perversity of violence" enacted by him (Rose 64).

> 'Lookit, I could have killed the bitch, but I didn't, did I? And you know why? Because I'm a good guy. Nobody gives me credit. Bibianna has to learn not to fuck with me, I told you that. You think I like this? She'd done what I said to begin with, we wouldn't be here.' (259)

Millhone reflects on Maldonado's behavior: "His view of the world was so skewed there was no reasoning with him. He really seemed to see himself as innocent, the victim of circumstances in which everybody else was responsible for his behavior except him" (259-60). Millhone absolves Diaz of her responsibility for male criminal behavior and by focusing attention on Maldonado, Grafton refuses to fetishize the victim's damaged body. In the process of exposing the crime, the female detective undercuts the voyeuristic nature that is an intrinsic part of the genre. In doing so she "removes the obscenity from the bodies of the victims and places it back where it belongs" in the acts of the criminal (Jouve 37). In this way the female detective can act as a liberating agent; she uncovers male violence and in the purging process, she returns to the victim her subjectivity.

Each of Grafton's novels ends with an epilogue where loose ends are tied up and Millhone makes awkward peace with the process of the law. The tone of humorous acceptance, tempered with the aggression that Millhone's language relays, suggests she is less than happy with the apparent completion of the investigation. The legal resolution to the criminal acts within the narrative is often the primary focus of this conclusion; however, the brevity and largely factual nature of the language does not give the epilogue the weight of finality. In *H is for Homicide* Millhone informs the reader that Diaz has survived Maldonado's attempt to kill her and she has been reunited with her husband. She goes on to say "[w]hether they lived happily ever after or not, I really couldn't say, as all this happened just three weeks ago" (228). The reference to a "'happily ever after'" closure for Diaz would appear to package her into the traditional narrative resolution, as well as the conservative institution of marriage. However, the processes of completing the story, one that fits into the hard-boiled detective narrative formula, does not diminish the textual gest of Millhone's relationship with Diaz. The strength of Millhone's commitment to Diaz means she is willing to put herself at risk in order to protect Diaz: "If Raymond killed Bibianna, he was going to have to kill me, too" and bring Maldonado to justice (88). While the narrative symmetry of this action does not appear to allow an engagement with the horrors of domestic violence, female detectives such as Millhone offer individual responses to the effects of violence and the objectification of women as victims, confirming Betz's assertion that the female detective can assign value to the marginalized in society (175).

Negating the power of violence

Grafton's failure to accord valor to the act of violence further breaks down the narrative trajectory. In the conventional male authored texts, the willingness of the detective to enter into the violence of the criminal act is defined as courageous and noble. As a consequence, the representation of violence by feminist detective writers is a particular focus of academic criticism. Knight argues that "the violence of language and action of the private eye . . . seems contrary to the tenet of feminism" (163). Chandler's detective, Marlowe, lays claim to his mythology through his assumption that whatever the odds he will remain the hero. In *Farewell My Lovely*, Marlowe is drugged and imprisoned; when he regains consciousness, he assesses his physical state and works to regain his self-control. Despite the fact that he is exhausted, he persists until he is well enough to overcome the guard. He maintains a constant dialogue with himself as a means of focusing his mind and encouraging recovery. Alongside this assessment of his physical incapacitation is an ongoing humorous reference to his toughness and his assumption that he will prevail: "I'm weak. I couldn't knock over a flower vase. I couldn't break a fingernail. Nothing doing. I'm walking out of here. I'm tough. I'm getting out of here" (151). The humor diminishes the pain, the vulnerability he is experiencing and allows the reader to focus on his expected return to "toughness." His reference to "I couldn't break a fingernail" establishes his degree of weakness, in that it implies a stereotypical depiction of femininity which he then rejects with "I'm tough." While the violence of detective fiction can offer a form of indulgent fantasy, where the reading process allows access to an equation that does not exact a price for the horrors that it portrays, Grafton's work operates differently. Often her representation of physical violence allows no opportunity for the reader to separate themselves from the effects of violence.

    In *B is for Burglar* Grafton's depiction of Millhone in a similar situation to Marlowe does not give the reader any opportunity for relief: "I hunched, taking the blow on the shoulder this time. The pain was like a heat licking up my side. I hung on to the stairs for dear life. A bright cloud was reducing my vision to a pinpoint, and I knew once the aperture closed, I was dead" (226). Grafton's language is unrelenting with no suggestion of humor; there is no courage or nobility in the description of "I hunched," "I hung on to the stairs for dear life." Millhone talks of herself and her attacker as "snuffling like wounded animals looking for a way to crawl off and hide" (227). The textual gest of "snuffling" and "crawl off and hide" eliminates any suggestion of heroic behavior; rather, Millhone positions herself as a "wounded animal." While Marlowe frees himself and moves on to the next violent physical encounter, Millhone acknowledges the ongoing trauma that the violence has caused: "I hurt just about every place. I look in the mirror and I see someone else's face. ...I'm feeling some other kind of pain as well and I don't know quite what that is made of" (229). Grafton fails to characterize violence as simply part of the job description. When Millhone comments, "I'm feeling some other kind of pain," she is accepting the long-term effects of physical violence. The opening of the next novel, *C is for Corpse*, establishes this reality when Millhone firstly outlines the fitness routine designed to get herself back into shape and then admits, "I was feeling emotionally battered and I needed a rest" (1). Grafton rejects the portrayal of sanitized violence delivered for entertainment and engages instead with its physical and emotional impact.

In *A is for Alibi* when Millhone shoots a man, she uses the phrase: "I blew him away" (253). The language is reminiscent of *Black Mask* writer and later contributor to the genre, Mickey Spillane, whose glorification in violence meant his work was described by Knight as "sadistic" (123). In *Kiss Me, Deadly* Hammer describes the killing of a man as "good": "It wasn't quite the way I wanted it but it was just as good...the muzzle rocketed a bullet into his eyeball and in the second before he died the other eye that was still there glared at me balefully before it filmed over" (436). The apparent casual reference to killing on the part of Grafton is disquieting if taken at face value because it conforms to archetypal representations of violence in the genre. Cawelti categorizes this representation when he comments, "The hard-boiled detective is first and foremost a tough guy. He can dish it out and he can take it," establishing the primacy of violent exchange (149). In this way, the early male authors "celebrate a tough and brutal hero" (Cawelti

155) one who is prepared to meet "violence with violence" (157). Grafton's language suggests she is replicating this characterization: when Millhone is threatened by a man who has already killed twice, she meets "violence with violence." However, the final phrase, "I blew him away," needs to be understood as the culmination of a six-page chase during which Millhone flees across a beach, over a rocky promontory, into the sea, and finally hides in a trash bin. Millhone is terrified that she will be found and killed:

> I flew across the yard.... He was staring straight down at me. I propelled myself forward, nearly flinging myself through the waist high water... .I reached the rocks, slippery and sharp.... I slipped once and something bit into my left knee. ... I crouched, shifting my gaze to the left. Now that I was forced into immobility, the fear took up where it had left me, ice spreading across my lungs, pulse beating in my throat.... I darted towards the trash bin, lifted the lid. ... Surely he could hear me. Surely he knew now where I was. (246-52)

The language is a mixture of factual commentary and emotive description which effectively evokes the textual gest of Millhone's flight and her fear. Many of the verbs give a sense of her physical responses, her momentum: "flew," "propelled," "slipped," "darted." The frequent use of monosyllabic words creates pace. There is no self-satisfaction in the possibility of meeting violence with violence; instead there is a palpable sense of Millhone's distress. Once in the trash bin and stationary, Millhone waits for the man to find her. The cramped space and the waiting remind her of childhood games of hide and seek: "I'd never been good at that as a kid. I always jumped right out when anyone got close because the tension made me want to wet my pants" (252). The memory makes her start to cry, as if she has returned to a state of child-like vulnerability, unable to control even her bodily functions. When the lid of the bin is lifted and the murderer is revealed holding a ten-inch knife, the four-word sentence "I blew him away" seems inadequate as a response to the tension and fear that Grafton has created. Unlike Spillane, there is no glorification in the act of violence and the shooting is by no means "good."

Grafton identifies both the immediate and the ongoing horror of violence. She also challenges the limitations inherent in failing to acknowledge the reality of violence. In *I is for Innocent*, Millhone investigates the death of a woman who has been shot. She states: "It is hard to have faith in your fellow man when you're forced to look at some of his handiwork" (16). Grafton's approach is not to dwell on the killer but to give voice to the dead: "The dead are mute....The final testimony from Isabelle Barney was framed in the language of her fatal injury, a devastating portrait of waste and loss" (16). In the process of agreeing to take on the case Millhone accepts the role of "voice" or adjudicator to the dead woman. At the close of the novel Millhone is confronted by David Barney, who has killed his wife, and Millhone shoots him. Her response to the shooting makes reference to and then discards the comic book effect that such violence takes on in film: "In the movies, you shoot someone and they're either blown back a foot or they keep coming at you, up from the bathtub, up from the floor, sometimes so full of bullet holes their shirts form red polka dots" (282). Having rejected this imagery, Millhone observes the reality of pain: "The truth is, you hit someone and it hurts like hell. I could testify to that. David Barney had to sit down with his back to the wall and think about life" (282-83). For Millhone, the investigation is about giving justice to the dead, but equally it is about commenting on the way that violence is defined. The imagery of "had to sit down with his back to the wall" operates to diminish a man who has already killed three people and taunts Millhone about how he is going to kill her. Having shot Barney, Millhone disarms him: "I leaned down and took the gun, which he offered up without resistance" (283). The lack of bravado here defines a particular type of understated gest. The language is simple, minimalist, with no claim to heroic behavior. "I leaned," "took," "without resistance" refuses to fetishize violence. The use of understated language takes the potency of violence away from the killer. Millhone's rejection of societal expectations about violence generates an alternative representation of femininity, one that rejects dominant portrayals of women as victims. Such a response determines a fundamental structuring of Grafton's female detective, one that recognizes that death, despite being part of the genre, is not trivial. Grafton's observations on the process of dying references iconic action and thriller films of the 1980s and early 1990s. The novel clearly intersects with a particular time and place and its cultural and social determinants, but Grafton's language here sets her apart from both the mundane acceptance of popular media portrayals and the encoded expectations of the genre. As a consequence, the language of death and its determining textual gest alienates the familiar to create a femininity that is at once vulnerable and powerful.

The argument that the hard-boiled genre is determined by the norm of male behavior is challenged by Grafton's portrayal of Millhone. The everyday textual gest of Millhone works to fracture the centrality of a masculine narrative order and diminishes the primacy of a conservative structural resolution. While it is clear that each of Grafton's novels closes with a formulaic resolution, what Munt calls the "dominant...cultural location," Grafton's revisions alter the reading process and the formulaic narrative logic (30). The trajectory or weight of the narrative is no longer simply bound by a need to arrive at a closure, particularly one that functions to reinforce the status quo. Within this alternative narrative, the victim is not simply the means to decode the whodunnit; rather, she is given status and the acts of the criminal do not take narrative precedence. Grafton does not use her texts as a platform to advocate gender politics; she offers ways of seeing how women's lives are molded by social expectation through the experiences of her detective. The detail of the social event is filtered through the textual gest of Millhone's life, and the common man of the original mythology is undercut with the messy-everyday.

Grafton's writing reveals a pragmatic and subtle examination of gender and power in relation to her detective and the crimes she works to solve. The textual gest uncovers what Adrienne E. Gavin calls "women's experiences in the face of patriarchal systems of both crime and justice" (265). The role of Millhone is not a simple representational figure. She does not identify solutions to the discriminations that women face; however, she does as part of the investigative process examine inequality and questions how femininity is defined. By examining the textual gest of the detective's habits and her humorous attention to the personal details of her life, the distinctiveness of her characterization counters the mythology of the "tough guy" and simultaneously refuses to offer a fantasy woman. In addition, the physical violence that is typically part of this literary form is not lionized. What is perceived as its potency is negated, firstly, through the acknowledgment that the detective is vulnerable to its ravages and, secondly, through a language that does not ascribe value to the use of violence. Millhone, through the textual gest of her private life and her personal responses to the investigations that she undertakes, gives the reader access to an interpretative process that exposes not just the criminal act but the complexities and contradictions that women live with daily.

Works Cited

Babener, Liahna. "Uncloseting Ideology in the Novels of Barbara Wilson." *Women Times Three*, edited by Kathleen Gregory Klein, Popular P, 1995, pp.143-61.

Betz, Phyllis M. *Lesbian Detective Fiction: Woman as Author, Subject and Reader.* McFarland, 2006.

Brecht, Bertolt. *The Development of an Aesthetic.* Hill and Wang, 1964.

Cawelti, John. *Adventure, Mystery and Romance.* U of Chicago P, 1976.

Chandler, Raymond. *Farewell My Lovely.* Penguin, 1940.

Clark, Danae. "Cagney and Lacey: Feminist Strategies of Detection." *Television and Women's Culture,* edited by Mary Ellen Brown, Sage, 1990, pp. 117-33.

Coward, Rosalind, and Linda Semple. "Tracking Down the Past: Women and Detective Fiction." *From My Guy to Sci-Fi: Genre and Women's Writing in the Post-Modern World,* edited by Helen Carr, Pandora P, 1989, pp. 39-57.

De Lauretis, Teresa. *Technologies of Gender: Essays on Theory, Film and Fiction.* Macmillan, 1987.

Gavin, Adrienne E. "Feminist Crime Fiction and Female Sleuths." *A Companion to Crime Fiction,* edited by Charles J. Rzepka and Lee Horsley, Wiley-Blackwall, 2010, pp. 258-69.

Gerard, Nikki. "Sleuth Sayings." *The Observer,* 27 June 1993, p.62.

Glover, David. "The Stuff That Dreams Are Made Of: Masculinity, Femininity and the Thriller." *Gender, Genre and Narrative Pleasure,* edited by Derek Longhurst, Unwin Hyman, 1989, pp. 67-83.

Grafton, Sue. *A is for Alibi.* Macmillan, 1982

---.*B is for Burglar.* Macmillan, 1985.

---.*C is for Corpse.* Macmillan, 1986.

---.*D is for Deadbeat.* Macmillan, 1987.

---. *E is for Evidence*. Macmillan, 1998.

---. *F is for Fugitive*. Macmillan, 1989.

---. *G is for Gumshoe*. Macmillan, 1990.

---. *H is for Homicide*. Macmillan, 1991.

---. *I is for Innocent*. Macmillan, 1992.

---. *J is for Judgement*. Macmillan, 1993.

---. *K is for Killer*. Macmillan, 1994.

---. *Y is for Yesterday*. Marian Wood, 2017.

Grimes, Larry E. "Stepsons of Sam: Re-Visions of the Hard-boiled Detective Formula in Recent American Fiction." *Modern Fiction Studies,* vol. 29, no. 3, 1983, pp. 537-44.

Hammett, Dashiell. *The Maltese Falcon*. Orion, 2002.

Jouve, Nicole Ward. *The Street Cleaner: The Yorkshire Ripper Case on Trial*. Marion Boyers, 1986.

Klein, Kathleen Gregory. *The Woman Detective: Gender and Genre*. U of Illinois P, 1988.

Knight, Stephen. *Crime Fiction 1800 - 2000: Detection, Death, Diversity*. Palgrave Macmillan, 2004.

Munt, Sally. *Murder by the Book: Feminism and the Crime Novel*. Routledge, 1994.

Nolan, William F. *The Black Mask Boys: Masters in the Hard-Boiled School of Detective Fiction*. The Mysterious Press, 1989.

Plain, Gill. *Twentieth Century Crime Fiction: Gender, Sexuality and the Body.* Edinburgh UP, 2001.

Rose, Jacqueline. *Why War?* Blackwell, 1993.

Spillane, Mickey. *Kiss Me, Deadly.* Alison and Busby, 1952.

Walton, Priscilla L., and Marina Jones. *Detective Agency: Women Rewriting the Hard-boiled Tradition.* U of California P, 1999.

Wright, Elizabeth. *Postmodern Brecht: A Re-Presentation. Critics of the Twentieth Century.* Routledge, 1989.

Temporality and Contemporary Crime in Sue Grafton's Later Alphabet Series

Nicole Kenley

Abstract

Over the course of its publication run, Sue Grafton's alphabet series enters into a temporal disjunction. That is, Grafton's decision to set her novels in monthly installments creates an ever-growing lag between the dates of the novels' publication and setting. *A is for Alibi* is set in 1982, the year in which it was published, and thereafter, Grafton sets each novel within months of the previous entry in the series, such that the series' final novel, *Y is for Yesterday*, is set in 1989 and published nearly thirty years later in 2017. This disjunction works counter to much contemporary crime fiction, which frequently races to include the newest technology as a means to solve previously-unimagined global crimes. Kinsey Millhone, meanwhile, continues to type her reports on a portable Smith-Corona as she tracks down more conventional murderers, rapists, and thieves.

This article argues that Grafton uses her later fiction, set in the late 1980s but written in the 2000s and 2010s, to make two broad points about contemporary crime fiction. First, the twentieth century cannot be nostalgically depicted as a simpler time despite a more complex technological methodology being brought to bear on crimes in the twenty-first century. Second, Grafton utilizes temporality to indicate that contemporary crimes are frequently informed by their lack of change, rather than their distance from the crimes that preceded them. In these ways, then, Grafton uses the setting of the 1980s as a platform from which to offer historically-informed commentary on the information technologies of the new millennium.

While much strong scholarship from the 1980s and 1990s exists on Grafton's early work and her progressive use of gender, sexuality, and refigured hardboiled tropes,[1] something of a decrease in critical attention concerns her later work. With the exception of scholarship from Sue Penuel, Carol McGinnis Kay, and Heath Diehl, who all consider the stylistic differences between early and late Grafton, many critics seem to find little difference between Grafton's work in the early 1980s and the late 2010s. The fact that Grafton writes about the same character for thirty-five years forces the issue such that, as Gary Hubbell puts it, "The real mystery becomes, how will Grafton develop Kinsey Millhone's character and still return to [the] independent loner she begins with" (15). This waning interest may be explained by Grafton's choice to maintain her series setting before two major changes in the genre. As the genre more broadly became more invested in forensic and digital technologies,[2] some of those scholars interested in gender and detection turned towards the more technologically savvy detectives for whom Grafton's Kinsey Millhone is a clear forebear. Kinsey provides an archetype for the tough, technologically engaged female detectives that follow her—first, Patricia Cornwell's Kay Scarpetta and Kathy Reichs' Temperance Brennan, both of whom utilize forensic technology—and then in the next iteration, Stieg Larsson's computer hacker, Lisbeth Salander. In one sense, Scarpetta and Brennan are the 2.0 versions of Kinsey Millhone, and Salander the 3.0. However, as these newer iterations of female detectives begin to take shape and their authors differentiate them from

Grafton's creation through their application of forensic and digital technologies, Grafton's position on the cutting edge of contemporary detective fiction begins to erode. Though Grafton's work does continue to grow and change, the relative drop-off in critical attention seems to indicate that, while it appeared at a rapid pace well into the 2010s, Grafton's work was no longer considered at the vanguard of contemporary crime fiction.

At first glance, such a perception seems to fit with the novels Grafton wrote. Many of Kinsey's hallmarks of detection seem quaint rather than innovative: an insistence on using a portable Smith-Corona typewriter instead of a computer, or taking straightforward notes on index cards, may lack the efficiency of DNA evidence or computer hacking. Many of the later series' plots and subplots, too, seem directed at an aging readership, as they focus either on older victims or Kinsey's octogenarian landlord Henry Pitts and his cozy interests. While Jean Swanson points out as early as 1998 that Santa Teresa, in general, is "a setting reminiscent more of the cozy subgenre of mysteries than of the hard-boiled school" (442), a notable uptick in time spent visiting Henry's softer world does occur in the later novels. *X*, for instance, devotes many pages to Henry's obsession with irrigating his yard; *W is for Wasted* fixates on whether Henry or his brother William will get a cat. *T is for Trespass* centers on a case of elder abuse, depicting the myriad ways in which its villain, Solana Rojas, can mistreat Kinsey's eighty-nine-year-old neighbor Gus after he takes a hard fall and requires home care. Solana's list of criminal misdeeds includes sedating Gus, stealing his money, appointing herself his conservator, convincing him that he suffers from dementia, and verbally and sexually abusing him. These crimes are threatening regardless of the reader's age, but they do seem geared toward an aging readership. At least *Trespass* retains some of Kinsey's signature intense physical fighting; in this novel, she bites her assailant's crotch and rips off his arm all while in a moving car. By the time Grafton reaches *Wasted*, Kinsey's dramatic fight scene involves her fending off an assailant while armed only with a potting trowel and a bag of sphagnum moss. Perhaps it is little wonder, then, that scholars have largely not considered Grafton's work as part of the larger conversation on contemporary crime.

Yet the slackening of critical attention obscures the fact that Grafton's work provides a valuable counterpoint to other contemporary crime fiction by serving as a much-needed foil and even caution to a fiction often racing to depict the next wave of technological trends. In retaining her 1980s setting, Grafton both offers commentary on the present from a now-fictional past and gives the lie to the notion of a pre-digital past as a simpler time.

"'You're missing the boat'": Metafictionality and Futurity

Grafton has always employed humor in her writing, as Peter Rabinowitz and Rachel Schaffer both point out, but in her later work she uses it to poke fun at her privileged position of commenting on the past with the benefit of hindsight. Through a series of metafictional winks[3] to the audience as the contemporary timeline moves farther from that of her novels, Grafton signals that she is in on the joke. In *Wasted*, Kinsey browses "the October 10, 1988, issue" of *People* magazine to read an article "about Jersey Girl Patti Scialfa" coupling with Bruce Springsteen. Kinsey thinks skeptically "Oh yeah, right. Like that marriage would last" (148). When *Wasted* was published in 2013, Springsteen and Scialfa were still married; Grafton uses this joke to acknowledge the humor inherent in her position of being able to comment on the past. In *Trespass*, she takes the joke a step further, making fun of Kinsey's lack of foresight and, perhaps, her own in not considering the technological changes that would soon impact her genre. *Trespass* uses the repartee between Kinsey and a computer repair technician to highlight her protagonist's lack of foresight:

'What do you have?'

'A portable Smith-Corona.'

He half-smiled, as if I were making a joke, and then he wagged his finger at me. 'Better catch up with reality. You're missing the boat. Time's going to come when computers will do everything.'

'I have trouble believing that. It just seems so *unlikely*.'

'You're not a believer like the rest of us. The day will come when ten-year-olds will master these machines and you'll be at their mercy.'

'That's a depressing thought.'

'Don't say I didn't warn you.... And if you change your mind about becoming computer literate, you know where I am. I could get you up and running in no time.'

'How much?'

'Ten grand.'

'You lost me there. I don't want to pay ten grand for something that makes me feel inadequate.' I left thinking, *Ten-year-old kids? Get serious.* (329-331, italics in original)

Here, Grafton makes fun of the past and present simultaneously with the outrageously high 1980s price for a computer, Kinsey's utter incredulity, and her own refusal to quite literally '"catch up with reality"' by writing a novel in 2007 set twenty years prior in 1987.

Grafton also obliquely pokes fun, in this moment and elsewhere, at the writerly and readerly craze for detective fiction so focused on digital and forensic technologies. In the exchange above, she stresses how "*unlikely*" it is that "'the rest of us'" would become ardent "'believer[s]'" in not only "'a day'" but a school of crime writing wherein "'computers will do everything.'" In *X*, she teases herself further, writing about a librarian who cannot acclimate "'to a newfangled electronic system: words, pictures, and graphics, including maps. Don't ask me how it's done. I have no idea. . . . All way over my head. . . . Might be time to retire'" (140). Kinsey empathizes with this woman, commiserating with "'I don't even own a computer'" (140). This exchange might well be read as a parodic exchange between writer and character in the series' penultimate installment, suggesting that with the genre's ever-increasing dependence on a "'newfangled electronic system'" to which Kinsey has no access, it "'might be time to retire.'" Forensic detective fiction, too, gets a light spoofing in *X*, as Kinsey finds that to threaten her, someone has defecated in her trash can. She contemplates, "A forensic specialist would not perform a DNA analysis on the turd left in the wastebasket, nor would the turd data be entered into the National Crime Information Center database for comparison to criminal turds nationwide" (196). Grafton teases both forensic writers for their reliance on "DNA analysis" and herself for being unable to genuinely include the kinds of forensic details so popular with readers. In essence, Grafton approaches her increasing distance from the setting of her novels with metafictional good humor that signals to the audience her intentional use of that distance to comment on eras both past and present.

"'Too bad you don't have a time machine'": Faulty Memories of a Difficult Past

Part of Grafton's project in setting her novels nearly three decades prior to their publication date is surely to highlight the ways in which overly nostalgic memories obscure truths about both the present and a seemingly pre-digital, pre-forensic past. *U is for Undertow* begins with the words "[w]hat fascinates me about life is that now and then the past rises up and declares itself" (1). Several of Grafton's later novels, *Undertow* especially, present exactly this notion of the past declaring itself through Grafton's fictionalization. The declaration that the past makes, in this case, is that it has often been misremembered from a contemporary vantage point. In *V is for Vengeance,* a security guard tells Kinsey that, since her memory is poor, it is "'too bad you don't have a time machine'" (209). While detective fiction suggesting that memory is unreliable is nothing new, Grafton works towards a broader purpose here. Essentially, her novels provide readers with that time machine because, as she stresses again and again, their memories of the now decades-past 1980s are inaccurate and misconstrued by nostalgia.

In much of contemporary crime fiction, digital technology is presented as one of the driving forces of the twenty-first century. By contrast, in Grafton's novels, Kinsey's world remains largely analog and, as a result, might be thought to contribute to a recollection of the 1980s as a simpler time. With much contemporary crime fiction featuring flashy forensic technologies or social media as a motive for murder, Kinsey's late 1980s Santa Teresa setting seems practically pastoral. Grafton warns against this tendency to misremember the past as a less complicated era in *X*, writing, "I had no access to the past except for other people's recollections, which are often telling, but not always to be trusted. Memory is subject to a filtering process that we don't always recognize and can't always control. We remember what we can bear and we block what we cannot" (291). In suggesting the unreliability not only of Kinsey's memory but also of the reader's through the use of the plural pronoun "we," Grafton reminds readers that their own memories of the 1980s are out of their "control" and subject to "filtering" out the negative aspects that the reader cannot endure. In *Trespass,* the manipulation of memory is figured as a vicious and criminal attack, but in *X* Grafton reminds readers that they too are subject to misremembering without outside intervention. The most harmful aspect of the past, in Grafton's formulation, is its ability to recur in memory with many of its most deleterious aspects edited away.

Undertow effectively functions as a large-scale case study into the harmful effects of misremembering the past. The novel intertwines an investigation in April of 1988 into the events April 1963, twenty-five years prior. Narrated from the perspectives of three additional characters besides Kinsey, *Undertow* is an exercise in representing the widespread unreliability of past memory. The frequent flashbacks to the 1960s, for example, depict the era of hippies as deeply problematic rather than idealistic. Grafton parodies certain beliefs of the decade through representing hippies as out-of-touch, negligent parents who malnourish and abandon their children while giving themselves names like Destiny and Sky Dancer. In this way, she represents the dangers of misremembering any decade, not just the 1980s.

Further, all three major characters in the novel confront the realization that memory can be deeply flawed. One side plot involves Kinsey continuing to uncover some of her family roots. As a child she believed that none of her extended family members besides her Aunt Gin cared for her, but *Undertow* presents her with a supply of letters proving otherwise. To her shock, these letters show her conniving maternal grandmother, Grand, trying to wrest Kinsey from her Aunt Gin's guardianship via blackmail. Kinsey's perception of her childhood, it turns out, was dramatically skewed. In attempting to uncover the truth about her upbringing, Kinsey contacts another private investigator, Hale Brandenburg. Meeting him, she senses a familiarity, but she cannot place him. Only after discovering a cache of photographs does she recall that Brandenburg was her Aunt Gin's boyfriend. In both cases, Kinsey realizes that her memories of her own past were distorted and unreliable. Another primary character in *Undertow*, Walker, sees the fragility of memory through his experiences with alcohol. After going on a drinking binge, Walker wakes up in the hospital with no memory of his actions. To his horror, his wife informs him that he hit and killed a girl while driving drunk and then fled the scene of the crime. For the rest of the novel, Walker tries unsuccessfully to reconstruct his own memory of events, which forces him to confront the notion that his memories are outside of his control. In other words, both characters, have their pasts (distant or recent) reconfigured in this text.

The ultimate study of the unreliability of memory though, comes from Kinsey's client Michael. After reading a story in the newspaper about a girl who went missing 25 years prior, Michael remembers seeing a girl-sized body buried in the woods as a child—leading him to contact the police who refer him to Kinsey. On the surface, this recollection seems akin to Kinsey's own childhood recollections in that it is shown to be ultimately unreliable. While Michael did see two men burying a large bundle as a child, virtually everything else about his recollection, from the location to the date to the circumstances, is proven to be incorrect over the course of the text. However, Grafton is not merely reiterating the point she makes about Kinsey's childhood; she goes a step further to suggest that memory can be manipulated through external influences. Michael's sister Diana Alvarez, a journalist, comes to Kinsey and reveals that her brother Michael falsely accused their father of sexual assault based on false memories implanted by a psychotherapist who "'was using hypnosis and guided imagery to help him recover his "repressed" memories, sometimes with the aid of sodium amatol'" (*Undertow* 120). After months in treatment, the therapist "'persuaded him it would be "healing" if he confronted the past... He had these shadowy memories that he knew were real. Soon his hazy mental movie came into focus and he "remembered" my mother was also in on the abuse. Next thing you know, my younger brother Ryan was added to the list. We're talking nasty stuff—claims of satanic ritual, bestiality, animal sacrifice, you name it'" (120-21). In this version of events, "'confronting the past'" can reveal extremely "'nasty stuff,'" "'hazy'" and "'shadowy memories'" that paint a wildly exaggerated picture. Michael's reminiscences are proven to be phony and he apologizes to his family, but the irreparable damage caused by attributing false memories to a prior time remains. Grafton provides a hyperbolic counterexample to remembering the past too fondly, complete with "'satanic ritual, bestiality, animal sacrifice, you name it'" to illustrate the danger inherent in looking to the past to provide truths about the present.

Undertow depicts even Kinsey's stalwart index cards as a guard against using foggy memories to reconstruct the past. These cards, a stylistic hallmark of Grafton's since *A is for Alibi*, certainly provide a tool to aid readers in keeping the facts in order as they try to unravel mysteries alongside Kinsey. In *Undertow*, though, Grafton stresses their preventative function: with the facts consigned neatly to cards, the faulty memory that shrouds the past, recent or distant, can be kept at bay. Kinsey muses at some length on the dangers of relying on memories of the past:

> I had a lot of ground to cover, consigning everything I'd learned to note cards, one item per card, which reduced the facts to their simplest form. It's our nature to condense and collate, bundling related elements for ease of storage in the back of our brains. Since we lack the capacity to capture every detail, we cull what we can, blocking the bits we don't like and admitting those that match our notions of what's going on. While efficient, the practice leaves us vulnerable to blind spots. Under stress, memory becomes even less reliable. Over time we sort and discard what seems irrelevant to make room for additional incoming data. In the end, it's a wonder we remember anything at all period. What we managed to preserve is subject to misinterpretation. (255)

Again, Grafton stresses the tendency toward "blocking the bits we don't like and admitting those that match our notions of what's going on," and again she uses the first person plural pronoun, warning readers against becoming "vulnerable to blind spots" by indulging in "misinterpretation" of decades past.

Grafton insists so strongly and consistently that recollections of the past should not be limited to faulty memory because, in her depiction, the 1980s were fraught with social problems. Grafton has not necessarily been considered a socially progressive author outside of her obvious feminism (Svoboda points out that, "unlike Warshawski...[Millhone] does not view her profession as tilting at the structures of society" [262]). In particular, her position on homosexuality has been questioned in her early work. Ann Wilson points out a strain of latent homophobia in *E is for Evidence*, and Heather Humann points out that while in *D is for Deadbeat* Grafton does address "a still taboo subject (cross-dressing), she does so in a way that conforms to widely held societal attitudes, rather than challenging them" (65).[4] However, with the case of *Trespass*, Grafton's position on homosexuality represents a change in perspective on the social issue front as well, underscoring Diehl's point that *Trespass* in particular signals that "Grafton suggests that storytelling within hardboiled fiction must evolve to accommodate ever-malleable notions of criminality and 'justice'" (2016, 1). Further, *Undertow* depicts the social mores of the era as regressive through Kinsey's encounter with Hale Brandenburg, the P.I. hired by her grandmother to investigate her Aunt Gin. At Kinsey's insistence, Hale reveals that Kinsey's "'grandmother believed Virginia was a lesbian'" (342). If Hale could confirm this notion, it would be enough to suggest that Virginia was an unfit guardian for Kinsey. He explains, "'You asked about the leverage. That was it. In those days, the accusation was damaging, even if there wasn't any proof. That's why I wouldn't give her written reports. I didn't want Mrs. Kinsey to have anything to hold over Virginia's head'" (343). While it would be simple to depict 1988, when the novel is set, as an easier time than 2009, when the novel was published, Grafton resists that impulse. Instead, she depicts 1950s as an era when a child's legally appointed guardian and biological aunt could be sued for custody of that child were she found to be a lesbian and the 1980s as a time when that secret would still be considered shameful. Early readers of *Undertow* may have noticed the timeliness of Grafton raising the issue: in California in 2007, Proposition 8, a ballot measure banning same-sex marriages, had been added to the upcoming 2008 ballot via a signature petition campaign in the 2006 gubernatorial election. The hotly-contested debate about marriage equality was a state and national news item for much of that year. The comparison between past and present may have been evident to Grafton's audience—while in the year before the novel's publication marriage equality was being debated, in the year of the novel's setting, the suspicion of homosexuality would still be a shocking secret. Grafton stresses two points here: that the past was more challenging with regard to certain social issues, and that, in retrospect, not as much had changed as might have been expected in the three decades between setting and publication.

Grafton also tackles the notion that the advent of the digital era is responsible for the lack of privacy that seems to pervade twenty-first-century culture. Grafton's later work debunks the idea that the Internet and other digital technologies are responsible for eroding privacy, suggesting instead that privacy has always been a myth. *Trespass*, for example, presents the issue of identity theft as an evergreen opportunity for criminals rather than a product of personal information made readily available by the Internet. The criminal in *Trespass* steals the identity of her coworker, Solana Rojas, in a few easy steps. After lifting the driver's license of her target, whom she refers to as the Other, the criminal explains that "[w]hen the Other noticed her license was gone, she'd assume she'd left it somewhere. It was always this way. People blamed themselves for being careless and absentminded. It seldom occurred to them to accuse anyone else" (8). From there, Solana simply waits for an opportune moment to lift the Other's job application materials in order to find that "the two-page form contained all the data she would need to assume her new life: date of birth, place of birth, which was Santa Teresa, Social Security number, education, the number of her nursing license, and her prior employment" (9). All this highly sensitive information, Grafton demonstrates, has always already been accessible to those who wish to access it. Solana Rojas does not need Internet access to steal the Other's identity, but only a few minutes.

Kinsey's detective skills, too, take the point even further by highlighting the range of information available not through thievery (though as Mary Freier notes, Kinsey has few ethical qualms when it comes to obtaining the information of others) but rather through public records. One of Grafton's stylistic hallmarks is her description of Kinsey's research methods. As these techniques have remained largely static since the series' beginning, they may initially seem dated in relationship to twenty-first century information-gathering strategies. However, as Grafton continues to include these descriptions, she forces them into relief with the more technologically-driven methods of other contemporary detective fiction. The descriptions of Kinsey's methods reveal that, before the advent of search engines, vast quantities of personal information were still widely available. In *Wasted*, Kinsey describes using the Polk and Haines directories to find a wealth of information in a relatively short time. She explains that the Polk directory includes "both an alphabetical listing of residents and an alphabetical listing of street addresses, with names of the occupants included," while the "Haines directory, also known as a crisscross, is a mechanical reversal of the information in the phone book, its listing ordered by street names and by telephone numbers in sequence" (195), such that possession of either a phone number or an address can reveal a wide amount of personal data. For example, a brief "finger walk through the pages" of the Polk directory" reveals "Sterling Dace (Clara): util wrk, PG&E, (h) 4619 Paradise" and "Randall J Dace (Glenda): srvc rep, PG&E, at 745 Daisy Lane" (196). In essence, Kinsey (or any interested party) does not need computer technology to learn the name of a person, that person's spouse, profession, employer, home address, and telephone number; this information exists for quick reference in directories and public records. It follows, then, that digital technology cannot be solely responsible for a lack of privacy, since as Grafton demonstrates, such personal information was already readily available.

"It looked like things were as bad as they were going to get": Addressing the Contemporary Moment through Juxtaposition with the Past

Having established that writing from the vantage point of the 2000s allows her to realign perspectives about the 1980s, Grafton then uses the 1980s to comment on the nature of the time in which she writes. Just as Grafton warns about the dangers of misremembering the past by blocking or filtering out problematic memories, she also uses the difficulties of that past to comment on issues in contemporary society and crime. Sometimes, as before, she uses metafictional commentary to establish a knowing hindsight which allows her to give perspective on contemporary affairs. In *Wasted*, Kinsey explains, "This was October 7, 1988, and it looked like things were as bad as they were going to get. On the national front, congressional spending was a whopping $1,064.14 billion and the federal debt was topping out at $2,601.3 billion. Unemployment hovered at 5.5 percent and the price of a first-class postage stamp had jumped from twenty-two cents to twenty-five" (3-4). Certainly the numbers Kinsey quotes serve the dual function of simultaneously reminding readers of the state of affairs in 1987 and shocking them into realizing how much congressional spending, the national debt, and unemployment had grown by 2013. At the same time, by so clearly inviting comparison to the present by beginning "it looked like things were as bad as they were going to get," Grafton announces that *Wasted* can and will provide commentary on the contemporary moment and that its 1980s setting does not restrict its relevance to the twenty-first century.

X provides a similar level of commentary, this time linked to the changes in media between the 1980s and the present. The same librarian who cannot acclimate to the "'newfangled'" system expresses her concern to Kinsey that:

> 'One day soon newspapers will be a thing of the past.'

'That can't be true. You think? I mean, people want to know what's going on in the world. A television broadcast is never going to take the place of hard news.'

'All I know is there was a time when a newspaper was the heartbeat of the city. Now, not so much It's like the lifeblood is draining out.' (142)

Here as well, the dialogue provides commentary on past and present simultaneously; Grafton highlights the beginning of a change that will come to pass in ways neither Kinsey nor the librarian can fully grasp, with television wresting dominance from newspapers only to itself be toppled by the unnamed usurper in this dialogue, social media. Grafton cannot have her characters speculate about a form that does not yet exist, but she does conjure the specter of social media for readers in 2015, when *X* appeared in print. Indeed, Grafton extends her practice of using the past to comment on present phenomena she cannot name in her final novel, *Y is for Yesterday*.

"While the girl lay passive and unresisting": *Y is for Yesterday*, Steubenville, and Contemporary Crime

Yesterday centers on a murder that results from an attempt to cover up an extremely damaging teenage sex tape. In the tape, three male students from the elite prep school Climping Academy are shown sexually assaulting their highly intoxicated and sometimes unconscious female classmate. The tape gets out around the school, a murder is committed to cover it up, and it reappears years later as a blackmail attempt. Kinsey gets involved when one boy's wealthy family hires her to help track down the blackmailers and save their son. Grafton has written about rape previously and, as Diehl (2016) notes, even relatively recently with *Trespass* and the rape of the nursing patient Gus by his caretaker Solana Rojas. *Yesterday*, though, moves her engagement farther from the realm of fiction and closer to reality. Even from this brief description, striking similarities to a recent rape emerge. The notorious Steubenville, Ohio, case parallels the events of *Yesterday* in many details. According to Danielle Keats Citron, "In August 2012 a sixteen-year-old girl was gang-raped while she was unconscious. The night of the rape, the perpetrators, members of the Steubenville, Ohio, high school football team, posted incriminating videos, tweets, and photographs, which were soon deleted. One photo featured two football players carrying the unconscious woman" (114). In both the Steubenville case and *Yesterday*, a high school girl was raped by multiple classmates while unconscious, and the recording of the assault was distributed among other students. Further, as Bronwyn Winter writes, "The abused teenager was drunk to the point of vomiting and passing out on the night in question and recalls little to nothing of events. Her attackers... not only repeatedly raped her, vaginally and orally, but also urinated on her and photographed her" (132). This account includes the additional steps the assailants took to humiliate the victim. In *Yesterday*, Grafton describes the viewing of the tape from two perspectives, Kinsey's and Lauren McCabe's. Lauren, the mother of one of the boys on the tape, in an effort to protect her son, hires Kinsey to help her track down blackmailers when the tape resurfaces. The graphic description of the tape from Lauren, cited here at length but eliding descriptions of all the participants, indicates the similarities to the Steubenville case:

> [Iris, the victim] reached for a beer bottle and chugged it, clutching the towel to her chest. She seemed to be as goofily drunk as the boys, which made Lauren uncomfortable even if the three were mugging for effect....As the scene continued, the girl stumbled and nearly fell....The camera panned. Lauren caught her breath, her heart suddenly pounding, and her posture stiffened with dismay. 'Oh lord no,' she said. She put a hand over her mouth, her cheeks burning with shame.

Both boys were naked and fully erect. The girl, Iris, had apparently passed out on the pool table while the boys showed off for each other, egging each other on. Troy was the first to approach the girl, wagging his stiff penis while Fritz sidled up to her and fondled one of her bare breasts. What followed was a full-on sexual assault. They seemed to do anything that occurred to them while the girl lay passive and unresisting. She might have been acting, but Lauren doubted it. The boys flipped her over on her stomach, her bare butt occupying much of the screen. Lauren stared as though hypnotized, grimacing as the tape rolled on. She knew she should shut the machine down, but she still held out the perverse expectation that this was all in good fun. It was tacky and in bad taste, but if the girl was a willing participant, that might make all the difference. From the left of frame, Fritz appeared with an open can of Crisco, which he held aloft, pretending to twist an imaginary mustache like the villain in a melodrama. Fritz held out the can to Troy, who dug his fingers into the white grease. The scene jumped to Troy with his back to the camera as he pumped away at the girl on the pool table.

Lauren covered her mouth as though to repress all sound, shaking her head in horror. Meanwhile, Fritz picked up a pool stick and stuck it in the girl. Austin Brown's looking on, so cold and unconcerned, made it all the worse. Lauren pressed the Off button. Hands shaking, she pushed the button that ejected the tape. . . . She turned the VCR off and sat without moving, trying to collect herself. She felt ill. (117-19)

Of the many similarities to the Steubenville case at play here, several stand out. The girl's level of intoxication leading to her stumbling around, the boys encouraging each other, the unconscious girl being used as an object, and the Crisco-covered pool cue as a stand-in for the denigrating effect of urinating on the victim all work to recall the Steubenville case. Grafton's detailed level of description here is of note as well. She cannot give readers the literal experience of watching the tape, but she can describe it in excruciating detail and narrate the viewer Lauren's increasing discomfort and disgust with what she witnesses. Further, she can narrate Lauren's thought process as she continues to hope that the video depicts a consensual sexual encounter even as the possibility becomes more remote.

Lauren's visceral response to the tape highlights a crucial component of Grafton's narration. For Lauren, as for Kinsey, there is no doubt that the video shows sexual violence. Lauren concludes that "what followed was a full-on sexual assault" and later confirms that "the two had raped and sexually abused the girl" (119). Kinsey's description, too, calls the tape a recording of "an ongoing sexual assault" and "clearly criminal" (39). This unequivocal description is crucial because, in *Yesterday* as in the Steubenville case, multiple alternative explanations are offered. Kinsey observes, "I could picture the boys boasting of their sexual conquest, probably blaming Iris for being promiscuous and therefore deserving of their treatment" (40). With the Steubenville case and the addition of social media, Bronwyn Winter writes, a survey showed that "roughly one-fifth of respondents believe that a victim is responsible for rape and abuse if she is drunk or drugged, is particularly chilling, especially given that the survey was done after the international scandal of the Steubenville rape. One might have expected, if nothing else, that the horrors of the Steubenville story might have caused sufficient outrage to change public perceptions about victim blaming. But, in fact, no, it did not because the media fully participated in the victim-blaming exercise" (132). Grafton's representation of the response to this tape, with Kinsey all too aware that the assailants might be "blaming Iris for being promiscuous and therefore deserving of their treatment," can be read as a form of counter-media participation to the kind Winter reports, using her fiction as an effort to answer Winter's call, retroactively, for "sufficient outrage to change public perceptions."

Indeed, Grafton's depiction, whether meant as a direct response to the public's response to Steubenville or not, attacks multiple aspects of contemporary rape culture. When one participant tells the murder victim, Sloan, that the tape "'wasn't meant to be taken serious. We were just horsing around,'" she responds that "'It doesn't look like 'horsing around'. . . It looks like full-on sexual assault.'" When the boy claims that he "'couldn't see the harm,'" again the murder victim responds with incredulity. "She looked at him in disbelief. 'Honestly? You screw the poor girl when she's completely out of it and you can't see the harm?'" (263). The repetition of Lauren's prior phrase "full-on sexual assault," as well as her talking back to the rapist's feckless rejoinder that he "'couldn't see the harm,'" presents a wish-fulfillment dialogue, with the rapist forced to confront his actions. Of course, Grafton does not shy away from the potential danger Sloan puts herself in by responding so strongly and, indeed, it is her refusal to destroy the tape that leads to her murder. As Sloan herself remarks, the tape is damning— "'If the cops get hold of that tape, you and Fritz will end up in jail'" (264). The boys and their friends who know about the tape, as well as the parents who hire Kinsey, work to keep the tape from coming out. Lauren, who fully recognizes her son raping the girl on the tape, still works to protect him. The efforts to protect the futures of the wealthy boys also echoes the Steubenville case. Carine Mardorossian recounts that "The Steubenville case, however, led to disturbing media reports focused on how the guilty verdict 'ruined the promising lives of the Steubenville rapists'" (54). Carrie James, too, notes that in the case of Steubenville, "Although the parents, teachers, and coaches of the youths involved tried to trivialize the incident, it became difficult to do so in the face of these digital artifacts" (102). In *Yesterday*, the perpetrators and their friends attempt to "trivialize" the rape as a "'pornographic spoof'" (250), while their parents use their considerable economic means to protect their sons from being "'held accountable by law'" (39). Again, the parallels are striking—in both *Yesterday* and the Steubenville case, justice for the victim is portrayed as secondary to the needs of the perpetrators. Erica Meiners notes that, in the case of Steubenville, "perceptions of socioeconomic status contributed to produce an initial narrative that the sexual activity was consensual" (254). *Yesterday*, too, shows a deep desire on the part of the rapist's mother to believe that the act was consensual and on the part of the rapists to believe that it was a "spoof." Grafton also highlights the socioeconomic status of the boys as relevant to their parents' ability to hire Kinsey in the first place.

Again, whether or not Grafton works to recall Steubenville to her readers specifically matters less than her inclusion of so many familiar beats of the narrative that Steubenville represents: victim-blaming, prioritization of the perpetrators over the victims, damning video evidence designed to humiliate the victim and spun to exonerate the rapists. Many critics read Steubenville as a cautionary tale about the long life of artifacts in the digital age; James writes that it represents the "double-edged nature of the Web—the opportunities for both good and evil at our fingertips. The Steubenville story, along with the other extreme cases described in this book, represents both a horrific offline incident and the worst-case scenario of how social media and the Internet can be used" (122). Grafton, though, refuses to depict the actions of *Yesterday* so matter-of-factly. By taking a narrative about the afterlife of a video tape that refuses to disappear and setting in in 1989, she reminds readers again that such media, and the actions depicted within it, existed well before "social media and the Internet." Further, she insists that the Steubenville case and the events of *Yesterday* are not isolated incidents but rather representations of an ongoing problem that has changed remarkably little in the time between the novel's 1989 setting and its 2017 publication. Kinsey remarks that she "had heard of similar situations, where still photographs of a sexual assault had been circulated among the perpetrators' friends.

What possessed anyone to record such vile behavior was beyond me" (40). Grafton refuses to let the case of *Yesterday* stand as an isolated incident, rather situating it in a chain of behavior that persists through 2017 and beyond. Throughout her later work, then, Grafton uses the past to offer trenchant commentary on the present.

While Sue Grafton's alphabet series might not be the first work thought of as depicting contemporary crime, the later installments in the Kinsey Millhone novels contribute to the landscape of twenty-first-century detective fiction in several significant ways. First, they reject the nostalgic notion of the 1980s as a simpler time, forcing a consideration of the ways in which the 2000s do and do not differ from previous decades. In showing the potential harm that comes from relying on memories of the past to reconstruct it, Grafton also insists that to oversimplify the past as the backwards cousin of a fast-paced techno-future neglects the crucial similarities between crimes in the new millennium and those of the 1980s. Lastly, Grafton works to depict those similarities as essential to understanding the way that contemporary crimes do function analogously to those of the past, just as the rape in *Yesterday* echoes the Steubenville case. Her fiction demonstrates that ignoring the ongoing trajectories of these crimes muffles an understanding of how long certain criminal patterns and responses to those patterns have existed. To ignore those patterns, Grafton demonstrates, risks minimizing the need for thoroughgoing change.

Notes

1. Grafton scholarship on feminism and the hardboiled tradition, gender's relationship to that tradition, and sex and sexuality's relationship to that tradition thrived for a decade, with work from Maureen Reddy (1988, 1990), Patricia Johnson (1994), Priscilla Walton (1995), Scott Christianson (1995), Louise Conley Jones (1995), Frederic Svoboda (1995), Timothy Shuker-Haines and

Martha M. Umphrey (1998) and Jenny Blade (1998). In the 2000s, scholarship of this type began to taper, though Lisa Cook (2004), Linda Mizejewski (2004), Heath Diehl (2012), and William Klink (2014) did continue to consider how Grafton operated in relation to the hard-boiled paradigm. Even those critics who take a different angle on Grafton, as is the case with Sue Matheson's creative approach to another long-running Grafton theme, food consumption, or Russel Gray's interest in the metaphysical aspects of Grafton's literary style, typically find a way to connect Grafton back to the hard-boiled.

2. I discuss the relationship between these two trends in crime fiction in greater depth in the "Digital Technology" chapter in the *Routledge Companion to Crime Fiction*.

3. Grafton has employed such metafictional humor before, Penuel points out, as in the "arch detective-genre joke" wherein Kinsey "frequently dines on 'hard-boiled' egg sandwiches" (75).

4. It is worth noting that Grafton may not have changed her position on cross-dressing much from *Deadbeat* to *Trespass,* as the latter novel features Kinsey engaged in a fight to the death with a man wearing a nurse's uniform and hose. During the altercation, Kinsey has time to derisively quip, "Any clothing other than panty hose would have offered him protection—heavy jeans or sweats serving as a jock strap or a codpiece of sorts—shielding his nuts. But he was turned on by the feel of silkiness against his naked skin. Such is life. We all have our preferences" (408).

Works Cited

Blade, Jenny Elizabeth. "Grafton's Progression from the Hard-Boiled Tradition." *Clues: A Journal of Detection*, vol. 19, no. 2, 1998, pp. 69-77.

Christianson, Scott. "Talkin' Trash and Kickin' Butt: Sue Grafton's Hard-Boiled Feminism." *Feminism in Women's Detective Fiction*, edited by Glenwood Irons. U of Toronto P, 1995, pp. 127-47.

Citron, Danielle Keats. *Hate Crimes in Cyberspace*. Harvard UP, 2014.

Cook, Lisa A. "The Female Private Detective: Kinsey Millhone—America's New Hero." *The Image of the Hero in Literature, Media, and Society*, edited by Will Wright and Steven Kaplan, Colorado State UP, 2004, pp. 135-40.

Diehl, Heath A. "Innovation and Hardboiled Fiction." *TEXT*, vol. 37, 2016, pp. 1-13.

---."W' is for Woman: Deconstructing the Private Dick in Sue Grafton's Alphabet Series." *Murdering Miss Marple: Essays on Gender and Sexuality in the New Golden Age of Women's Crime Fiction*, edited by Julie H. Kim, McFarland, 2012, pp. 120-42.

Freier, May P. "Information Ethics in the Detective Novel." *Clues: A Journal of Detection*, vol. 24, no. 1, 2005, pp. 18-26.

Grafton, Sue. *A is for Alibi*. Bantam, 1982.

---. *D is for Deadbeat*. Bantam, 1987.

---. *E is for Evidence*. Bantam, 1988.

---. *T is for Trespass*. G. P. Putnam's Sons, 2007.

---. *U is for Undertow*. G. P. Putnam's Sons, 2009.

---. *V is for Vengeance*. G. P. Putnam's Sons, 2011.

---. *W is for Wasted*. G. P. Putnam's Sons, 2013.

---. *X*. G. P. Putnam's Sons, 2015.

---. *Y is for Yesterday*. G. P. Putnam's Sons, 2017.

Gray, W. Russel. "Flow Gently, Sweet Grafton: 'M' Is for Metaphysical (or at Least Metaphor) in '*C' Is for Corpse*." *Clues: A Journal of Detection*, vol. 20, no. 1, 1999, pp. 63-9.

Hubbell, Gary. "All You Have Left in the End: Conclusions and the Series Character in Sue Grafton's 'Alphabet Series.'" *Clues: A Journal of Detection*, vol. 18, no. 1, 1997, pp. 15-24.

Humann, Heather Duerre. *Gender Bending Detective Fiction: A Critical Analysis of Selected Works*. McFarland, 2017.

James, Carrie. *Disconnected: Youth, New Media, and the Ethics Gap*. MIT P, 2014.

Johnson, Patricia E. "Sex and Betrayal in the Fiction of Sue Grafton and Sara Paretsky." *Journal of Popular Culture*, vol. 27, no. 4, Spr. 1994, pp. 97-106.

Jones, Louise Conley. "Feminism and the P. I. Code: Or, 'Is a Hard-Boiled Warshawski Unsuitable to Be Called a Feminist?'" *Clues: A Journal of Detection*, vol. 16, no. 1, 1995, pp. 77-87.

Kay, Carol McGinnis. "Sue Grafton." *American Hard-Boiled Crime Writers*, edited by George P. Anderson and Julie B. Anderson, Gale, 2000, pp. 175-87.

Kenley, Nicole. "Digital Technology." *The Routledge Companion to Crime Fiction*, edited by Janice Allan et al., Routledge, 2020.

Klink, William R. *The Hard-Boiled Female Detective Novel: A Study of a Popular Literary Genre.* Edwin Mellen Press, 2014.

Mardorossian, Carine M. *Framing the Rape Victim: Gender and Agency Reconsidered.* Rutgers UP, 2014.

Matheson, Sue. "Food Is Never Just Something To Eat: Sue Grafton's Culinary Critique of Mainstream America." *Journal of Popular Culture*, vol. 41, no. 5, Oct. 2008, pp. 809-22.

Meiners, Erica R. "Offending Children, Registering Sex." *Women's Studies Quarterly*, vol. 43, nos. 1/2, Spr/Sum 2015, pp. 246-63. *ProQuest*, doi:10.1353/wsq.2015.0021.

Mizejewski, Linda. *Hard Boiled and High Heeled.* Routledge, 2004.

Penuel, Suzanne. "In Poor Taste: Morality and Sue Grafton." *Class and Culture in Crime Fiction: Essays on Works in English since the 1970s*, edited by Julie H. Kim, McFarland, 2014, pp. 69-87.

Rabinowitz, Peter J. "'Reader, I Blew Him Away': Convention and Transgression in Sue Grafton." *Famous Last Words: Changes in Gender and Narrative Closure*, edited by Allison Booth, U of Virginia P, 1993, pp. 326-44.

Reddy, Maureen T. "The Feminist Counter-Tradition in Crime: Cross, Grafton, Paretsky, and Wilson." *The Cunning Craft: Original Essays on Detective Fiction and Contemporary Literary Theory*, edited by Ronald G. Walker and June M. Frazer, Western Illinois UP, 1990, pp. 174-87.

---. *Sisters in Crime.* Frederick Ungar, 1988.

Schaffer, Rachel. "Armed (with Wit) and Dangerous: Sue Grafton's Sense of Black Humor." *Armchair Detective: A*

Quarterly Journal Devoted to the Appreciation of Mystery, Detective, and Suspense Fiction, vol. 30, no. 3, 1997, pp. 316-22.

Shuker-Haines, Timothy, and Martha M. Umphrey. "Gender (De)Mystified: Resistance and Recuperation in Hard-Boiled Female Detective Fiction." *The Detective in American Fiction, Film, and Television*, edited by Jerome H. Delamater and Ruth Prigozy, Greenwood P, 1998, pp. 71-82.

Svoboda, Frederic. "Hard-Boiled Feminist Detectives and Their Families: Reimaging a Form." *Gender in Popular Culture: Images of Men and Women in Literature, Visual Media, and Material Culture*, edited by P.C. Rollins and S.W. Rollins, Ridgemont P, 1995, pp. 247-72.

Swanson, Jean. "Sue Grafton." *Mystery and Suspense Writers: The Literature of Crime, Detection, and Espionage*, edited by Robin V. Winks and Maureen Corrigan, Scribner's Sons, 1998, pp. 439-48.

Walton, Priscilla L. "'E' is for En/Gendering Readings: Sue Grafton's Kinsey Millhone. *Women Times Three: Writers, Detectives, Readers*, edited by Kathleen Gregory Klein, Popular P, 1995. pp. 101-15.

Wilson, Ann. "The Female Dick and the Crisis of Heterosexuality." *Feminism in Women's Detective Fiction*, edited by Glenwood Irons, U of Toronto P, 1995, pp. 148-56.

Winter, Bronwyn. *Women, Insecurity, and Violence in a Post-9/11 World*. Syracuse UP, 2017.

Peanut Butter and Pickle Sandwiches: Sue Grafton's Alphabet Series and Everyday Life

Eric Sandberg

Abstract

Despite their enduring popularity and consistently high quality, Sue Grafton's Kinsey Millhone novels have not attracted their due measure of critical attention. In part, this may be because they do not respond particularly well to some of the critical paradigms frequently applied to crime fiction. While Grafton's position as a trailblazer of the feminist hardboiled alongside writers like Marcia Muller and Sara Paretsky has been generally acknowledged, her work is not obviously what Beverly G. Six calls a "literature of dissent" (144). This essay proposes an alternate reading by examining the Alphabet series' focus on everyday life, on ordinary places, experiences, and routines. The Millhone novels are fascinated with the banal realities of the quotidian — an interest that contrasts strongly with the hardboiled's typical reliance on investigative plotting and violent action. This essay thus draws attention to a neglected facet of Grafton's work and connects it to literary production beyond its genre.

The first page of the first novel in Sue Grafton's Alphabet series, *A is for Alibi*, presents a dichotomy that becomes a defining element of the series from its 1982 inauguration to its untimely conclusion with *Y is for Yesterday* in 2017. Although private investigator Kinsey Millhone admits at the outset that she has "killed someone," she also points out that apart from the danger concomitant with her profession, her "life has always been ordinary, uneventful, and good" (9). This contrast between the exposure to violence that is a part of her job and the ordinariness of her life is central to the series, and offers not just a different way of reading Grafton's work, but also a different way of thinking about crime fiction more broadly.

Critical approaches to crime fiction take many different forms.[1] Some scholars focus on its reliance on clear and relatively predictable narrative structures to generate and maintain readerly interest. From this perspective, it is a type of fiction in which we can productively "speak of the plot and of the plot alone," as G. K. Chesterton said of Dicken's unfinished novel *The Mystery of Edwin Drood* (viii). Other critics focus on the centrality of violence to crime fiction, the way it dwells on physical crimes and their grotesque impact on the (frequently female) body in ways that border on, at times, "prurient excess" (Stewart 695). The genre is also frequently read as a form of social critique, a literary form that allows for, or even encourages, engagement with important and frequently unpleasant social realities, from child-abuse to government corruption, and more broadly, with the overall power hierarchies prevailing in a given society (Messent 11-12).

What these diverse ways of reading the genre have in common, however, is their shared focus on the *crime* of crime fiction. In some forms of crime writing, like the classic detective stories of the Golden Age, criminal behavior is represented as exceptional, an aberration from a peaceful norm, a shocking eruption of violence, cruelty, or evil into the world. In other traditions—for instance, the hardboiled detective novel—violence and criminality permeate or underlie normal life. Understandably enough, these moments of criminal transgression have operated as focal points for critical attention. However, what is lost here is the very everyday reality that is disturbed by crime, what Michel de Certeau describes in his landmark study *The Practice of Everyday Life* as "the open sea of common experience that surrounds, penetrates, and finally carries away every discourse" (15). To paraphrase Roland Barthes' *Camera Lucida*, when we talk about crime fiction we tend to discuss the *punctum* rather than the *studium*, the "element which rises from the scene, shoots out of it like an arrow, and pierces" rather than its "average" state (26).

This is, I want to argue, a one-sided way of reading crime fiction, which, between its scenes of violence, detection, and punishment is deeply invested in the representation of the quotidian. Grafton's work is a perfect example of this dual nature. Consider, for example, the structure of the titles of the Millhone novels: *A is for Alibi, B is for Burglar, C is for Corpse*, etc. Grafton traces this naming convention to her enjoyment of mystery series with linked titles, like John D. MacDonald's color-coded Travis McGee novels or Harry Kemelman's day-of-the-week Rabbi Small series ("Interview: A Conversation"). It also has obvious associations with Lawrence Treat's pioneer police procedurals (e.g. the 1945 *V as in Victim*). But what is most important here is the way Grafton's titles balance the two levels of textual reality that co-exist in her work: the everyday of the alphabet itself, and the exceptional terms that follow "is for" — the murder (*H is for Homicide*) and danger (*P is for Peril*) that punctuate the calm, everyday tenor of Millhone's life. Certeau's project has been described as an attempt to direct critical attention towards everyday cultural practices, and this is very much the goal of this paper (Buchanan 98). It is, in other words, an attempt to turn our attention away from the second half of Grafton's titles towards the first.

Everyday Interpretation

De Certeau argues that all societies, and their "normative institutions," tend to foreground certain cultural practices; this means that others "remain 'minor,' always there but not organizing discourses" (48). The critical community of crime fiction scholars has, to some extent, functioned in this way, directing attention towards a certain set of textual practices at the expense of others. In the case of Grafton's work, the bulk of critical attention has fallen on her relationship to feminism.

Grafton is almost always associated with a group of women writers (Marcia Muller and Sara Paretsky are most frequently mentioned, but the list also includes Amanda Cross, P. D. James, and Patricia Cornwell) who re-purposed and re-invigorated the hardboiled tradition by having a female detective occupy the male-gendered subject position of the private investigator (Gavin 264),[2] thus remaining, as Ann Wilson writes, "faithful to the tradition of tough-guy detective fiction while disrupting its gender codes" (148). This approach certainly provides powerful critical traction for reading Grafton, who describes herself as "a feminist from way back," and ascribes her motivation in adopting the PI genre to the fact that she "like[s] playing hardball with the boys" — and no doubt beating them at their own game (Taylor 128). As Sue Matheson points out, the critical analysis of the Alphabet series has largely focussed on the ways the novels "feminize" the traditionally masculine hardboiled novel, or more broadly what Glenwood Irons calls the "the phallocentric world of genre narrative" (810; Irons 128). For Scott Christianson, for instance, the key is the way Grafton's appropriation and transformation of the hardboiled idiom changes the genre into a "place from which a woman can exercise language as power," while simultaneously problematizing its traditional posture of male toughness (129, 137). Other critics have focussed on Kinsey Millhone's rejection of chauvinist beauty standards, and the way her appreciation of other women undermines sexist versions of female competitiveness (Walton 107-108). This interpretive heritage has led to a certain amount of controversy, with a number of critics pointing out that there is a tension between the overtly feminist content of the Millhone novels and the fact that despite the female PI's rejection of patriarchy — not just Kinsey's but any female detective's — her work ultimately supports it (Klein 201). As Peter Rabinowitz writes, "narrative structures continue to assert power over author and character" in ways that illuminate how the "resilience of genre, its resistance to revisions, may hide out in places where authors have little control" (Rabinowitz 327-328).[3]

Yet these feminist readings of Grafton's work become arguably less relevant as the series progresses. Despite the slowed-down narrative chronology of the series, and its reliance on what Johanna Sandberg describes in another context as "creative stasis," *A is for Alibi* and *B is for Burglar* are in some respects very different works from later novels like *U is for Undertow* or *Y is for Yesterday*. One such difference is the fact that assertions of feminist positions and sentiments are much more prominent in the earlier novels: in *Burglar*, for example, we learn that Kinsey left the police because "back then, policewomen were viewed with a mixture of curiosity and scorn" and that her unmarried, child-free state, while perfectly acceptable to her, "seems to piss people off — especially men" (1, 64). This is a novel in which her client's husband is perfectly comfortable telling Kinsey, ". . .it amuses me to think about a girl detective" (142). This sort of direct engagement with chauvinism and misogyny is much less common in the later novels. Certainly it is true that female investigators are now far more common in crime narratives, and this type of bland, everyday misogyny would likely seem jarring to contemporary readers and viewers. But misogyny has not disappeared from public discourse since the early 1980s, and its comparative scarcity late in the series is interesting — and may account for difficulty applying traditional critical tools to the series as a whole.

Another major difference may at first seem superficial: Grafton's earlier novels are substantially shorter than her later ones. *Alibi* is, for instance, approximately seventy-five thousand words long, while *Undertow* approaches a hundred and thirty thousand.[4] This point is in itself not particularly interesting; what is interesting is what fills the "extra" pages of the later novels. The additional length comes in part from the "inter-chapters" narrated in the third person dealing with the lives of characters at the time the crime occurred, a regular feature of the series after *S is for Silence*. But the main factor is the space dedicated to descriptions of the everyday routines, objects, and practices of both Kinsey and other characters.

Everyday Practices

As Henri Lefebvre points out in his landmark study *Everyday Life in the Modern World*, "everyday life is made of recurrences": it consists of a whole repertoire of repeated "gestures of labour and leisure" as well as a range of "mechanical movements both human and properly mechanic," which take place within a temporal framework that is itself built around the repetition of "hours, days, weeks, months, years" (18). The range of activities that fall under the category of everyday life, then, is vast. But one of the most obvious places to look here is to the dinner table, for what could be more normal, more daily, than eating?

While food has an important place in some versions of the crime novel (Manuel Vázquez Montalbán's detective Pepe Carvalho, for instance, has his own cookbook, while Patricia Cornwell's forensic detective Kay Scarpetta has two), it is not a major component of the hardboiled PI tradition that Kinsey Millhone arises from. In *The Maltese Falcon*, Dashiell Hammett's Sam Spade eats, but the fact that he puts away "scrambled eggs, bacon, toast and marmalade" and "two cups of coffee" with Brigid O'Shaughnessy and Gutman does not indicate much in the way of narrative interest in the event (207). The characters, like the reader, are waiting for morning and the arrival of the titular bird, and the consumption of food is a footnote. Compare this with Kinsey Millhone's description of her not dissimilar breakfast: "I ate a big breakfast in a little diner across the road from the motel, washing down bacon, scrambled eggs, and rye toast with fresh orange juice and three cups of coffee" (*Alibi* 96). While this is still a brief narration, it is an event in itself, and a highly pleasurable one, for both character and reader: the breakfast is not just a breakfast, but a big one, the toast is not just toast, but rye toast, and the coffee and juice are not merely drunk, but wash down the food. In

S is for Silence, Kinsey eats an identical breakfast, again at a diner, but here even more narrative attention is dedicated to the experience: "She filled my coffee cup, set the cream pitcher within range, and moved down the line, offering refills and warm-ups before she put in my order. My breakfast arrived and I focused my attention on my orange juice, rye toast, crisp bacon, and scrambled eggs. This was my favorite meal, and I wasted no time putting it away" (171). This pattern of "excess" narrative attention to the consumption of food reappears throughout the series.

In the second volume of *The Practice of Everyday Life* Luce Giard points out that, unlike animals, we rely on "*cultured* foodstuffs, chosen and prepared according to laws of compatibility and rules of propriety unique to each cultural area" (168). This means that food does not simply nourish, but signifies, and this is certainly true of the representation of food in narrative. Matheson, for example, has offered a feminist reading of the representation of food and eating in the Alphabet series, arguing that as the culinary realm is traditionally gendered as female, its depiction in feminist writing is particularly important (810). Kinsey's love of fast food associates her with male characters and traditionally male characteristics; her landlord and friend Henry Pitts' love of baking and cooking also inverts normative gender roles (812). While this reading is sound, it seems to only partially account for the persistent return of the alimentary in the series.

Giard describes "*doing-cooking,*" or our total engagement with food from preparation to serving to consumption, as "the medium for a basic, humble, and persistent practice that is repeated in time and space, rooted in the fabric of relationships to others and to one's self, marked by the 'family saga' in the history of each, bound to childhood memory just like rhythms and seasons" (157). In some ways, Kinsey's "doing-cooking" operates in direct contradistinction to this association of food and family, food and place. Matheson points out that eating in the hardboiled tends to highlight the PI's isolation, their separation from the sort of social context Giard discusses (810). From this perspective, when Kinsey eats lunch at her desk in *R is for Ricochet*, "feasting on an olive-and-pimento-cheese sandwich on wheat bread, cut in quarters," it would be an indication of generically typical isolation; she is not, after all, having lunch with friends or colleagues (2). But there is none of the bleak, alienated sensibility of traditional hardboiled here, both because of Grafton's diction (feast instead of eat) and the exuberant oddity and specificity of Kinsey' sandwich, and because, as the immediately following sentence indicates, this isolation is a choice: "So what was the problem? I had none. Life was great" (2). Similarly, the fact that this particular sandwich is her "third-favorite sandwich in the whole world" will immediately remind the reader of her other two sandwiches of choice — the "hot hard-boiled egg sandwich with mayo" and the "peanut butter and pickle sandwich" (*Ricochet* 2; *Vengeance* 422; *Silence* 318). The routineness of this sandwich-eating makes it the type of "persistent practice. . .repeated in time and space" to which Giard refers. It is also important that these sandwiches are connected for the orphaned Kinsey to her memories of her mother, and thus function as signifiers of domestic intimacy in however attenuated a form (*Innocent* 57). Indeed, through repetition across the series, these meals come to be shared with a "family" that consists of Kinsey and her readers.

The representation of food in the Millhone novels can be seen as part of a larger pattern in which the repeated representation, or re-presentation, of everyday activities moves from the background of narrative to the foreground. Rather than looking, then, at the diversity of Kinsey's modes of engagement with food — which could be subdivided into a number of categories including breakfast, fast food, Henry Pitts' home cooking, occasional luxurious meals on dates, and her friend Rosie's Hungarian cooking — each of which could be read in terms of its own signifying capacity (as Matheson does in relation to feminism), the fact that these multiple categories recur throughout the series means that each type of "doing-cooking" gradually acquires the patina of familiarity that makes them so important for Kinsey herself as a character, and for her readers.

Pierre Mayol has pointed out that "ordinary culture hides a fundamental diversity of situations, interests, and contexts under the apparent repetition of objects that it uses" (256). I want to effectively reverse Mayol's argument and claim that in Grafton's case the diversity of ordinary culture and cultural practices masks its primary function — that of being ordinary.

In some ways, it is difficult to see food as ordinary, because of both individual and cultural preferences, and its corresponding freight of personal and social significance. How ordinary are peanut butter and pickle sandwiches, after all? The Alphabet series' interest in the ordinary may become clearer, then, if we turn to other elements of Millhone's daily routine, to which she dedicates an astonishing level of narrative interest. As she claims in *V is for Vengeance*, "Sometimes I think routine is everything in life" (142). The following passage from *S is for Silence* is typical of the series' interest in the trivial, repeated actions of everyday life: "I went into the bathroom, floor squeaking as I walked, and pulled my toothbrush, toothpaste, and a change of underpants from my shoulder bag, where I keep them for such occasions" (169). Having relocated for investigative purposes to a motel in the small town of Serena Station, Kinsey not only maintains her daily routine and includes it in her narration, but she also contextualizes it in a second pattern of repetition, her habit of keeping the necessities of daily life on her person at all times, a habit that will be recognizable to any reader of the series.

This emphasis on routine is one of the primary factors shaping the prose style and narrative structure of the Alphabet novels. *B is for Burglar*, like many other novels in the series, contains detailed descriptions of Millhone's daily life: "I came home, showered, washed my hair, napped, got dressed, sneaked in a little grocery shopping, and then I sat down at my desk and worked on note cards while I drank a glass of white wine and ate a warm, sliced-hard-boiled-egg sandwich with loads of Best Food's mayo and salt, nearly swooning at the taste" (114-115). In *Modernism and the Ordinary*, Liesl

Olsen argues that ordinary experience is both "a mode of organizing life"—we build our lives around highly structured sequences of repeated activities—and a way of presenting it. In other words, it is a style associated with "aesthetic forms such as the list, or linguistic repetition..." (6). Kinsey's narration of her daily routines approaches very closely to Olsen's notion of an ordinary style: the passage quoted above, with its string of sequential domestic activities, is essentially a list. In other cases, Grafton relies on structural repetition to indicate routine, as in this passage describing one of Kinsey's regular morning jogs:

> By the time I reached the jogging path, I was sufficiently warmed up....After that, I only had to cope with my protesting body parts,....I was home again forty minutes later....I let myself into the apartment, stripped off my sweats,....I was out and drying myself when the telephone rang. I took the call while turning the towel into a makeshift sarong. (*Ricochet* 56)

While the passage has been edited to emphasize its repetitive structure, the changes do not over-emphasize the fact that this run, like so many of Kinsey's routine activities, is described in a series of repeated first-person declarative sentences. In another example from *R is for Ricochet*, Kinsey describes a quiet evening at home watching television and snacking, followed by a short excursion. In a two-paragraph, fifteen-sentence passage that begins when Kinsey arrives home ("I let myself into my place...") and ends when she returns home ("I went back to my place..."), ten sentences begin with an "I + past tense verb" structure (72-73). While this is admittedly a typical feature of first-person retrospective narratives, Grafton's extensive use of it draws attention to itself. Grafton's prose is not just representing routine, but, as Olsen claims in her discussion of "ordinary style," using lists and repetition to "embody the ordinary, to perform it" (6).

On a larger scale — at the level of novel rather than paragraph or sentence — this performative routineness is also very much part of the Alphabet series. The novels begin with (or include somewhere in their first pages) an introduction to Millhone, including information about her professional activities, marital status, living arrangements, and personal preferences. As Fiona Peters points out, each of these ritualistic self-introductions differs slightly (129), but they are highly repetitious, indeed stylized, and make a powerful appeal to our sense of the ordinary and familiar. This passage from *W is for Wasted* — "My name is Kinsey Millhone. I'm a private investigator, female, age thirty-eight. I rent office space in a two-room bungalow with a kitchenette and a bathroom on a narrow side street in the heart of Santa Teresa..." — differs very little from a much earlier example from *D is for Deadbeat*: "My name is Kinsey Millhone. I'm a private investigator, licensed by the state of California, operating a small office in Santa Teresa, which is where I've lived all my thirty-two years. I'm female, self-supporting, single now, having been married and divorced twice" (*Wasted* 3; *Deadbeat* 1). This routine presentation of routine information offers new series-readers access to required information, and to habitual series-readers the pleasure of familiarity and recognition. Narrative closure is achieved through a similarly repetitious pattern, with the now iconic last words "Respectfully submitted, Kinsey Millhone" (*Trespass* 372). These patterns, like the more detailed narration of daily life, contribute to the series' aesthetics of the ordinary.

Everyday Investigation

My argument to this point has focused on the parts of Grafton's novels that have nothing to do with crime, detection, or punishment. This is, of course, one of the central claims I am making about the Millhone novels: that despite their clearly marked generic status and the rich paratextual apparatus that situates them as crime novels, despite the fact that readers are told repeatedly that Kinsey is a private eye, and that she solves at least one major crime in every novel, these works are at least as engaged with everyday life as they are with murder. Nonetheless, a reading that simply opposed the quotidian *studium* to the abrupt *punctum* of crime would indicate that Grafton's work operates on two disparate and perhaps irreconcilable planes. This is not, however, the case, for Millhone's investigations are frequently as mundane as her life and are narrated in a style that emphasizes ordinariness.

It is possible to connect the everydayness of Millhone's investigations with traditions of feminist interpretation. Grafton's self-conscious evocation and appropriation of the gendered voice of the hardboiled narrator has been widely remarked on (Walton and Jones 125), as has her non-traditional, independent lifestyle (Peters 129). But the re-gendering of the investigative processes around which the plots of the novels develop has gone generally unremarked. This is surprising, as the link between the feminization of the everyday and the everydayness of the private eye's activities is very much in evidence in the early novels of the series. In *A is for Alibi* Kinsey notes that "the basic characteristics of any good investigator are a plodding nature and infinite patience. Society has inadvertently been grooming women to this end for years" (30). This is followed by a description of investigative activity that relates "personal errands" to the work of investigation: "checking and cross-checking, filling in blanks, detail work that was absolutely essential to the job but scarcely dramatic stuff" (30). In *B is for Burglar*, Kinsey links private investigation not just to women in general, but to housewives in particular, thus yoking a cultural icon of extreme masculinity to the central icon of feminine domesticity: "There's no place in a P.I.'s life for impatience, faintheartedness, or sloppiness. I understand the same qualifications apply for housewives" (*Burglar* 34). Grafton's point here is that, to adapt a phrase from another pioneer of the feminist hardboiled, being a PI is indeed a suitable job for a woman, not because she can shoot a gun or take a beating (or dish one out) every bit as well as her male peers, though she certainly can, but because the nature of the job is tailored towards a set of skills, inclinations, and attitudes that have been socially constructed as feminine.

This aspect of Grafton's emphasis on the routine aspects of private investigation, like other instances of overt feminism, is less prominent in later novels in the series. But the insistence on the normalcy of investigation persists. This is evident, for example, in her signature investigative techniques. While details vary from novel to novel, Millhone spends a great deal of time talking with people — not interrogating them, or taking witness statements, or trying to break their alibis, or any of the other typical interaction patterns of crime fiction, but talking to them. In *S is for Silence*, for example, Kinsey tries to solve the disappearance of Violet Sullivan thirty-four years ago largely by "making the rounds, asking about Violet," a process that a bartender tells her "must be frustrating" (173). Kinsey's reply emphasizes the ordinariness of the process, and of the information she obtains from it: "Monotonous is more like it. People are trying to be helpful, but information is scarce and the story tends to be the same. Violet had a trashy reputation and Foley beat her. Try to make something out of that" (173).

Trying to make something out of a mass of ordinary facts and opinions is precisely what Kinsey does in another characteristic investigative technique, the use of index cards to record and review information. This process is sometimes presented as a way of seeing a case in a new light — the physical manipulability of the cards allows for unusual and unforeseen combinations of facts that can, at least in theory, spark an unexpected insight. But this technique is also an indication of the ordinariness of Millhone's investigations: "I got out my index cards and reviewed my notes, which were beginning to bore me senseless. None of the items were monumental. I'd been asking the same six to eight questions for two days, and while nothing revolutionary had come to light, I had to admit I was better informed" (*Silence* 170). The cards record Millhone's incremental investigative progress and at the same time emphasize the fact that investigation is normal, not an adventure, so normal, in fact, as to be boring. Of course, the conclusions of Millhone's investigations tend to be much more dramatic than this discussion suggests, and the novels generally end with scenes of suspense and violence. But these compensatory bursts of terminal action cannot conceal the fact that Millhone's detective practice is highly routine.

One way of thinking about this investigative everydayness is to see it in light of the norms and patterns of twentieth-century American working life: as the frequent reliance on index cards indicates, Millhone's work is in many respects an office job. This perhaps explains the narrative interest displayed in Kinsey's physical office spaces over the course of the series, which are frequently described in ways that emphasize their status as ordinary spaces. In *Q is for Quarry,* for instance, we learn that her office has two rooms: "The larger I designated as my office proper; the smaller I was using as a combination library-and-reception area. In addition, there was a galley-style kitchen, where I kept a small refrigerator, my coffee pot, and my Sparkletts water dispenser. There was also a small fusty half-bath with a sorrowful-looking toilet and sink" (2). This description is overwhelmingly neutral, and (until the modest adjectival modification of the bathroom) operates as a functional description of a functional workspace in a way that is generically atypical. It is entirely free, for example, of the "imagistic descriptions" typical of Raymond Chandler's prose, and thus of the rich evocativeness of the hardboiled PI's office (Hilgart 369). In Chandler's *Farewell, My Lovely*, for instance, Marlow's office is decorated with a calendar image of Rembrandt: "His face was ageing, saggy, full of the disgust of life and thickening effects of liquor. But it has a hard cheerfulness that I liked, and the eyes were as bright as drops of dew" (193). The connection between this self-portrait and Marlow's self-image is clear, and contributes to the sense of the office as a space in which both external and internal dramas are played out, where we are unsurprised to find moments of pure aestheticism, as when we read that "a wedge of sunlight slipped over the edge of the desk and fell noiselessly to the carpet" (194). There is no equivalent of this in Grafton's descriptions of Millhone's office spaces, which remain resolutely banal, "devoid of personal touches," the "desktop. . . clear, all the paperwork consigned to folders tucked away in the file cabinets lining one wall" (*Wasted* 40).

This bland, anodyne, and functional office is the ideal setting for Millhone's professional life. Her status as a professional, as a person who exercises a particular set of skills for monetary remuneration, is emphasized throughout the series. As Millhone puts it, "If I don't work, I don't eat" (*Wasted* 13). What this professional imperative means is that while the novels are frequently directed towards major crimes in terms of their large-scale plotting — frequently the re-investigation of unsolved crimes from the past — these investigations are embedded within routine professional activity. This sort of work appears both when Millhone introduces herself and her job towards the beginning of the novels ("I operate on a modest scale, supporting myself by doing missing-person searches, background checks, witness location, and the occasional service of process" (*Wasted* 3), and during the actual narratives, as in *T is for Trespass,* when Millhone serves a restraining order on one Vinnie Mohr. Millhone's narration here goes beyond even the limited drama available from the actual process of locating, identifying, and serving Mohr, which has at least the potential for generating narrative interest — Mohr could refuse to identify himself, try to escape, or even resort to violence (none of which occurs). The same cannot be said of the aftermath, narrated by Millhone with equal attention to detail:

> In the car again, I logged the time I'd spent and the mileage on my car.
>
> I drove back into downtown Santa Teresa and parked in a lot near a notary's office. I took a few minutes to fill out the affidavit of service, then went into the office, where I signed the return and had it notarized. I borrowed the notary's fax machine and made two copies, then walked over to the courthouse. I had the documents file-stamped and left the original with the clerk. (30)

This is exactly the sort of activity that leads Millhone to describe the "big threat" of her job as "being bored half to death" (*Wasted* 8).[5]

Of course, Grafton is carrying out a sort of narrative sleight of hand by emphasizing the routine nature of Millhone's work: any reader of the series is aware that her professional life is anything but ordinary. Indeed, due to the compressed time frame of the series, with each novel, particularly later in the series, set within a few weeks or at most months of the previous one, Kinsey's actual career, as opposed to her presentation of it, is improbably exciting, with life-threatening incidents and major investigations occurring with the regularity demanded by the genre. Yet Grafton is consistent in highlighting the everyday nature of the investigative process, and indeed, of the crimes themselves. In *A is for Alibi*, for example, Millhone points out that "except for cases that clearly involve a homicidal maniac, the police like to believe murders are committed by those we know and love, and most of the time they're right—a chilling thought when you sit down to dinner with a family of five. All those potential killers passing their plates" (*Alibi* 13). This is of course an oblique reference to Millhone's own profound discomfort with traditional family structures, but it also relocates the criminal from the outside—the stranger who threatens our familiar world—to the inside. As Millhone claims later in the same novel, "there is less tendency to violence among the institutionalized insane than there is in the citizenry at large" (171). And throughout the series, while generically-typical crimes do occur, they are contextualised, even insulated, by a layer of everyday crimes, those that "take place daily that don't generate a smidge of interest in the public at large" (*Vengeance* 36). Crime here becomes, in other words, normal.

Conclusion

To this point I have argued that Grafton's Alphabet series displays an unusual level of interest in the routines, patterns, and textures of everyday life, in terms of both Millhone's private life, and perhaps more surprisingly, her professional life as a PI. These are, in other words, crime novels that are more concerned with the representation of everyday life than with the depiction of crimes and investigations. Raymond Williams famously claimed that "culture is ordinary" (6). The argument I have put forward here indicates that crime fiction, too, can be ordinary, despite its association with the abnormal, the exceptional, and the unusual, and in this very ordinariness be fascinating. As Jorge Luis Borges writes, "...the lodestone mountain and the genie sworn to kill the man who released him from the bottle were, as anyone will admit, wondrous things, but not much more wondrous than this morning and the fact of being" (176).

This focus on the everyday sheds light on the persistent success of Grafton's series. While her early novels were engaged with a feminist re-thinking of the hardboiled detective novel, this element of her fiction has moved steadily into the background, and thus cannot alone explain her success. Nor has Grafton's work kept pace with developments in crime fiction more generally. The intense, graphic violence that plays such a prominent role in Scandinavian noir, for example, has little place in her work. We must look elsewhere, then, for reasons for the success of the series, and their emphasis on the quotidian is a plausible explanation for their popularity. These are novels that are read for the pleasures of recognition, of familiarity, of routine, for the satisfaction that comes from seeing mundane aspects of our own lives—eating, house cleaning, office work—transformed through narrative.

It may also help us resituate crime fiction, at least in some of its many forms, alongside the mainstream novel from which it sprang in the nineteenth century, and alongside which it has developed. The first point to recognize is that the nineteenth century novel was itself, in its dominant forms, a genre of the ordinary: De Certeau describes these novels as "indexes of particulars" full of the "poetic or tragic murmurings of the everyday" (70). The plot function of a given novel is, in this reading, merely an excuse or pretence: "'stories' provide the decorative container of a *narrativity* for everyday practices" (70, italics in original). This link between the novel and the everyday is, as Franco Moretti argues, of a special quality: it is not directed towards a revelation of the squalidness, or inequality, or transience of life, but simply what he describes as "*a culture of everyday life*" (35, italics in original). Grafton's Alphabet series can thus be seen as an instance of the novel's historical role as both repository and example of the ordinary. It is an ordinary genre that deals with ordinary people and events and assumes a position as an ordinary part of culture.[6]

Another way of conceptualizing Grafton's interest in the ordinary would be to see it as emerging, albeit circuitously, out of the modernist revolution. While de Certeau and Moretti look to the nineteenth century novel, for Lefebvre modernist writing is the place where the ordinary comes into its own, with James Joyce's *Ulysses* representing "the momentous eruption of everyday life into literature," the point at which the "traditional novel recounting the story of the hero's progress, the rise and fall of a dynasty or the fate of some social group" gives way to the quotidian, the everyday, the ordinary, which now "steals the show" (2-3). Joyce was not, of course, alone in this reconceptualization of what Virginia Woolf calls "the proper stuff of fiction": there is a strong tradition of female modernists who also made the experience of the ordinary central to their fiction (154). Woolf's own work deals largely with what she calls in her seminal essay "Modern Fiction" the experience of "an ordinary mind on an ordinary day," or the "life of Monday or Tuesday" (149,150). But we could also think about writers like Dorothy Richardson, whose 13-volume *Pilgrimage* can be seen as a compendium of the everyday, or Gertrude Stein, whose experimental 1912 novel *Tender Buttons* is organized into sections dealing with food, objects, and rooms. These writers, and many other modernists, question the presumption that, as Woolf writes, "life exists more fully in what is commonly thought big than in what is commonly thought small" (150). The same can be said of Grafton's approach to writing crime fiction.

A number of critics have noted the formal parallels between modernist experimentation and detective fiction (Hilgart 368). Fredric Jameson's work on Chandler approaches the "modernism" of detective fiction, however, from another direction, arguing that the structure of the detective story is a "pretext" or "organizational framework" for moments of "isolated perception" (*Detections* 4). "There are," he writes "certain moments in life which are accessible only at the price of a certain lack of intellectual focus: like objects at the edge of my field of vision which disappear when I turn to stare at them head-on" (*Detections* 4). These moments are not the red-letter events, the marriages, funerals, and accidents that draw attention to themselves, but the smaller, less obviously significant moments of daily life, the random encounters, the moments of boredom, the routines. These are what the detective form is able to save from narrative oblivion by, as it were, looking aside to focus on the exceptional states of crime and investigation, a process which, counter-intuitively, makes the ordinary states of daily life visible. As Ludwig Wittgenstein writes in the 129th aphorism of his *Philosophical Investigations*, "[T]he aspects of things that are most important for us are hidden because of their simplicity and familiarity. (One is unable to notice something—because it is always before one's eyes.)" (50). The focus of Grafton's novels on the everyday experience of life challenges the invisibility of the familiar, making that which is closest to us, so close as to be imperceptible, visible again. In *V is for Vengeance* Kinsey Millhone asks "what could be more banal" than her daily routines (20). We might well reply by asking what could be more important?

Notes

1. See Heta Pyrhönen's *Murder from an Academic Angle: An Introduction to the Study of the Detective Narrative* (1994) for a comprehensive account of the development of crime fiction studies.

2. This is a very partial list: at the end of the twentieth century Priscilla Walton and Manina Jones estimated that the number of fictional female investigative figures in print had risen from roughly a dozen in the late 1970s to over three hundred in the mid-1990s (28-30).

3. More specific criticism has been directed at Grafton based on the idea that Kinsey's "latent feminism is individual rather than communal" (Klein 206). See Priscilla L. Walton's "E is for En/Gendering Readings: Sue Grafton's Kinsey Millhone" for a response to both Irons' and Rabinowitz's attempts to complicate feminist readings of Grafton.

4. I am relying here on the *Renaissance Accelerated Reader Bookfinder* for word counts (http://www.arbookfind.com/default.aspx).

5. This emphasis on the professional nature of her work can be linked to Grafton's own "self-conscious status as a 'professional' writer," and thus back to her participation in a feminist assertion of women's abilities and rights (Walton and Jones 1).

6. While the nineteenth-century context referred to here may seem remote from Grafton's novels, the same principle of ordinariness is at work in contemporary writing. Consider, for example, the embrace of the everyday so central to auto-fiction, perhaps best exemplified by Karl Ove Knausgård's six-volume *My Struggle*, in which the minutiae of everyday life are recorded in detail that should be boring but is instead captivating.

Works Cited

Barthes, Roland. *Camera Lucida: Reflections on Photography*. Translated by Richard Howard, Hill and Wang, 2010.

Borges, Jorge Luis. "The South." *Collected Fictions*. Translated by Andrew Hurley, Penguin, 1998, pp. 174-79.

Buchanan, Ian. "Introduction to Part III Other People: Ethnography and Social Practice." *The Certeau Reader*, edited by Graham Ward, Blackwell, 2000, pp. 97-100.

Chandler, Raymond. *The Big Sleep and Other Novels*. Penguin Books, 2000.

Chesterton, G. K. "Introduction." *Edwin Drood & Master Humphrey's Clock*, by Charles Dickens, J. M. Dent and Sons, 1915, n.p.

Christianson, Scott. "Talkin' Trash and Kickin' Butt: Sue Grafton's Hard-boiled Feminism." *Feminism in Women's Detective Fiction*, edited by Glenwood Irons, U of Toronto P, 1995, pp. 127-47.

De Certeau, Michel. *The Practice of Everyday Life*. Translated by Steven Rendall, U of California P, 1984.

Gavin, Adrienne E. "Feminist Crime Fiction and Female Sleuths." *A Companion to Crime Fiction*, edited by Charles J. Rzepka and Lee Horsley, Wiley-Blackwell, 2010, pp. 258-69.

Giard, Luce. "Part 2: Doing-Cooking." *The Practice of Everyday Life Volume 2: Living and Cooking*, by Michel de Certeau, Luce Giard, and Pierre Mayol. Translated by Timothy J. Tomasik, U of Minnesota P, 1998, pp. 149-248.

Grafton, Sue. *A is for Alibi*. Macmillan, 1986.

---. *B is for Burglar*. Papermac, 1988.

---. *D is for Deadbeat*. St. Martin's Paperbacks, 2005.

---. *I is for Innocent*. St. Martin's Press, 2008.

---. "Interview: A Conversation with Sue Grafton 1996." *Sue Grafton: Author of the Kinsey Millhone Series*, web.archive.org/web/20061231203224/http://www.suegrafton.com/interview.htm. Accessed 8 November 2018.

---. *Q is for Quarry*. Berkley Books, 2003.

---. *R is for Ricochet*. Berkley Books, 2005.

---. *S is for Silence*. G. P. Putnam's Sons, 2016.

---. *T is for Trespass*. Berkley Books, 2008.

---. *V is for Vengeance*. G. P. Putnam's Sons, 2016.

---. *W is for Wasted*. Berkley Books, 2014.

Hammett, Dashiell. *The Maltese Falcon, The Thin Man, Red Harvest*. Alfred A. Knopf, 2000.

Hilgart, John. "Philip Marlowe's Labor of Words." *Texas Studies in Literature and Language*, vol. 44, no. 4, 2002, pp. 368–91. *Academic Search Premier*, doi: 10.1353/tsl.2002.0022.

Irons, Glenwood. "New Women Detectives: G is for Gender-Bending." *Gender, Language, and Myth: Essays of Popular Narrative*, edited by Glenwood Irons, U of Toronto P, 1992, pp. 127-41.

Jameson, Fredric. *Raymond Chandler: The Detections of Totality*. Verso, 2016.

Klein, Kathleen Gregory. *The Woman Detective: Gender & Genre*. 2nd ed., U of Illinois P, 1995.

Lefebvre, Henri. *Everyday Life in the Modern World*. Translated by Sacha Rabinovich, Transaction Publishers, 1994.

Matheson, Sue. "Food Is Never Just Something to Eat: Sue Grafton's Culinary Critique of Mainstream America." *Journal of Popular Culture*, vol. 41, no. 5, 2008, pp. 809—22.

Mayol, Pierre. "Part 1: Living." *The Practice of Everyday Life Volume 2: Living and Cooking*, by Michel de Certeau, et al.. Translated by Timothy J. Tomasik, U of Minnesota P, 1998, pp. 5-148.

Messent, Peter. *The Crime Fiction Handbook*. Wiley-Blackwell, 2012.

Moretti, Franco. *The Way of the World: The Bildungsroman in European Culture*. Translated by Albert Sbragia, new ed., Verso, 2000.

Olsen, Liesl. *Modernism and the Ordinary*. Oxford UP, 2009.

Peters, Fiona. "Kinsey Millhone, Sue Grafton (1940-2017)." *100 Greatest Literary Detectives*, edited by Eric Sandberg, Rowman & Littlefield, 2018, pp.129-30.

Pyrhönen, Heta. *Murder from an Academic Angle: An Introduction to the Study of the Detective Narrative*, Camden House, 1994.

Rabinowitz, Peter J. "'Reader, I blew him away': Convention and Transgression in Sue Grafton." *Famous Last Words: Changes in Gender and Narrative Closure*, edited by Alison Booth, UP of Virginia, 1993, pp. 326-44.

Sandberg, Johanna. "Bernard Grimes Rhodenbarr, Lawrence Block (1938–)." *100 Greatest Literary Detectives*, edited by Eric Sandberg, Rowman & Littlefield, pp. 161-2.

Six, Beverly G. "Breaking the Silence: Sara Paretsky's Seizure of Ideology and Discourse in Blacklist." South Central Review, vol. 27, no. 1/2, 2010, pp. 144–58. JSTOR, doi: 10.1353/scr.0.0084.

Stewart, David M. "Cultural Work, City Crime, Reading, Pleasure." *American Literary History*, vol. 9, no. 4, 1997, pp. 676–701.

Taylor, Bruce. "G Is for (Sue) Grafton: From the Archives: This story was first published in *The Armchair Detective*, vol. 22, issue 1, Winter 1989." Murder & Mayhem, 8 August 2017, murder-mayhem.com/sue-grafton-interview. Accessed 15 November 2018.

Walton, Priscilla L. "E is for En/Gendering Readings: Sue Grafton's Kinsey Millhone." *Women Times Three: Writers, Detectives, Readers*, edited by Kathleen Gregory Klein, Bowling Green State U Popular P, 1995, pp. 101-15.

Walton, Priscilla, and Manina Jones. *Detective Agency: Women Rewriting the Hard-Boiled Tradition*. U of California P, 1999.

Williams, Raymond. "Culture is ordinary." *Studying Culture: An Introductory Reader*, 2nd ed., edited by Ann Gray and Jim McGuigan, Arnold, 1997, pp. 5-14.

Wilson, Ann. "The Female Dick and the Crisis of Heterosexuality." *Feminism in Women's Detective Fiction*, U of Toronto P, 1995, pp. 148-56.

Wittgenstein, Ludwig. *Philosophical Investigations*. Translated by G. E. M. Anscombe, Blackwell, 1992.

Woolf, Virginia. "Modern Fiction." *The Common Reader: First Series*, edited by Andrew McNeillie, Hogarth P, 1984, pp.146-54.

Christianity in Sue Grafton's Alphabet Mysteries

Peter Bush

Abstract

In an interview with *The Armchair Detective* while working on *F is for Fugitive*, Sue Grafton said, "I view the mystery novel as a vantage point from which to observe the world we live in. What I hope to do is engage in a kind of truth-telling about what I see....I have taken some potshots at religion, but I try to be fair in that I bad-mouth all of them equally." By the time she had reached *M is for Malice*, Grafton was more nuanced in her truth-telling about American Christianity. Millhone's world is populated with churchgoing people, as one would expect of Americans in the 1980s. While having brief and checkered relationships with Sunday school and church as a young person, Millhone is a careful observer of funeral services, in particular, and of clergy, in general. People's actions being congruent with their words is an important value for Millhone as she meets the faithful and hypocrites among church leaders and church attenders. *M is for Malice*, which this essay will explore in depth, can be viewed as a re-telling of Jesus's parable of the prodigal son, in which Grafton asks the question, what happens after the son returns home? This reading will explore the role church plays in the redemption of Guy Malek and the unusual theology Pastor Peter Antle espouses. *M is for Malice*'s portrait of church contrasts with the increasingly slick mega-churches which were appearing on the American religious scene in the 1990s.

    Detective fiction is replete with priests and ministers, pastors and clergy, even rabbis and imams who solve crimes and seek justice for victims. Religious leaders seek meaning and try to make spiritual sense of the world, skills enabling them to make sense of the disorder and violence inherent in crime. Further, leaders of religious communities need to be careful observers of people, intuitively reading behind words and actions. These skills are the very things that make for good detectives. Additionally, through their words and actions these religious leaders turned detective offer a religious commentary on the world. The Sue Grafton-created private investigator Kinsey Millhone offers a detective's view of Christian, primarily Protestant, churches and practice in American culture. Millhone in her work as a detective meets people grieving the death, the murder, of loved ones, moments when ministers are present visiting bereaved families and friends. Millhone also attends funerals to observe potential suspects. Millhone's experience of church life has an important relationship to her detective work.
    Millhone does not believe in Christianity, but neither is she an atheist. More accurately she could be described as an agnostic. Her upbringing and early experience in mainline Protestant churches left her skeptical of faith and she resists any attempt to convert her to Christianity. At the same time, she recognizes the helpful role church as an institution can play in the life of a community and the positive impact faith can have on the life of the individual. Millhone remains, throughout the series, an outside observer of Christianity, offering insightful description and at times critique while repeatedly affirming her unbelief.
    Grafton said in a 1989 interview, "I view the mystery novel as a vantage point from which to observe the world we live in. What I hope to do is engage in a kind of truth-telling about what I see….I personally don't feel it's the job of a mystery writer to convert anyone to anything." Through Millhone, Grafton spoke

truth about a variety of things in American culture: clothing and buildings, fast food restaurant menus and Hungarian cuisine, and the abuse of the elderly and the motivational power of revenge. Grafton did not avoid religion as part of the cultural matrix of Millhone's world. Grafton acknowledged her critiques of religion saying, "I have taken some pot-shots at religion, but I try to be fair in that I bad-mouth all of them equally" ("Interview with Sue Grafton"). The interview took place while Grafton was writing *F is for Fugitive* (1989), which includes the completely unsavoury pastor, the Reverend Robert Haws. A more accurate description would be that Grafton critiqued Christianity, most frequently Protestant expressions of Christianity. Other world religions are notably absent from the series. Natalie Hevener Kaufman and Carol McGinnis Kay in their *G is for Grafton* (2000), a handbook to the alphabet series, recognize the role religion plays in the series.[1]

Millhone insists, a number of times, she knows little about the various branches of Christianity with which she interacts. Yet as Kaufman and Kay note, Grafton's grandparents on both sides were Presbyterian missionaries in China. Grafton, because she knew Christianity "so well from the inside," can give Millhone a church vocabulary rare in someone who claims to know as little about Christianity as Millhone does (373).

Participation or non-participation in religious communities and religious practices is largely a matter of personal choice in contemporary America, allowing for religion to be moved into the private sphere. As a number of scholars have noted, one of the significant contributions of women mystery writers has been the complicating of the question of public and private spheres (Bertens and D'haen 28).[2] Grafton, through Millhone's presence at funerals and interactions with people who are religiously committed, demonstrates that in the area of religion private and public are intertwined even in the life of outside observers like Kinsey Millhone.

This discussion begins by piecing together Millhone's religious upbringing, which may be best described as a series of unfortunate incidents. The attention then turns to the variety of funerals

Millhone attends. Grafton's eye for detail and her ability to create an effect with her descriptions are skilfully used in describing the funerals. The focus then moves to the encounters Millhone has with clergy in other contexts. An analysis of *M is for Malice* (1996), which it will be argued is in part a retelling of Jesus's parable of the prodigal son, concludes the discussion.

Millhone's Religious Background

Kinsey Millhone was raised by her unmarried Aunt Gin, her mother's sister, following the death of Millhone's parents in a car accident. It being the 1950s in the United States, Aunt Gin saw value in Kinsey learning the basics of the Christian faith and sent her to Sunday school. But Millhone's "early religious training would have to be considered spotty at best, consisting as it did of sequential expulsions from a variety of church Sunday schools" (*P is for Peril* 202). Despite the unpleasantness of her Sunday school experience, some things made a lasting impression. During the three Sundays in Methodist Sunday School, before her aunt was asked to take her down the street to the Presbyterians, Millhone discovered the Song of Solomon which the Methodists thought "too smutty" for young children (*D is for Deadbeat* 120). Millhone, however, read enough of the Biblical book that more than twenty years later she recognized a passage being quoted by Essie Daggett in the throes of grief. While Millhone may have remembered the passage, that did not mean she had developed a religious conviction. As she told readers during a funeral sermon highlighting the need for salvation through the blood of Christ, "I don't believe in this stuff" (187).

Millhone's "most unfortunate" experience was in the Baptist Sunday School when, in the weeks leading to Christmas, the story of the birth of Jesus was recounted. As the teacher, Mrs. Nevely, began to explain how it was that Mary was "with child," Kinsey put up her hand and when called upon pointed out how incorrect Mrs. Nevely was about how babies came to be. "By the time Aunt Gin came to fetch me, I'd been set out on the curb, a note pinned to my dress, forbidden to say a word until she had picked me up to take me home" (*P* 302-03). The Virgin Birth is a predictable point of debate between the world of faith represented by Mrs. Nevely and Kinsey's recounting of Aunt Gin's explication of the scientific facts. Has Grafton intentionally chosen to give the teacher a name close in sound to "naively"? Kinsey being set outside the church and silenced serves as a metaphor for how some view the church's relationship with science.

By this point Aunt Gin was giving up hope there was a Sunday school where her niece could find a welcome. So "feeling huffy" on Kinsey's behalf, Aunt Gin "decided I was entitled to go to proper church services." Kinsey speculated, "I suppose her intention was to expose me to spiritual admonition." Kinsey did learn some religious rituals, such as how the offering is taken up and a pastime many children, and maybe not a few adults, have engaged in, counting the number of decorative pipes in the pipe organ (*N is for Noose* 159). Millhone describes her relationship with things spiritual in this way: "I've never been taught proper prayer etiquette. As far as I can tell, it consists of folded hands, solemnly bowed heads, and no peeking at other supplicants. I don't object to religious practices, per se. I'm just not crazy about having someone else inflict their beliefs on me" (*F* 99). In a 2010 interview, Grafton identified this unwillingness to be told what to believe and to do, saying of her editors, "They leave me alone. I don't like editorial interference....I still have the attitude that I know what I'm doing, and I want to be left alone to do it" ("Interview with Sue Grafton"). This desire for independence in her writing and, by extension, in her beliefs, Grafton was prepared to extend to others; she said, "I am not trying to persuade anybody of anything" ("W is for Writer"). In the same interview, Grafton described Millhone as "a stripped down version of me....Her biography is different, but our sensibilities are identical. At the core, we're the same," so it is not a stretch to say that the author's beliefs coincide with her character's ("Interview with Sue Grafton"). Grafton wished to be left alone to be an outside observer of religion, a "sensibility" Millhone has also expressed.

For many who as children attended Sunday school in the 1950s and early 1960s, organized religion became a memory of a past time, rather than a present-tense lived experience of faith. This left many, like Millhone, outside the church in adulthood, able to recognize the hymns and the other acts of worship but not understanding the church's message and unwilling to join its mission. Despite being "expelled from numerous denominations of Sunday Schools, I bore no grudge," says Millhone (*S is for Silence* 72). She is more forgiving than many of her generation. The generational loss of faith is made clear in *Q is for Quarry* (2002). Millhone meets members of her mother's family she knew nothing about, since Millhone's mother and Aunt Gin were alienated from their mother and father and the rest of the family. When contact is made, portions of Millhone's family history are revealed, including that her great-great-grandfather (her mother's great-grandfather) was a Presbyterian minister. Three generations later, Aunt Gin had no particular loyalty to the Presbyterians, never mentioning Kinsey's great-great-grandfather's vocation. As a result, Millhone, sitting in a Presbyterian church building, told readers, "I don't know much about the Presbyterian faith" (*P* 299). Learning this family history had no impact on Millhone's faith or religious practice. The religious convictions of the ancestors did not impact the religious practices of present generations.

Despite a limited religious background, Millhone demonstrates a functional church vocabulary which she uses accurately. In fact, in her use of certain theological terms, such as "atonement," Grafton has given Millhone a more sophisticated theological vocabulary than her checkered childhood experience with church would offer her. Millhone may have a sophisticated theological vocabulary, but she does not believe.

Millhone's Professional Interactions with Religion

In her professional life Millhone encounters Christianity, primarily Protestantism, in a variety of contexts. From attending funerals where religious rites are practiced, through observing clergy care for parishioners, through needing to fit her interaction with people around their participation in church life, people's religious lives impinge on Millhone's work.

Readers catch glimpses of religion's wide-ranging impact on the lives of ordinary Americans through Millhone's reporting of her cases. Church people offer care to John Daggett's widow, supporting her in her grief through donations of "tuna casseroles and chocolate cakes" and providing an audience for the expression of that grief (*D* 109-10). This occurs because Essie Daggett is part of a church community. Church communities also provide a context for people to gather in groups, to initiate projects, and fund-raise as Selma Newquist does in *N is for Noose*. Churches have a physical presence beyond their church buildings, as demonstrated in the references to a church camp in *Y is for Yesterday* (2017, 177). Yet, even as people's religious lives appear in Grafton's work, it is with the awareness of declining church attendance. For example, Sloan Stevens, who works at a church camp in the summers and goes to church almost every Sunday, is regarded as a Miss Goody Two-Shoes by her peers (177). Congregation members and church groups and programs provide background to Millhone's investigations, but it is church clergy who at times appear in the foreground of Grafton's writing.

Notably, all the clergy in the 25 Millhone mysteries are men. A number of American Protestant denominations, including Presbyterians, by the 1980s had ordained women to serve as congregational pastors. Grafton's decision to have only male clergy in the series contrasts to Millhone, a woman fulfilling a role traditionally regarded as a man's job. Those clergy who demonstrate care and compassion, who engage in the lives of people, who observe and respond to those in need, are described most sympathetically by Grafton. These clergy develop characteristics often identified as feminine traits. Clergy who are aloof, not observant of others' emotions, or who possess an aggressive male sexuality are described negatively by Grafton. Clergy fulfill a helpful role when they adopt the traditional female role of caregiver.

Later in the series, Millhone worries about people who have no connection to church. As people's connection to church becomes more tenuous or is non-existent, where do they find support and spiritual services in a time of crisis? Grafton writes poignantly about this in the aftermath of the death of Jon Corso's mother. Jon's father being away, the hospital tries to find someone to care for 13-year-old Jon until his father returns. Jon does not know how to reach his brother who lives out of town and he does not know of any other relatives in the area: "His parents didn't go to church, so there wasn't even a minister to call" (*U is for Undertow* 155). On another occasion, while attending a funeral led by a Rev. Anderson "with no church affiliation specified," Millhone wonders about the "protocol." "Was there a Rent-a-Reverend agency for folks who weren't members of a proper congregation?" (*V is for Vengeance* 105). Millhone does not define what constitutes "a proper congregation." The clergy of "proper congregations" have important roles to play at times of death, supporting people when a loved one dies and providing appropriate funeral rites. A funeral, while emotional and at times filled with rituals that are uncomfortable, is an important part of responding to a death and finding healing. A funeral in Millhone's world means the presence of a minister; despite her unbelief, she feels that funerals provide ritual closure, if not a rite of faith.

Funerals

Millhone's lack of belief in Christianity does not mean she has no connection with people of faith or religious institutions and their clergy. Funerals are a place where religious practice is on display. In her professional life Millhone frequently attends funerals to support clients, to observe suspects, and to pay respects to the deceased.

Bobby Callahan's funeral in *C is for Corpse* (1986) provides Grafton her first opportunity to describe funeral rituals. Funerals, Millhone notes, can become for some mourners a reminder of all previous deaths, saying of her own response, "It was more than this loss. It was all death, every loss—my parents, my aunt" (130). Funerals, as times of deep emotion, are best when they are "mercifully short." The graveside service preceding the burial was less "potent" since it lacked organ music, for "even the most banal of church hymns can rip your heart out at times like this" (131). This funeral leaves Millhone charting her own emotional space. In attending the funeral in her public, professional capacity, she is brought face-to-face with private life.

The introspective experience of attending Callahan's funeral contrasts with Millhone's observer and commentator role at John Daggett's funeral in *D is for Deadbeat*. The funeral takes place in "the sanctuary of some obscure outpost of the Christian church" (187). Readers never learn the denominational affiliation of the church. Millhone sees a clear distinction between what are referred to as "mainline" churches and other Christian churches. In *X* (2015), she notes the community of Burning Oaks had a St. Elizabeth's Roman Catholic Church: "All of the other churches were outposts of off-brand religions. Apparently, the good citizens of Burning Oaks did not hold with the Baptists, the Methodists, or the Presbyterians" (263). Brand-name and, by implication, more trustworthy churches include Baptists, Methodists, and Presbyterians along with the Catholics. It is not clear why the "mainline" (or "brand-name") Roman Catholics are present in Burning Oaks. The others, those without brand names, are suspect.

Grafton heightens the dubious nature of the church hosting Daggett's funeral: this "Kmart of churches" was "the sort of chapel you glimpse through the bushes when you're going someplace else" (*D* 186). As Millhone walks towards the one-story yellow stucco building, which gave no outward sign of being a church, she could hear the electronic organ "thumping out in a style better suited to a skating rink than a house of God." Millhone's "discomfort" is evident as she describes worrying whether the congregation was "keen on converts." The funeral director's demeanor indicates his view that "the services were spiritually second-rate." Millhone dismissively describes the opening hymn as "a ditty that went on and on about blood and sin." Inside the building there are folding chairs instead of pews. The stained-glass windows "depicted forms of spiritual torment," making Millhone "squirm." Her fears regarding conversion appear legitimate as she notes, "I could feel a burgeoning urge to repent" (*D* 188).

Millhone is "curious" what Pastor Howard Bowen will say about John Daggett, "whose transgressions were many and whose repentances were few." After describing all present as "wretches," Bowen succeeds in making the link to Daggett through Deuteronomy 28:44: "He shall lend to thee, and thou shalt not lend to him; he shall be the head, and thou shalt be the tail." Bowen does not avoid Daggett's sin, speaking directly to the wrong he had done. Portraying Daggett as an example of everyone's need of forgiveness, Bowen issues an invitation to all to repent and find salvation. The concluding hymn becomes an emotional outpouring, as the congregation "was really getting into the spirit of things and hosannas were being called out on all sides....This was beginning to feel like soul-aerobics" (*D* 189). The emotion and energy are too much for Millhone, who tries to leave.

The energy and emotion of Daggett's funeral contrasts with the spareness of Olive (Wood) Kohler's funeral depicted in *E is for Evidence* (1988). Olive, killed by a bomb, is remembered in "a Spartan ceremony in a setting stripped of excess" at the Unitarian Church (225). The sanctuary's "floors were red tile, glossy and cold. The pews were carved and polished wood, without cushions. The lofty ceiling of the church lent a sense of airiness, but the space was curiously devoid of ornamentation and there were no religious icons at all" (225). In this spare space a spare "ceremony" takes place: "Unitarians apparently don't hold with zealousness, piety, confession, penance, or atonement. Jesus and God were never mentioned, nor did the word 'amen' cross anybody's lips. Instead of scriptures, there were readings from Bertrand Russell and Kahlil Gibran" (225-226). The service has no space for an expression of hope linked to the resurrection of Jesus, a common theme for Christian funerals. Millhone notes none of the family and friends give a eulogy, "but the minister chatted about Olive in the most conversational of tones, inviting those congregated to stand up and share recollections of her. No one had the nerve" (226). The content provided by the minister is informal and warm contrasting with the Spartan coldness of the space. The minister's conversational tone does not provide enough warmth for anyone to share memories.

Placing two such contrasting funerals in consecutive books suggests intentionality on Grafton's part. Not only does she contrast the styles of the funeral, but also the socio-demographic backgrounds of those present at each service. A number of times in her description of Daggett's funeral Millhone references the cheapness of the service: a "Kmart" church with brown vinyl flooring and a mimeographed funeral program. The cemetery "felt like a cut-rate country club, low membership fees for the upstart dead. The rich and respectable were buried someplace else." Yet the congregation is supportive of Daggett's widow, Essie, who is "nearly borne aloft like a football coach after a big win" (*D* 189). At Olive Kohler's funeral the mourners are among the well-to-do of Santa Teresa who, over champagne following the ceremony, make empathetic comments like, "'he'll never recover from the loss...,'" to comments critical of the dead, such as, "'He worshipped the ground she walked on, though I never could quite see it myself...'" (*E* 226-27). Below their external façade, the elite have a rough nature as well. The open display of care and compassion present at the "Kmart" church is absent from the ceremony attended by the elite.

In describing these two funerals, Grafton places theological extremes present in American Christianity in juxtaposition. While Daggett's funeral is excessively emotional for Millhone, she recognizes an honesty present in the emotion that was lacking in Kohler's funeral rites. While not believing in the theology Bowen preaches, she does not find the Unitarian service helpful either.

Millhone attends the funeral of friend and fellow private investigator, Morley Shine, in *I is for Innocent* (1992). The service takes place in a funeral home's "generic chapel designed to serve just about any spiritual inclination you might favor in death." The space is "vaguely churchlike" having a "faux apse" and "faux nave" and a stained-glass window made up of "blocks of rich color." No religious symbols are present—"no angels, no crosses, no saints, no images of God, Jesus, Muhammad, Brahma, or any other Supreme Being" (173).[3] Millhone, later attending another funeral in this same space notes, "Even an atheist would have felt right at home" (*V* 104). The reader may wonder if, in addition to providing description, there is here also a hint of wistfulness that holding a funeral in a space, "stripped of religious symbolism and sacred ornamentation" takes away from the spiritual experience.

In this generic space, an unnamed rent-a-reverend leads a generic service for Morley Shine which includes passages "from some new version of the Bible with every lyrical image and poetic phrase translated into conversational English" (*I* 174). Through Kinsey, Grafton quotes this "conversational" version of the opening verses of Psalm 23: "'The Lord is my counselor. He encourages me to go birding in the fields. He leads me to quiet pools. He restores my soul and takes me along the right pathways of life. Yes, even if I pass by Death's dark wood, I won't be scared...'" (174). On hearing this version, Henry Pitts, Millhone's octogenarian landlord, gives Millhone "a look of consternation." The literary beauty of the nearly 400-year-old King James Version translation of the Bible is missing. By 1992, when *I is for Innocent* was published, a plethora of contemporary English translations of the Bible were on the market. Grafton mocks them for not providing the spiritual comfort of the well-known words. The rent-a-reverend twice refers to Morley as Marlon and in his remarks gives Morley attributes Millhone does not recognize as being part of Morley's make-up. Millhone, signaling her feelings about this funeral, concludes with the words "when we were finally liberated." This contemporary funeral is unsatisfying due to its informality and disconnection from the life of the deceased.

As she discovers at Dr. Dowan Purcell's funeral at a Presbyterian Chapel in Montebello, traditionalism can be equally dissatisfying and disconnected from the lived life of the deceased. The church building is described as follows:

> The sanctuary was narrow, with high stone walls, a beamed ceiling....Outside, the day was damp and grey and the six stained-glass windows, done in tints of deep scarlet and indigo, reduced most of the available light to a somber gloom. I don't know much about the Presbyterian faith, but the atmosphere alone was enough to put me off predestination. (*P* 299)

The architecture reinforces the environment of gloom. While not knowing much about Presbyterians, Millhone knows enough to link predestination and the gloominess often associated with it to Presbyterians. The formality and somberness of Presbyterian worship are emphasized by the arrival of the minister "in a robe like a judge, accompanied by his spiritual bailiff, who intoned the corollary of the courtroom "All rise." "We stood and sang. We sat and prayed" (302). The judge-like minister speaks, making "the sort of generic remarks that were safe for any but the most depraved decedent" (303). Again there is relief when "the service finally ended." A traditional funeral with little connection to the deceased is no more satisfying than the contemporary approaches. What Millhone seeks in a funeral is honesty about the deceased; such honesty is possible when the minister leading the service has some knowledge of the deceased, a knowledge that grows from personal connection with the deceased and their loved ones.

Clergy in Other Contexts

The most common place to meet a minister, pastor or priest besides a funeral would be a Sunday worship service or similar congregational gathering. Millhone in her professional role, however, never attends a Sunday worship gathering in a church. The closest she gets is standing outside Quorum Baptist Church on Easter Sunday hearing the music through the open windows. Her connection with ministers, besides funerals, is through meeting them in the course of her investigative work.

The Reverend Robert Haws, minister of the Baptist Church in Floral Beach, pushes himself into the foreground of Millhone's investigation in *F is for Fugitive*. He and his wife, June, arrive to provide comfort to Ori Fowler as the police search for Fowler's son, Bailey, who has escaped police custody. Haws is wearing a black shirt and clerical collar for the pastoral visit which Millhone found "an affectation for a Protestant" (103). After an "interminable prayer" Haws reads some passages of scripture including "an alarming passage from the Old Testament full of beseigedness, pestilence, consuming locusts, and distress. Ori's lot must have seemed pretty tame by comparison, which was probably the point" (102). None of this does Millhone appreciate.

She is particularly turned off when Haws arrives at her motel room door to introduce himself and invite her to the Baptist Church, noting that "[h]e had all the easy charm of someone who spent his entire adult life on the receiving end of pious compliments." She shakes his "moist" hand and "he held on to mine and gave it a pat making lots of Christian eye contact." Millhone's impression of Haws is solidified when he inquires if Millhone's husband is traveling with her. When she replies he is not, Haws "put his hands in his pants pockets, subtly adjusting himself....'I hate to see you run off so soon'" (104). His actions may have indicated he is interested in more than just another parishioner.

Millhone's investigation reveals the teenage murder victim, Jean Timberlake, had a sexual relationship with Haws. Millhone's informant answers her inquiry about who it was that Timberlake was intimate with, saying "'The Right Reverend Haws. What a pal he turned out to be. He knew I lusted after her, so he counseled me in matters of purity and self-control. He never mentioned what he did with her himself'" (*F* 184). The informant goes on to describe the nature of the sexual activity between Haws and Timberlake. Haws is a sexual predator, whose prominent position in the small community of Floral Beach protects him from exposure.

Millhone, at one point in the investigation, thinks Haws is responsible for Timberlake's death, confronting him with what she knows about his extra-marital activities, using a crude hand gesture "he seemed to grasp right away." Having confronted "this plague, this poison ivy of the soul" (251), Millhone departs as Haws's "smile was losing wattage" (254).

The detective's disdain for Haws is evident in her discussion of the "modest-sized white frame" Baptist Church. Having seen this design before, Millhone comments, "One thing about the Baptists, they're not going to waste the congregation's money on some worthless architect," imagining the same set of blueprints being used in multiple locations (249). The implication is that Haws uses people in both his public and private life. While Haws is not guilty of murder, his actions create and permit an environment in the community where the school principal can have a sexual relationship with a student. In the process Haws destroys any number of people.[4]

Father Luevanos in *H is for Homicide* (1991) is a very different figure from the Rev. Haws. While both their arrivals draw attention, their interactions with people are contrasts in style. Chago, a gang member, is killed and Millhone is present at the wake. Father Luevanos, the parish priest, arrives "in clerical black, a hyphen of snowy white collar visible at his neck." Luevanos, in his sixties, is the prototypical Catholic priest, "like St. Francis of Assisi only minus the birds." He offers comfort to his parishioners, knowing them and acknowledging them. He does this not by reading lengthy passages of Scripture aloud, but through quiet one-on-one conversations. Father Luevanos does not seek the attention of the crowd; he focuses on the needs of the grieving. When Raymond comes up to him, Luevanos "took his hands and the two murmured together in a mixture of English and Spanish. I could see Raymond's grief surface in response to the priest's compassion" (245). Similarly, with Bibianna, "[s]he was close to tears and her mouth began to tremble when he took her hands. He leaned toward her, murmuring something in Spanish. She must have felt an almost overwhelming impulse to unburden herself" (245). The priest offers comfort in the midst of sorrow, providing a place for people to express their grief and have it authenticated. Millhone's reference to "an almost overwhelming impulse to unburden herself" raises the question, was Luevanos blind to who these parishioners were? Whether or not Luevanos is aware of what his parishioners do, he is good at providing pastoral care, because following his visit to the wake, and the comfort he brought, "the mood of the place began to lighten" (245).

Other clergy Millhone meets are either blind to the actions of their parishioners or unwilling to address parishioners' actions. This lack of awareness or unwillingness to see the deeper things going on in people's lives is one of Millhone's critiques of clergy. In *Q is for Quarry*, the McPhee family hide a dark secret, poisoning relationships within the family and between the McPhees and the surrounding community. The McPhees are influential members of Quorum Baptist Church, yet their unnamed pastor has not confronted the McPhees with the dark cloud hanging over the family. Similarly, Father Xavier in *X* fails to recognize the dynamics at work between Ned Lowe and his wife Lenore. Lenore seeks the priest's help as Ned cuts her off from every source of support in her life, but Ned succeeds in turning the priest into an ally against Lenore. During her interview with Father Xavier, Millhone has to suppress a laugh of derision at the priest's misreading of the situation. Father Xavier genuinely wants the best for his parishioners, but is easily deceived by Ned Lowe. Some clergy in Millhone's world are either naïve, being blind to the reality before them, or cowardly, unwilling to address situations in their congregations.

Not all the clergy Millhone observes are blind or cowardly; some are deeply engaged in helping people confront their inner demons and offering grace, which many people around them regard as undeserved. The pastor of Cromwell Presbyterian Church in *S is for Silence* is one such clergyperson. The pastor remains unnamed, a sign of how uninterested he is in being the center of attention. He is an anonymous caregiver, not seeking reward, but he and the church building he serves from are places of welcome to those who need a place of security.

Millhone's eye for detail extends to a lengthy, and at times nostalgic, description of the Cromwell Presbyterian Church building, which was "plain in the nicest sense of that word, white frame with a steeple, set on a wide lawn of green" (*S* 70). The sanctuary "was bathed in quiet," the pews "gleaming in the light." As she enters the "large social hall" Kinsey wonders if the congregation still had potluck suppers like those she remembered as a child: "Where else could you get beef-and-macaroni pies and green-bean casseroles made with cream of mushroom soup?" (71-72), she wonders. The quiet simplicity of the building is matched by the quiet simplicity of the hospitality given to those in need.

The person in need of such hospitality is Foley Sullivan, who most people in the area believe was responsible for the death of his wife Violet over thirty years earlier. Sullivan says,

> "You can ask anything you like, but I want to say this first: Pastor of this church is the only man in town with any charity in his heart. After Violet left, I got laid off and I couldn't get work. I did construction before, but suddenly no one would hire me to do anything. Based on what? I was never arrested. I was never charged." (74)

While Sullivan has been ostracized by the entire community, the pastor has taken the risky step of offering Sullivan not only a job as janitor but also a small apartment in the church where Sullivan could live. Sullivan is not a saint; during the interview with Millhone he admits he physically hit Violet. But he did not kill her. As Millhone's investigation continues, Sullivan is beaten and taken to the emergency room where he is patched up. His daughter, Daisy, unwilling to take him home to her place cannot let him return to his apartment at the church, for he needs on-going care. In the middle of the night, the Presbyterian pastor dressed in slippers, pajamas, and a robe opens his door to provide a place, for Sullivan, taking him into his home (285). The pastor shows a grace which is in short supply in Cromwell and the surrounding community. Grace is undeserved and yet is still offered. This is part of the church's message.

M is for Malice

M is for Malice is a deeply theological book. Two Biblical metaphors are woven into the narrative: Jesus's parable of the prodigal son and the image of the scapegoat. In her re-telling of the prodigal son story, Grafton explores what happens in the days following the prodigal's return, interrogating the dynamics of the family when the lost has been found. Jesus's original story suggests such a return could be difficult but leaves an open question for the hearer to ponder. Grafton provides readers with the results of her pondering. In the process of answering the question at the end of Jesus's parable, Grafton gives an example of the theological concept of scapegoat.

In Jesus's parable, the younger (second) son asks for his portion of the family inheritance while his father is still alive and then the son leaves for a far country. In that place the son wastes his funds and ends up doing the lowliest of jobs, feeding pigs. Meanwhile the older brother has served the father in the family business. The younger son in a moment of insight decides to return home, hoping to find a place to eat and sleep. To the surprise of both the younger son and his older brother, their father throws a welcome-home party for the lost son. The older brother is irate at the father's action, and the father pleads with him to come join the party. The unanswered question is: What did the older brother do? How would he treat his brother who had come home?

Bader Malek through dint of hard work and entrepreneurial acumen built a successful construction business in Santa Teresa. Bader had four sons. Guy, the second son, gives his parents "years of aggravation and grief" by always getting into trouble; "like James Dean, rebellious and tragic...misunderstood" (176). Millhone says of Guy, "[a]s an adolescent...he was a bad kid, lawless and self-destructive, one of life's lost souls" (48). In his early twenties Guy disappeared, having taken, it was assumed, a collection of valuable letters containing signatures of a number of famous people. The collection was the financial base the Maddison family intended to use to support college educations for of their children and to help their parents in their retirement. Guy having disappeared eighteen years earlier meant the three brothers who remained at home considered themselves the only heirs to the business. When Bader dies leaving a will naming Guy among those who were to share the inheritance, the family is shocked. It falls to Donovan, the eldest, who "was always working for his dad" (208) and loves "the company more than any man alive" (176), to manage the company and the estate so that it will not be harmed by Guy "the trouble-maker" (208). While the three sons, all adults still living at home, are irate about Guy's inclusion in the will, they cannot inherit until Guy is found. Millhone is called in to find the lost son.

A younger son, who did drugs and got in trouble, disappeared taking a significant amount of money to support his lifestyle. The thought of his return draws anger from the remaining brothers including the eldest who has spent his life working for his father and the father's business. The parallels to Jesus's parable are evident.

Within a day of being hired Millhone finds Guy working as the maintenance man for a church and doing odd-jobs for people in the tiny community of Marcella, about eighty miles north of Santa Teresa. Guy's story is that when he disappeared eighteen years earlier he had headed for San Francisco hitch-hiking. He was picked up by the pastor of the church in Marcella, Peter Antle, who took Guy in as he rode a bad drug trip. Guy's family was not religious; his parents, having read Philip Wylie's *Generation of Vipers* with its attack on religion, did not expose their children to religious teaching.[5] The Antles, Peter and Winnie, were the first clergy Guy had interacted with. Antle committed himself to helping Guy even though Guy would "backslide...you know get drunk and take off..." (51, ellipses in original). Finally, realizing the Antles would never give up on him and would keep on seeking him out, as Guy said, he "took a stand and found Jesus in my heart. It really turned my life around" (51).

Here Grafton's re-telling of the parable breaks with Jesus's original. Following his conversion, Guy does not return home to be welcomed by a gracious and forgiving father; instead that grace and forgiveness are found in Peter and Winnie Antle. Guy makes no effort to let his family know he is alive; he remains in his lowly position of doing odd-jobs for people and living in humble circumstances.

Earlier in her series Grafton, as noted, was critical of churches not affiliated with a recognized denomination, but here she portrays Peter Antle in a very positive light. Antle ministers to an unnamed congregation in Marcella. The church building is simple but as Millhone walks in "something about its plain appearance spoke of goodness" (53). This small, simple church, which made such an impact on the life of Guy Malek, lost soul that he was, stands in contrast to the mega-church movement which arose on the American religious scene in the 1990s.[6] For Grafton, the small unnamed church in Marcella is where goodness could be found. There grace is lived.

Having run away from home, a perennial question in Guy's life is whether he should make an overture towards reconnecting with his family or if he should wait, hoping his family will make an overture towards him. When Millhone tells Guy she has come at his family's request, Guy replies, "'You don't know how hard I prayed for this….The pastor of my church…he swore up and down it would come to pass if it was meant to be. No point in praying if it isn't God's will'" (50). Antle's guidance is unexpected. A pastor saying don't pray for what you want, rather trust God's will to unfold in God's time and wait, is unusual. This approach stands as markedly different from the Health, Wealth, and Prosperity Gospel, which encourages followers to name in their prayers the things they want and to claim the promises of God's blessings for the believer and those the believer prays for. Antle does not regard prayer as a way to get God to do what the pray-er wants; instead Antle affirms God will do what God will do. Human beings are invited to trust the goodness of God to bring goodness to human beings.

Guy has done nothing to let his family know that he is alive, let alone seeking to return home. When Guy learns the rest of the family has done nothing to find him and the hiring of Millhone is about legal requirements, not because they were "burdened by a lot of warm, gooey feelings" for Guy, he is hurt (51). As Millhone leaves Guy to report to the rest of the family on her work, she reflects on a question Guy has not asked: "How large his inheritance was going to be." While the easy way Guy speaks of his conversion is off-putting to Millhone, Guy's humility and integrity are attractive. She comments, "I happened to believe that Guy had changed his wicked ways" (72).

Upon hearing that Guy is alive, Donovan extends an invitation to Guy to come to a family meeting at the Malek house in Santa Teresa. Guy telephones Kinsey for her opinion about accepting the invitation, saying, "'I want to be connected again. I screwed up, I admit that and I want to make it up to them. Peter [Antle] says there can't be any healing unless we sit down together'" (96). Kinsey, fearful of what might happen at this gathering, tries to dissuade Guy from attending. Against her advice, Guy arrives in Santa Teresa for the meeting, which gets delayed. During the delay Guy and Kinsey talk; Guy says, "I'm trying to show 'em I've changed and then I find myself feeling like I always did.... maybe this is some kind of test of my faith." Kinsey's responds, "Oh, it is not, it may be a test of your patience, but not your faith in God." Kinsey, the outsider to faith, sees the strength of Guy's faith in God in a way that he does not (130). Finally, Kinsey returns to her car and drives away leaving Guy behind: in hindsight, she notes, "Guy Malek was doomed and I delivered him into the hands of the enemy" (110). In retrospect Kinsey explores her traitorous behaviour.

Guy is murdered that night by Claire Maddison, who is seeking revenge for the destruction of her and her family's life and security. As the investigation into his death unfolds, it is revealed Guy did not steal the inheritance of valuable papers; rather his younger brother, Jack, who had artistic skills, did it with the help of a friend. Guy, who was the scapegoat for his family when he was away, becomes the scapegoat sacrificed for the family. In the ancient Hebrew practice two goats were placed among the people of Israel who were to touch both animals, symbolically placing their sins upon the animals. One goat was driven out of the camp into the wilderness and the other goat was killed on the altar. The goat that was killed was a sacrificial payment for sins, and the one that was driven out of the camp symbolized that the sins were gone from the people. Guy, in running away, had taken the sins of the family with him; when he returns home he is killed for the sins of others.

Kinsey is devastated by Guy's death, for there had been a connection: "If he'd lived, I am not sure we would have had a very strong relationship. Kinsey Millhone and a born-again was probably not a combination that would have gone anywhere. But we might have been friends," she thinks (217). Millhone is again left outside looking in at faith. She realizes a long-term relationship with Guy would mean she could not remain an outsider to faith. She would need to cross a line she is not willing to cross, for she is not willing to become a faith insider. Yet in the epilogue Kinsey describes a spiritual experience which offers her closure; through her tears she says "a prayer for the dead." Having no expectation of seeing any of the deceased in her life again, Millhone says good-bye. Being an observer and outsider does not preclude Millhone from having spiritual experiences or engaging in religious practices, like prayer, which she finds helpful in this context.

In *M is for Malice*, Grafton gives readers a theological narrative wrapped up in a murder mystery. In the character of Peter Antle a particularly appealing picture of a minister is drawn.

Standing Outside the Church

Kinsey Millhone's insights into Christianity, more particularly Protestantism, are from the perspective of someone standing outside the church. In *Q is for Quarry*, Millhone and Stacey are outside Quorum Baptist Church on Easter Sunday: "Some of the church windows were open, we were treated to organ music and an assortment of hymns. The sermon itself didn't carry that far" (290). Millhone describes parts of a worship service correctly, but the church's message is unclear. Millhone remains a knowledgeable outsider, not a believer, an observer, never a participant.

In writing about religion in this way, Grafton practices her particular kind of truth-telling about Christianity. The truth told is nuanced, being both critical and appreciative. It is always told from the perspective of an outside observer. Millhone's childhood encounters provide opportunity for both critique of religion and for memories of hospitality and religious knowledge. Through attending funerals and interacting with clergy, Millhone gives readers a window through which to see faith. She applauds the church and clergy when they are hospitable, gracious, and engaged with the hurting and the lost. She is critical when the church and clergy are distant, naïve about the lives of people, and have not made a connection with the people they are to care for. As an observer, Millhone holds a position similar to the majority of Americans who, while aware of church and clergy, remain outside hearing only the music but never really understanding the message.

Notes

1. See, for example, comments on pp. 62-64 and 372-73.

2. The authors demonstrate the descriptive gendered eye Millhone employs. Grafton's background as a screenwriter serves her well in writing description for effect. As she says of her writing, it is "economical and concrete." Elsewhere, D'haen further develops the point about the gendered eye in "Plum's the Girl! Janet Evanovich and the Empowerment of Common America," pp. 145-58.

3. While Grafton is usually correct with her religious references, here she makes an error. Muhammad, while central to Islam, is not divine as the list implies. Muhammad is a prophet of God. This error aside, Grafton effectively makes clear the chapel's generic nature.

4. *F is for Fugitive* was published in 1989, the same year as Marie Fortune's *Is Nothing Sacred?* was released.

Fortune's book caused many denominations to face the truth that among their clergy were sexual predators. No claim is being made that Grafton was aware of Fortune's book, but the timing of the two books does point to a growing awareness in the public mind of the sexual harassment and abuse in which some clergy engage.

5. Wylie's *Generation of Vipers* (1942) is described in *Kirkus Review* that same year: "This is a 'sermon' to a materialistic America which has lived neither according to science nor according to Christianity, and which, in gaining a world, has lost its soul. This is iconoclastic invective, against sexual promiscuity, against narrow educational systems, against certain American prototypes (the doctor, the business man, the statesman, the American 'mom')."

6. *M is for Malice* was published in 1996 and Grafton would have been aware of mega-church congregations like Willow Creek Church in South Barrington, Illinois, and Saddleback Church in San Diego, which were grabbing headlines by building churches seating thousands, as the future of American Christianity. See Barbara Dolan's article.

Works Cited

Bertens, Hans and Theo D'haen. *Contemporary American Crime Fiction*. Palgrave, 2001.

D'haen, Theo. "Plum's the Girl! Janet Evanovich and the Empowerment of Common America."*Investigating Identities: Questions of Identity in Contemporary International Crime Fiction*, edited by Marieke Krajenbrink and Kate M. Quinn, Rodopi, 2009, pp. 145-58.

Dolan, Barbara. "Full House at Willow Creek." *Time Magazine*, vol. 133, no. 10, 6 March 1989, content.time.com/time/magazine/article/0,9171,957169,00. Accessed 31Dec. 2018.

Fortune, Marie. *Is Nothing Sacred?: When Sex Invades the Pastoral Relationship*. Harper & Row, 1989.

Grafton, Sue. *C is for Corpse*. 1986. St. Martin's, 2005.

---. *D is for Deadbeat*. 1987. St. Martin's, 2005.

---. *E is for Evidence*. 1988. St. Martin's, 2005.

---. *F is for Fugitive*. 1989. Bantam Books, 2005.

---. *H is for Homicide*. 1991. Ballantine Books, 1992.

---. *I is for Innocent*. Henry Holt, 1992.

---. *M is for Malice*. Henry Holt, 1996.

---. *N is for Noose*. 1998. St. Martin's, 2011.

---. *P is for Peril*. 2001. Ballantine Books, 2002.

---. *Q is for Quarry*. 2002. Berkley Books, 2003.

---. *S is for Silence*. G. P. Putman's Sons, 2005.

---. *U is for Undertow*. 2009. Berkley Books, 2010.

---. *V is for Vengeance*. G. P. Putman's Sons, 2011.

---. *X*. G. P. Putman's Sons, 2015.

---. *Y is for Yesterday*. G. P. Putnam's Sons, 2017.

"Interview with Sue Grafton." *The Armchair Detective*, vol. 22, Issue 1, Winter 1989, murder-mayhem.com/sue-grafton-interview. Accessed 30 December 2018.

Kaufman, Natalie Hevener and Carol McGinnis Kay. *G is for Grafton: The World of Kinsey Millhone*. Henry Holt, 2000.

Review of *Generation of Vipers*, by Philip Wylie. *Kirkus*, 31 Dec. 1942, kirkusreviews.com/book-reviews/philip-wylie/generation-of-vipers/. Accessed May 6, 2019.

"W for Writer: A 2010 Interview with Sue Grafton (1940-2017)." *Writer's Digest*, Feb. 2010, writersdigest.com/editor-blogs/there-are-no-rules/interviews/w-writer-2010-interview-sue-grafton-writers-digest. Accessed 30 December 2018.

Wylie, Philip. *Generation of Vipers*. Rinehart, 1942.

Narrative Technique in Sue Grafton's Kinsey Millhone Short Stories

Ramie Tateishi

Abstract

The Kinsey Millhone short stories by Sue Grafton remain largely underrepresented in discussions of her body of work. These stories, written and published between 1986 and 1992 in the developing years of the Alphabet novel series, provide an opportunity to examine Grafton's literary constructions of theme, character, and setting as conveyed through this concentrated, tightly focused form, each example of which shows her techniques honed down to their essence. Analyzing these succinct narrative snapshots can lead to different types of insights about Grafton's writing style, as she takes advantage of the properties of this shortened storytelling format to craft her depictions of Kinsey Millhone, her detection skills, and the world in which she operates.

Traits of the Kinsey Millhone novels

One of the key techniques seen in Grafton's approach to the novel is her inclusion of a subplot that directly or indirectly relates to the main plot. The length of the long form novel affords Grafton the space to carry out two parallel stories and, accordingly, she takes advantage of this expectation of length to add greater depth and dimension to the main plot through this technique. Kaufman and Kay describe how "the novels typically contain two story lines, one from the current primary case and a second one from a minor case being investigated at the same time or from Kinsey's personal life or the personal life of one of her friends. The ways in which the main plot and the subplot tie together either factually or thematically becomes clear by the novel's conclusion" (309). The subplot may be directly relevant to the outcome of the main plot "factually" or it may provide indirect commentary on the main plot "thematically," but both approaches allow Grafton to craft a more complex story beyond the strict confines of whatever Kinsey's central case may be.

On the rhetorical level, one of the outcomes of narrative length is a more in-depth approach to exposition, description, and reflection. An exemplary instance of this can be seen in the novel *F is for Fugitive*, where Grafton reveals how a case involving a dying father affects Kinsey personally by stirring memories of her own father, who was killed in a car accident along with Kinsey's mother. The inclusion of these thoughts characterizes the detective through lengthier passages of self-reflection, a quality afforded through the length of the long fiction form, in which consideration can be given to aspects of the story not directly related to the case at hand. Toward the end of the novel, Kinsey relates the events of her current case to her memories of the car accident.

> I thought about my papa. I was five when he left me... five when he went away. An image came to me, a memory repressed for years. In the car, just after the wreck, when I was trapped in the backseat, wedged in tight, with the sound of my mother's weeping going on and on and on, I had reached around the edge of the front seat, where I found my father's hand, unresisting, passive,

and soft. I tucked my fingers around his, not understanding he was dead, simply thinking everything would be all right as long as I had him. When had it dawned on me that he was gone for good? When had it dawned on Ann that Royce was never going to come through? And what of Jean Timberlake? None of us had survived the wounds our fathers inflicted all those years ago. Did he love us? How would we ever know? He was gone and he'd never again be what he was to us in all his haunting perfection. If love is what injures us, how can we heal? (260)

The reflection is fleshed out through Kinsey's remembrance of sensory images (touch and sound) as well as her perception of the claustrophobic space, focusing on details going beyond a reporting or summarizing/stating of the mere fact that the accident occurred. Similarly, Grafton uses a series of rhetorical questions to convey Kinsey's connection between aspects of the case and her own personal thoughts. This technique reflects the detective's thought process of pondering and her attempts to find answers for herself, more so than simply positing the fact that she perceives a connection between the case and her own issues.

Another technique seen in the novels is the epilogue at the end of each story, which takes the form of a brief write-up in which Kinsey presents the last pieces of factual information related to the conclusion of the case, as well as her closing thoughts on it. Structurally, an important aspect of these epilogues is that they must take place at some point after Kinsey's direct narration of the events of the story. These epilogues are thus the product of time taken to reflect upon and summarize the case under stable conditions, rather than to respond and react directly to events. In the *F is for Fugitive* epilogue, Kinsey writes that "two weeks had passed" since she wrapped the case (261). In those two weeks, her thoughts on the case have come to affect her everyday relationships, as seen in her write-up:

> I find that I'm looking at Henry Pitts differently these days. He may be the closest thing to a father I'll ever have. Instead of viewing him with suspicion, I think I'll enjoy him for the time we have left, whatever that may be. He's only eighty-two, and God knows, my life is more hazardous than his. (261)

An unspoken quality of the epilogues is that they contain what Kinsey feels is the most befitting or proper manner of presenting the conclusion of a case, given the benefit of collecting her thoughts as opposed to simply reacting to events. In this epilogue, Grafton shows that the case continues to affect Kinsey, as the thoughts that it generated have changed her perception of her landlord Henry — a character that does not appear in the short stories. The presentation of these concluding thoughts after the passage of time, along with more instances and lengthier examples of description, exposition, and reflection, are techniques used by Grafton in the Kinsey Millhone novels that are either absent in the short stories (as in the case of the epilogues) or are perceived in different ways (as the lengthier paragraphs, which are used sparingly in the short stories, stand out more and may seem to take on greater significance and rhetorical weight).

Traits of short fiction

In the preface to *Kinsey and Me*, an anthology featuring the collected Kinsey Millhone short stories, Grafton describes her outlook on short mystery fiction. She explains that "while the mystery novelist has room to develop subplots and peripheral characters, as well as the leisure to flesh out the private life of the protagonist, in the short story such indulgences are stripped away. The subtleties of the artfully disguised clue and the placing of road signs pointing the reader in the wrong direction may be present in the short story, but pared to a minimum" (xiv). In her work, this approach takes the form of limiting the agency of characters—which in turn reduces the possible actions they might take within their setting—and narrowing first-person rumination and reflection to a mere sentence or two (or often eliminating such reflection entirely). Because of this, described actions and statements made in the first person take on heightened significance, and narrative analyses of story conception/plot construction (manipulation of time/pacing) and rhetorical analyses of detail (manipulation of information) can lead to a more nuanced understanding of how Grafton crafts her short fiction with these parameters in mind.

Grafton's explanation of the mechanics of mystery short fiction resonates strongly with the work of various scholars. In summarizing Norman Friedman's key claims about the properties that define the length of the short story, Charles May writes that "a short story is short because the action is static or dynamic, because the author chooses to present in a contracted scale by means of summation or deletion, or because the author chooses a point of view that lends itself to brevity" (*Short Story* 121). Applying this formulation to an analysis of Grafton's work leads to a focus on the length of time/amount of words spent on different types of actions, and the degree to which Kinsey provides or does not provide personal reflection/commentary on that which she narrates.

The effect of such abbreviation upon characterization — and the ways in which characterization relates to theme due to the handling of information in a story told in the first person — is that insight into motivation often has to be surmised from the briefest of clues, or taken at face value, with the tone stemming from the blunt succinctness of the statement to be interpreted as a part of the message. Jean Pickering writes that "in a short story, readers must grasp the nature of characters in a moment of revelation; we are called on to supply much of their context through imagination or experience" (51), and related to an analysis of Grafton's short fiction, the concluding lines often constitute such moments, when the accumulated experience of events leads Kinsey to encapsulate their import in a mere sentence or two. One such example comes in "A Poison That Leaves No Trace," in which a scheming daughter is outsmarted and double-crossed by her own mother. In the end, Kinsey sums up the case: "Ah well, I thought. Sometimes a mother's love is like a poison that leaves no trace. You bop along through life, thinking you've got it made, and next thing you know, you're dead" (*Kinsey* 143). The harsh, brutal impact of the sentiment is conveyed not only through her dismissive tone, but through the brevity of the statement itself, its very form serving as part of the expression of the sentiment.

Another important trait to consider in analyzing short fiction is the use of descriptive detail, which must be sparing and strategic in light of the limits on elaboration and expansion. The significance of minute detail is arguably of greater concern in the mystery than in any other genre, as it explicitly invites the reader to constantly note the specifics of any paragraph, sentence, phrase, or word that might serve as the slightest clue to the solution. Mary Rohrberger notes how the short form "reinforces close attention to detail, [and] a heightening of aesthetic intensity" (44), which we can apply to an analysis of Grafton's short fiction by looking at how specific word choices play a role in constructing the mystery to be solved, or the tone through which the tale is conveyed, and what effect that first-person voice might have upon our perception of events. These features of the short story can form the basis for analyzing techniques in Grafton's short fiction, specifically how she constructs and comments on character, theme, and genre.

Character: "Long Gone" and "Between The Sheets"

One aspect of Kinsey's persona fleshed out in the short fiction is her attitude toward children, which is given different treatments in two stories. While "Long Gone" introduces her general dislike of children which ends up shaping her perspective on the case of a missing woman, "Between The Sheets" depicts Kinsey's friendship with a precocious four-year-old girl that provides a new angle on Lewis Moore's claim that "seeing the world through community affects character....Composing the hard-boiled character thus requires an amalgam of gender roles which in the modern period realistically means reshaping the character of the detective in light of female experiences and attitudes" (180). In these tales, Kinsey's relationships with these children take the form of abbreviated reactions and responses more so than evolving, thoughtful ones based on the length of time afforded by the novel, thus offering little time for reflection and simply taking these interactions at their face value.

The introductory portion of "Long Gone," in which Kinsey is hired by Rob Ackerman to find his missing wife Lucy, establishes the centrality of Kinsey's perception of children to the case and her approach to it, with her scattered references to the Ackerman kids appearing steadily and constantly to inform her thoughts as a result of the short story's compressed narration, giving little time for lengthy reflection on other topics or diversion into other actions. In providing the portrait of Santa Teresa in the first paragraph, Kinsey conceives of the fall season through images of the start of a new school year:

> SEPTEMBER IN SANTA TERESA. I've never known anyone yet who doesn't suffer a certain restlessness when autumn rolls around. It's the season of new school clothes, fresh notebooks, and finely sharpened pencils without any teeth marks in the wood. We're all eight years old again and anything is possible. The new year should never begin on January 1. It begins in the fall and continues as long as our saddle oxfords remain unscuffed and our lunch boxes have no dents. (37)

Through either the use of adjectives or brief descriptive phrases associated with every noun that Kinsey calls upon, Grafton crafts a sense of the anticipation and newness that the detective perceives as part of her environment. This feeling is directly intertwined with images of childhood which are both specific (going so far as to place them in the time frame of being "eight years old"), yet general (in that they are not necessarily identifiable as her own personal memories, but rather commonly-held impressions attributed to a generalized "we/our"). This greatly compacted introduction to setting — contained in a single paragraph — sets up Kinsey's idealized notion of childhood so that it can be quickly and nearly immediately undercut by the reality of the Ackerman case.

Two paragraphs after the introductory setting paragraph, the case is initiated when Kinsey receives a phone call from Rob Ackerman soliciting her help in finding his missing wife. She notes how "in the background, I could hear whiny children, my favorite kind" (38). As Rob tries to elaborate on the situation, "[H]e was interrupted by a piercing shriek that sounded like one of those policeman's whistles you use to discourage obscene phone callers. I didn't jerk back quite in time. Shit, that hurt" (38). Her use of sarcasm and an unflattering analogy to convey the presence of the children, from the background noise to the intrusive shriek, stands in sharp contrast with the idyllic images which were used to craft the image of childhood a mere two paragraphs prior. Russel Gray's claim that Kinsey's "partiality to childhood and domestic tropes signifies parallel control of the rhetoric of her narration in registering distasteful realities and their implications" is an interesting one in light of Grafton's near-immediate juxtaposition of these opposite responses to children in "Long Gone," where the positive "childhood trope" clashes with one of these "distasteful realities" — specifically the distasteful reality of what Kinsey perceives as the negative dimension of childhood — as a result of the lack of reflection, exposition, and description between the general introduction and its specific introduction to the case that could have taken place in the novel (Gray 68).

The effects of Kinsey's outlook on children carry through consistently as she visits their home. Her summation of the surroundings is shot through with her continued negative tone as she notes how "little children had banged and scraped these floors and had brought in some kind of foot grit that I sensed before I was even asked to step inside" (39), her awareness of the dirt elevated to near precognition by her edginess. Similarly, Kinsey detects how, "like dogs, these infants sensed my distaste and kept their distance, eyeing me with a mixture of rancor and disdain" (40), reinforcing the primal nature of her reaction. When Rob feeds cookies to the kids, she imagines that "in fifteen minutes the sugar would probably turn them into lunatics. I gave my watch a quick glance, hoping to be gone by then" (40), her attitude toward the children affecting the course of this initial investigation into the case by shortening the time she is willing to spend at the house.

Kinsey's outlook on children predetermines her conclusion that Lucy ran away to escape her home life. As she looks at a photo of Lucy from two years ago, Kinsey ponders how "she looked beleaguered even then, and that was before the third baby came along. I thought about quiet little Lucy Ackerman, whose three strapping sons had legs the size of my arms. If I were she, I know where I'd be. Long gone" (43). The connection between Kinsey's phrasing of her "hoping to be gone" and her conclusion that Lucy was "long gone" acquires greater rhetorical weight due to the condensed time frame in which she makes these points, strengthening this connection in relation to the conclusion. Although Kinsey deduces that Rob killed Lucy after learning of her infidelity and her plans to leave him and the children, the question of Lucy's motivation remains unanswered. Despite this, Kinsey's initial attitude toward children strongly informs the conclusion and the reasoning behind Lucy's actions, so that Kinsey ultimately does not express anything about this topic at all in the end. Instead, the conclusion deals with Rob's breakdown and confession, with only her quip, "For once, I was glad to see Lieutenant Dolan amble into view," providing any indication of her feelings about resolving the case.

"Between The Sheets" is an interesting counterpoint to Grafton's technique of characterizing Kinsey through depicting her perspective on children. Whereas "Long Gone" established and concentrated the presence of the children at its beginning, "Between The Sheets" depicts Kinsey's relationship with Althea, the four-year-old daughter of her client, in a single scene, a continuous episode in time without any breaks in the action. In the first paragraph of the brief introductory section in which

Kinsey takes Emily Culpepper's case, Grafton establishes the presence of Althea before she actually appears: "I squinted at the women sitting across the desk from me. I could have sworn she'd just told me there was a dead man in her daughter's bed, which seemed like a strange thing to say, accompanied, as it was, by a pleasant smile and carefully modulated tone. Maybe I'd misunderstood" (7). The centrality of the little girl, seen literally in the placement of the victim specifically "in her daughter's bed" in the middle of this opening paragraph, will unfold throughout the course of the story, informing Kinsey's perspective on the case in a different manner than was seen in "Long Gone."

The attention that Grafton affords to Kinsey's first encounter with Althea is notable in its form as well as its precision. After Kinsey's initial interview with Emily, she goes to the apartment where the murder took place, initiating a continuous and uninterrupted episode in which she investigates the crime and becomes acquainted with Emily's daughter. The paragraph in which Kinsey first meets Althea is a lengthy passage that stands out in comparison to the other, much more concise paragraphs surrounding it:

> Ordinarily, I don't take to children. I'm an only child myself, raised by a maiden aunt who thought most kids were a nuisance, sometimes including me. But Althea had a strange appeal. Her sturdy four-year-old body was topped by an ancient face. I knew exactly what she'd look like as an adult. Her cheeks were plump and she wore plastic glasses with pink frames, the lenses so thick they made her gray eyes seem huge. She had mild brown hair, straight as a stick, caught up in pink barrettes that were already sliding off. She wore a Polly Flinders dress, smocked across the front, with short puffed sleeves biting into her plump upper arms. She seemed poised and humorless and I could imagine her, later in life, evolving into one of those mysterious women

> to whom men gravitate. In some terribly bossy, mundane way, she would break all their hearts and never quite understand their pain. (19-20)

This attention to detail, typically associated with describing her possible clues in a case, is used here to instead signify her fondness for the girl, placing the focus on how she notices the types of qualities that appeal to her (such as Althea's "ancient" face and Kinsey's ability to envision the girl looking like and acting like an adult rather than a child). Followed by a prolonged series of paragraphs consisting of little more than short lines of dialogue, Grafton signals the significance of Althea with the substantial paragraph. This approach to characterizing Althea continues with subsequent descriptions of the girl, as Kinsey perceives her thoughtfulness as being akin to the "solemnity of a cat" (20), another reference distancing her from being merely a child. When Althea tells a joke, Kinsey says, "I laughed, as much at the look on her face as the joke, which I'd told myself when I was her age" (21), again finding a link between the girl and herself, such as when she first notices that Althea is an only child, just as Kinsey once was.

This positive tone in the ways Kinsey thinks about Althea, in expressions both lengthy and brief, differs from the types of remarks that punctuate her impressions of the others in the case, such as when she reacts to Emily's initial consultation by noting how "my eyeballs began to bulge with pain. I wanted an Alka-Seltzer in the worst kind of way. I slid my desk drawer open a crack and spied a packet. I wondered what would happen if I opened the foil and slipped an Alka-Seltzer onto my tongue like a Necco wafer. I've heard it kills you to do that, but I'm not sure it's true" (13). Her distractedness contrasts with her keen eye when it comes to Althea. In describing Pat, the building manager of Emily's apartment complex, Kinsey sarcastically compares her voice to Minnie Mouse and someone who "just had a hit of helium" when condescendingly talking to Althea (22, 29), with the humorous references to her voice standing out as one of the few qualities allotted to Pat in the short form.

After emphasizing Kinsey's relationship with Althea in these ways, Grafton affirms its significance by turning it into the key to solving the case. Just as Kinsey's instinct regarding children played a role in the solution to the mystery of "Long Gone," her connection to Althea leads her to the steps necessary to resolve the case, but this time based on positive rather than negative associations. The brevity of her period of investigation and interviewing brings her back to Althea quickly, still in the same physical location with a minimal passage of time, as she concludes gathering clues and attempts to deduce the solution: "There was something about this setup that nudged at me. It was one of those situations I was sure had a simple explanation if I could only make the mental leap. I felt a tug and looked down to find Althea standing next to me, slipping her hand into mine" (29). The key to the "breakthrough," with the solution in Kinsey's grasp yet just out of reach, comes when Althea literally takes her by the hand and becomes her inspiration for rethinking her approach. At the end of this process, it is ultimately Althea herself who provides the solution by affirming that the victim was a golf pro and leading Kinsey to make the connection between his profession and a photograph of Pat at a golf tournament which she had noticed previously.

As with the conclusion of "Long Gone," the final lines of "Between The Sheets" provide no direct commentary or editorializing on Kinsey's part. The weight of the concluding sentences thus shifts to the significance of the final action, the last symbol of the bond between Kinsey and Althea:

> "Are you okay?" I asked.
>
> She nodded and then spoke up, her tone shy. "When I grow up, I want to be like you."
>
> Good plan," I said. "I'll tell you what. You come around to my office twenty years from now and we'll form a partnership."

"Okay," she said gravely and we sealed it with a handshake. (36)

The succinct, matter-of-fact exchange befits not only the short story form, but also the nature of Kinsey's relationship with Althea. The image of the handshake offers a sense of closure to both aspects of story and character with a simple yet profound gesture, invested with the intertwined values of Kinsey's perception of children as well as the resolution of the case.

Worldview: "The Parker Shotgun" and "Full Circle"

In hard-boiled detective fiction, the detective's quest for truth and desire for order are at odds with how the nihilistic, chaotic nature of the world seems to actively work against these goals, with events, circumstances, and actions impeding that quest at every turn. Kristen Garrison notes that "whatever the 'truth' of the case, it will likely come hard and explain very little....The problem becomes not so much the identity of the killer but of a reasonable account of truth, so that the hard-boiled novel explores the harsh reality of pursuing truth without the guiding light of absolutes" (106-07). Grafton uses aspects of the short story form to explore some of the implications of this condition in different ways. "The Parker Shotgun" reveals the murderer to be a stroke victim who will not live much longer, while the killer in "Full Circle" ends up dying in a car accident. Both feature a recurring object that provides Kinsey the opportunity to ponder very briefly the implications of the case each time the object appears, creating an explicit awareness of the passage of time that shapes her perceptions. Their conclusions showcase different responses to the hard-boiled milieu's lack of certainty and stability, with Kinsey as an active agent as well as an investigator. Her succinct remarks on both responses keep with the short story form that ultimately raises more questions than answers in the search for a satisfying resolution.

"The Parker Shotgun" uses the title object as a signpost that marks Kinsey's progression through her investigation of the murder of Rudd Osterling, whose widow Lisa hires Kinsey to find the murderer. Through the course of Kinsey's initial interview with Lisa, the subject centers on the circumstances behind Rudd's murder, which Lisa believes to be tied to his previous life as a small-time drug dealer. In the opening paragraph, "a woman walked in and tossed a photograph on my desk. My introduction to the Parker shotgun began with a graphic view of its apparent effect when fired at a formerly nice-looking man at close range. His face was still largely intact, but he had no use now for a pocket comb. With effort, I kept my expression neutral as I glanced up at her" (61). Grafton uses Kinsey's first-person voice to introduce the shotgun at the outset, with her mention of it in a scene where it does not yet become an object of interest (only its "apparent effects" as seen in the photograph). In this first appearance of the gun, the focus is on its expected function as a destructive tool, a superficial focus that belies its greater status and value — the value over which the murder actually took place.

Following the interview, the next use of the weapon as a framing device comes when Kinsey describes the start of her investigation at the Osterling house: "My second encounter with the Parker shotgun came in the form of a dealer's appraisal slip that I discovered when I was nosing through Rudd Osterling's private possessions an hour later at the house" (64). Grafton structures this section in a manner similar to the initial interview with Lisa, where lengthy interactions and dialogue relate to clues and leads connected to Rudd's past life, despite the signpost at the beginning of the section that signals the significance of the gun, which Rudd accepted in trade and was hoping to sell. The tension between the framing device and the unfolding of Kinsey's investigation in chronological steps comes back into play when the detective uncovers the appraisal slip that she introduced earlier: "On top of the chest was one of those brass-and-walnut caddies, where Rudd apparently kept his watch, keys, loose change. Almost idly, I picked it up. Under it there was a folded slip of paper. It was a partially completed appraisal form from a gun shop out in Colgate, a township to the north of us" (67). The nonchalant, seemingly inconsequential manner in which the slip of paper is introduced brings its significance into play (with Kinsey and Lisa discussing its history after uncovering it), while still maintaining the secret of its true value, in keeping with the thematic concern of differing versions of truth.

In terms of structure, with a conversation between Kinsey and the gun appraiser taking place at the midpoint of the tale, "The Parker Shotgun" literally centers on the revelation of the gun's worth. Avery Lamb, the appraiser, describes the reasons behind the shotgun's $96,000 appraisal value: "For one thing, the Parker's a beautiful shotgun. There are different grades, of course, but this one was exceptional. Fine wood. Some of the most incredible scrollwork you'll ever see. Parker had an Italian working for him back then who'd spend sometimes five thousand hours on the engraving alone. The company went out of business around 1942, so there aren't any more to be had" (71). In describing the properties of the gun, Grafton employs the sort of focus that might be seen when attempting to direct the eye to a vital clue, but here the technique is used to convey the authenticity and status of the Parker's worth.

The case unfolds as a series of attempts by various parties to deceive others as to the true worth of the shotgun. At two key moments, Kinsey summarizes what she believes to be the connections between the key players, explaining how their actions stemmed from attempting to conceal the true value of the gun's worth, which ended up in Rudd being killed in an attempt to get the gun back. In addition to Kinsey's final conversation with Lisa in which she reveals her working theory, the ending finds the detective confronting Bill, Rudd's killer (and the original owner of the gun), who has been immobilized by a stroke since committing the murder. The conclusion has Kinsey describing her actions as she switches the Parker for an ordinary shotgun in Bill's gun rack, foiling his wife's scheme to cash in the gun herself. The final use of the weapon comes in the last paragraph when Kinsey notes, "[T]he last I saw of the Parker shotgun, Lisa Osterling was holding it somewhat awkwardly across her bulky midriff. I'd talk to Lieutenant Dolan all right, but I wasn't going to tell him everything. Sometimes justice is served in other ways"

(84). The active role that Kinsey plays in the outcome of the case — and its repercussions for all involved — might on one hand go against her function as an investigator seeking the truth of the matter, but on the other hand, it befits Edward Wheat's definition of the hard-boiled detective as one whose actions do contain a constructive element: "In hard-boiled detective fiction the detective is presented with a version of the truth, a narrative, which he then deconstructs....The dick deconstructs the narrative given to him and reconstructs the truth as best he can. Society is not reordered; it remains corrupt; but at least there is a momentary stay against confusion. The modernist dick brings a personally constructed order out of social chaos. Call it 'justice'" (246).

"Full Circle" also uses the device of a recurring object to mark Kinsey's progression through the case, this time a photograph of Caroline Spurrier, the victim of a homicide. Kinsey perceives the girl's face differently at various stages in her investigation, which starts in the aftermath of an auto accident involving Kinsey herself. The story begins with Kinsey's recollection that "the accident seemed to happen in slow motion — one of those stop-action sequences that seem to go on forever though in truth no more than a few seconds have elapsed" (145). The juxtaposition of Kinsey's perception of the accident taking "forever" and the understanding that it actually took place within "a few seconds" starts the chain of events with an example of Grafton's manipulation of time as used to convey a sense of disorder. This technique is developed further throughout the next four paragraphs as the car next to her "veered abruptly," after which "suddenly, a dark green Mercedes appeared out of nowhere," further developing the contrast between the perceived speed at which the actions are taking place and the lengthy pace at which Kinsey relays the events.

Grafton emphasizes the chaotic nature of the accident consistently throughout its lengthy sequence, stressing how "brakes squealed all around me like a chorus of squawking birds and I could hear the successive thumps of colliding cars piling up behind me in a drumroll of destruction" (146). Kinsey is unable to escape the sensation, as that night "the jumble of images made sleep a torment of sudden awakenings, my foot jerking in a dream sequence as I slammed on my brakes again and again" (148). The connections between the repetitive elements of the actual incident and Kinsey's dream are strengthened through the proximity afforded to them by the short story form, with the chaos becoming a part of her and obligating her to take the case brought to her by Caroline's mother, who believes that her daughter was murdered. Grafton again takes advantage of the accelerated telling of the tale to draw a link between Kinsey's sensation of how "the weight of the young woman's death settled in my chest like a cold I couldn't shake" (148), and how "as a witness to the accident, I felt more than a professional interest in the case" (150). It is the firsthand experience with the chaotic nature of the world that drives Kinsey toward answers.

After initially seeing Caroline's photograph in a newspaper article about the accident, depicting her "shoulder-length blond hair, bright eyes, and an impish grin" (148), Kinsey keeps the photo by her desk, without any first-person explanation as to why. Grafton uses the photo as a reference to the passage of time as well as Kinsey's progress in the case, as with the gun in "The Parker Shotgun." Here, however, the object symbolizes the chaos of the world not through its stable identity amidst the chaos surrounding it, but through Kinsey's continually changing perception of the photo. At different steps in her investigation, she returns to her desk to find the picture that the picture of Caroline "looked down at me with a smile that seemed more enigmatic with the passing days" (156), and "her smile nearly mocking" after "a week passed with no results" (159). The references to the passage of time along with what Kinsey imagines to be Caroline's changing face in the still photograph depict the effects of chaos upon the detective, with the image of the girl representing Kinsey's frustrated lack of progress and its effects upon her.

At key moments in the investigation, including the break that ends up leading her to Caroline's murderer, Kinsey's instinct leads her to the necessary steps that help her to make progress.

Grafton emphasizes more of her intuitive qualities over logical reasoning in writing about these moments. The first of these steps comes when "I was sitting at my typewriter when an idea came to me, quite literally, in a flash" (157), leading her to find the newspaper photographer who took the photos at the site of the accident. The next moment comes when she investigates Caroline's roommate, and as she is about to leave: "I hesitated where I stood. There are times in this business when a hunch is a hunch — when a little voice in your gut tells you something's amiss" (160). Kinsey's discovery of Terry, the brother of Caroline's roommate, was a result of these intuitive insights, and the language used to describe them is more closely aligned with the chaotic rather than the logical.

Terry, infatuated with Caroline, murdered her, and the case concludes with Kinsey chasing him in a sequence closely resembling the opening accident, defining the chaotic nature of "zigzagging crazily" and Terry's car "hugging the shrubbery as he flew down the berm" (161), their actions going against the ordered structure of the environment. This parallel becomes the main point of the conclusion, as Terry crashes and Kinsey notes how "the road crew was replacing the big green highway sign sheared in half when Caroline Spurrier's car had smashed into it. Terry Layton died at the very spot where he killed her" (162). The ending thus plays out as a variant on Wheat's characterization of the "order out of chaos" aspect of the hard-boiled tale as well as Garrison's notion of the futility of ultimately finding the truth of the matter. In the final paragraph, Kinsey notes that "Caroline's smile had shifted back to impishness in the photograph above my desk. I keep it there as a reminder, but of what I couldn't say. The brevity of life, the finality of death—the irony of events that sometimes connect the two" (162). Although the changing picture of Caroline has stopped haunting Kinsey, the chaos that she encountered remains, manifesting itself in her inability to articulate the purpose behind keeping the picture visible, as well as the lingering presence of "irony" upon which her final thought hinges.

Genre: "A Little Missionary Work" and "Falling Off the Roof"

As noted in the introduction, Grafton herself has identified the plot points that constitute her approach to writing mysteries. If these points can be considered as conventions of the genre, "A Little Missionary Work" and "Falling Off the Roof" show Grafton toying with that notion of genre to produce a different type of Kinsey Millhone tale that makes reference to an awareness of those conventions in which both detective and author are working. These references stand out in the compacted space of the short story, with the manipulation of time, structure, and narrative properties coming to the fore.

At the outset of "A Little Missionary Work," Grafton utilizes the first-person point of view to introduce Harry, a key figure who would otherwise not enter into the chain of events until she calls upon his particular expertise in the course of pursuing the case. The method of introducing Harry establishes his importance without breaking the natural progression of events . In providing the *de rigueur* exposition of Kinsey's background and credentials in the first paragraph, Grafton writes, "I'm a licensed private eye, in business for myself, so I can't afford professional charity, but now and then somebody gets into trouble and I just can't turn my back" (163). The second paragraph then establishes time and place, with Kinsey in line at the bank, where "as usual, in the teller's line, I was thinking about Harry Hovey, my bank-robber friend, who'd once been arrested for holding up this very branch. I'd met him when I was investigating a bad check case. He was introduced to me by another crook as an unofficial 'expert' and ended up giving me a crash course in the methods and practices of passing bad paper. Poor Harry" (163). The connection between what appears to be the titular "missionary work" in the first paragraph and the sympathetic introduction to Harry in the second paragraph appears to identify the forger as the recipient of Kinsey's "charity," although this is just the first in a series of postponements that structure the story.

Grafton continues to structure the telling of the tale through manipulation of time with Kinsey's meeting with Jack Chamberlain, the bank manager who knows about her profession and introduces her to the case. As opposed to the near-immediate case introductions that occur within the first several paragraphs of these short stories, Chamberlain instead asks Kinsey to attend a party at which she will meet her prospective clients, telling her that "they don't want you appearing in any professional capacity. Time is of the essence, or we might go about this some other way. You'll understand when you meet her" (166). In addition to delaying Kinsey's involvement with the actual case by using Chamberlain as a go-between for the actual client, Grafton calls attention to this technique of postponement through the bank manager's ironic remark that "time is of the essence" in the midst of the prolonging of the specifics of the case.

The client turns out to be Karen Waterston, a well-known actress whose actor husband Kevin McCall has been kidnapped (thus, her desire for secrecy). Upon learning of her identity, Kinsey notes that the married couple is "starring in a new television series called *Shamus, P.I.*, an hour-long spoof of every detective series that's ever aired. I don't watch much TV, but I'd heard about the show and after seeing it once, I'd found myself hooked. The stories were fresh, the writing was superb, and the format was perfect for their considerable acting talents" (167). This moment can be seen as an explicit, self-aware referencing of the toying with genre conventions taking place on the more implicit level of story structure and pacing. The title of the Waterston/McCall series appears to reference both the Burt Reynolds detective film *Shamus* and the television series *Magnum P.I.*, making it a "spoof" specifically through pastiche. The positive attributes of the series might also be seen as a winking metacommentary on "A Little Missionary Work" itself, particularly the reference to the "format," with which Grafton is experimenting here.

A different approach to manipulating time through the first-person voice comes in the form of various summaries that Kinsey uses to relate key aspects of the case. Each instance of this technique sees Kinsey relaying information that would typically be conveyed in dialogue form, from the client's explanation of the case to key conversations between Kinsey and her client. Karen's explanation of the case is told entirely from Kinsey's point of view, beginning when she notes how Karen "got up and began to pace, describing in halting detail the circumstances of Kevin's abduction" (172). The next instance of a key plot point delivered through narration rather than dialogue comes when Kinsey decides to meet the kidnapper's ransom demands: "Time was short and the pressures were mounting every minute. If Jack and I didn't come up with *some* plan, Kevin would be dead. If the cash could be assembled, the obvious move was to have me take Karen's place during the actual delivery, which would at least eliminate the possibility of her being picked up as well" (176). Here, Grafton includes another reference to the urgency of the situation, perhaps linking this sense of increased pace to the choice to have Kinsey summarize this information. After a dialogue exchange in which the merits of Kinsey's plan are debated, she then describes the specifics of enacting this plan by running through the scenario in her head, starting with how "I'd return to the house on foot sometime after dark…" (177).

The build-up to the drop, which includes the solution to the mini-"mystery" of the nature of the case as well as Kinsey's meeting with Harry to procure the ransom money, seems to indicate the drop itself as the climax. However, the introduction to Kinsey's recounting of the event begins with her noting that "the drop played out according to the numbers, without the slightest hitch" (183). Despite a lengthy paragraph describing Kinsey's harrowing experience of carrying out the drop, Grafton undercuts the suspense of this potential climax, reversing expectations once more in order to set up the conclusion. Kevin and Karen are broke and perpetrated the kidnapping scheme in order to abscond with the ransom money themselves. In the final paragraph, Kinsey reveals that Kevin and Karen merely made off with a bag full of counterfeit bills, as she and Harry had plotted during their meeting. Aside from a factual recounting of this information, the only editorializing provided by Kinsey is that she refers to the whole plan as "my missionary work"

(189), having helped Harry in a genuine manner and having "helped" Kevin and Karen in an ironic fashion.

The first instance of genre subversion in "Falling Off the Roof" comes when Kinsey investigates the murder of Don Grissom at the behest of his brother, who believes that Don's wife, Susie, pushed him off the roof in order to collect the insurance money. Kinsey poses as an insurance investigator and visits Susie, rationalizing her guise by thinking that "while a cop is required by statute to identify himself (or herself) as a law enforcement officer, a private investigator is free to impersonate anyone, which is what makes my job so much fun. I'm a law-abiding little bun in most instances, but I've been known to tell lies at the drop of a hat. The fib I cooked up for Susie Grissom wasn't far from the truth, and I sounded so sincere that I half believed it myself" (111). Her own sense of personal enjoyment resulting from the deception, coupled with her own willingness to (half) believe her own deception, runs counter to the expected traits set forth in nearly every "standard" introductory paragraph given by Kinsey regarding her occupation.

The use of instinct/intuition as a tool in "Full Circle" is seen again here, but in this instance, Kinsey has her sense about Susie almost immediately: "From the moment I set eyes on this lady, I knew she was guilty. I've seen enough widows and orphans in my day to know what real grief looks like, and this wasn't it. This was pseudo-grief, counterfeit grief, or some reasonable facsimile, but it wasn't real sorrow" (112). Here, Grafton uses the greatly contracted interview, which lasts merely 11 lines of dialogue before Kinsey's summation of Susie, in order to strengthen the impact of her intuition, which in this case comes into play before any actual investigation or inductive/deductive practices. Her attempts to classify Susie's performance within a taxonomy of different types of feigned grief is an ironic counterpoint to her own act as she plays the role of the insurance investigator.

This irony is developed even further as Kinsey pretends to be a fan of mystery novels in order to work her way into the Santa Teresa Mystery Readers book club, which is run by Susie and other neighborhood residents. Grafton rapidly moves from the interview to the book club meeting, accelerating the pace at which the story progresses and intensifyng the degree to which Kinsey's lies are accumulating:

> "As a matter of fact, we're doing women writers this month. Would you like to come?"
>
> "I'd love it," I said. "What a treat."
>
> Which is how I ended up at a meeting of the Santa Teresa Mystery Readers. (113)

The abrupt change of setting and movement through time compounds the sensation of Kinsey's descent into Susie's world. Grafton further develops Kinsey's initial thoughts on lying and role-playing as she discusses how "we had tea and cookies and laughed and chatted about writers I'd never heard of. I kept saying things like 'Oh, the ending on that one scared me half to death!' or 'I thought the plot line was a bit convoluted, didn't you?' I lied so well, I worried I'd be elected to office, but all that happened was that I was invited back the next month" (113-14). In addition to taking pride in her own ability to deceive in the midst of her quest for truth, her lack of knowledge about the subject—the mystery fiction genre—creates multiple layers of irony.

The self-aware reference to the mystery fiction genre is nuanced further as Kinsey talks to Mrs. Hill, one of Susie's neighbors, in search of further evidence to support her conclusion. After several sentences of dialogue introducing herself to Mrs. Hill, Kinsey summarizes the remainder of the conversation: "I went through a series of questions. How well did she know the Grissoms? Was she home on the day of his accident? She was singularly uninformative, the sort who answered each query without editorial comment. When it was clear she had nothing to offer, I thanked her and excused myself, moving on" (115). Kinsey's awareness of the quality of "editorial comment" as an accompaniment to dialogue can be read as Grafton's own acknowledgement of this aspect of form in which Kinsey typically offers her own first person commentary—sometimes insightful, often sarcastic or humorous—on those she meets or on events that befall her.

As opposed to determining the identity of the person who pushed Don Grissom off the roof at the behest of Susie, Kinsey only gets as far as learning that a redhead in the book club perpetrated the actual murder, finally discovering that her name is Shannon when she introduces herself to Kinsey at the next book club meeting. This "group" culprit, with the book club members covering for each other in the style of Agatha Christie's *Murder on the Orient Express*, marks a departure from the types of conclusions that Grafton has used up to that point (by which Kinsey is able to eventually identify the guilty individual or persons after recognizing and pondering their key traits, having previously been given as clues). At that meeting, at which the book club members now realize that Kinsey is investigating Don's murder, she "could see fifteen to twenty women all seated on folding chairs. Several turned to look at me, their faces blank and curious and dead. My stomach gave a sudden squeeze, and I knew I was in trouble. We were playing an elaborate game and I was 'it'" (122). The uniformity with which Grafton describes the book club members depicts their collective nature, with their "blank" and "dead" features echoing their intent, is the main way in which Kinsey interprets their expressions.

The climax is a reversal of a typical conclusion involving an attempt to find and hunt down a culprit—instead, a chase scene ensues with Kinsey as the target of the Santa Teresa Mystery Readers. The chase is conveyed across four lengthy paragraphs that comprise the conclusion, in which Grafton demonstrates how Kinsey's panic heightens her awareness of everything taking place around her by showing her reactions to minute aspects of the ordeal. As in the car accident in the opening of "Full Circle," the actual length of the chase scene here is called into question as the prolonged descriptions depict Kinsey's perception of events rather than the passage of actual time, from longer reactions such as "headlights flashed around the corner toward me, and

I doubled my speed, feet flying as I raced across the street" to brief fragments such as "Dark houses. No foot traffic. No help" (123). In the last sentence, Kinsey reaches the steps of the Santa Teresa Police department, her final thought that she was "uncertain if I was laughing or crying when I finally burst through the doors," ending the case on a purely emotional rather than reflective note (123). This conclusion befits the unique nature of this short tale by focusing not on the implications of the case or judgments about it, but on Kinsey's own visceral, non-intellectualized reaction to the events that have transformed the detective story into an action/suspense thriller.

The Kinsey Millhone short stories are characterized both by a sense of distillation due to the condensed frame in which the tale occurs and, stemming from that condensation, a sense of exaggeration due to the increased awareness of detail that results from the brevity of the form. Charles May writes that the short story "demands an aesthetic rather than a natural or essential form" that comes from the sustained development over time which the novel allows ("Metaphoric Motivation" 66). It is this formal, aestheticized aspect of the structure of these tales that gives us a different way of looking at Grafton's construction and presentation of the world of Kinsey Millhone.

Works Cited

Garrison, Kristen. "Hard-Boiled Rhetoric: The 'Fearless Speech' of Philip Marlowe." *South Central Review*, vol. 27, nos. 1 & 2, Spring/Summer 2010, pp. 105-22.

Grafton, Sue. *F is for Fugitive*. Henry Holt and Company, 1989.

---. *Kinsey and Me*. Putnam, 2013.

Gray, W. Russel. "Flow Gently, Sweet Grafton: 'M' is for Metaphysical (or at least Metaphorical) in *'C' is for Corpse*." *Clues: A Journal of Detection*, vol. 20, no. 2, Fall-Winter

1999, pp. 63-69.

Kaufman, Natalie Hevener, and Carol McGinnis Kay. *"G" is for Grafton: The World of Kinsey Millhone*. Henry Holt and Company, 1997.

May, Charles. "Metaphoric Motivation in Short Fiction: In the Beginning Was the Story." *Short Story Theory at a Crossroads*, edited by Susan Lohafer and Jo Ellyn Clarey, Louisiana State UP, 1989, np.

---. *Short Story: The Reality of Artifice*. Prentice Hall, 1995.

Moore, Lewis D. *Cracking the Hard-Boiled Detective: A Critical History from The 1920s to the Present*. McFarland, 2006.

Pickering, Jean. "Time and the Short Story." *Re-reading the Short Story*, edited by Clare Hanson, Macmillan, 1989, pp. 45-54.

Rohrberger, Mary. "Between Shadow and Act: Where Do We Go from Here?" *Short Story Theory at a Crossroad*, edited by Susan Lohafer and Jo Ellyn Clarey. Louisiana State UP, 1989, np.

Wheat, Edward M. "The Post-Modern Detective: The Aesthetic Politics of Dashiell Hammett's 'Continental Op.'" *Midwest Quarterly: A Journal of Contemporary Thought*, vol. 36, no. 3, 1995, pp. 237-49.

The Street Was Hers: Deconstructing the Hardboiled in Megan Abbott's Noir Fiction

Nathan Ashman

Abstract

In her critical study *The Street Was Mine: White Masculinity in Hardboiled Fiction and Film Noir*, Megan Abbott offers a reconsideration of the archetypal "tough guy figure," illustrating what she perceives as hardboiled masculinity's parasitic reliance on the Femme Fatale for its own preservation. Within this hermetic structuring of masculinity, one dependent on "remaining free from contagion," Abbott argues that there is "no space for a woman who can volley masculine and feminine signifiers" (54). Via a reading of Abbott's first two novels, *Die a Little* (2005) and *The Song is You* (2007), this essay argues that these early works can be read as an active engagement with and response to her own literary criticism, as she repositions feminine identity, agency, and subjectivity from the delimited margins of the hardboiled crime novel to the narrative center. Focusing on Abbott's nuanced and complex reinterpretation of previously "passive" categorizations of femininity—such as the femme fatale, the voiceless victim, and the housewife—it suggests that Abbott's work operates to shift the dominant gaze of the genre, destabilizing masculinity's previously subjugating dependence on femininity for its own definition in the process. Consequently, the "house of cards" that is hardboiled masculine identity becomes severely under threat (Abbott 54). Although still relatively unexplored in critical discourse, this essay argues not only that Abbott's work not builds upon that of writers such as Sue Grafton and Sara Paretsky, but also that she is a unique and important new voice in contemporary American crime fiction.

In her critical study *The Street Was Mine: White Masculinity in Hardboiled Fiction and Film Noir*, Megan Abbott offers a reconsideration of the archetypal "tough guy" figure, illustrating what she perceives as hardboiled masculinity's parasitic reliance on "the other" for its own preservation. Far from reproducing the macho violence of Mickey Spillane's Mike Hammer, Abbott argues that most hardboiled heroes—particularly Chandler's Marlowe—are, in contrast, frequently characterized by a profound sense of "gender panic." For Abbott, this sense of "masculinity in crisis" underscores the broader strategies of paranoia, containment, and control that typify such narratives and is most forcefully exhibited via the hardboiled hero's ambivalence towards the figure of the femme fatale (Abbott and Adams 398). In these texts, the hardboiled hero finds himself caught in an irreconcilable and vacillating double bind, one that is marked by a concurrent "fascination with—and fear of—the feminine" (Abbott and Adams 399). These oscillating tropes of desire and destruction epitomize a hardboiled logic that continually situates women as threatening seductresses, with the femme fatale emerging as the ultimate embodiment of the temptation/peril dichotomy. For John Scaggs, it is the femme fatale's antithesis to the private eye hero that marks her threat, as "she reverses the normal dialectic of tough surface and sensitive depth" that punctuates the private eye's chivalric, masculine code (77). In other words, it is the femme fatale's transgression of the boundaries of gender that precipitates what Abbott identifies as a profound sense of panic. Within the hardboiled novel's hermetic structuring of masculinity—one entirely dependent on "remaining free from contagion"—there is ultimately "no space for a woman who can volley masculine and feminine signifiers" (Abbott 54). The reaffirmation of the hardboiled hero's identity thus derives from the defeat of the femme fatale and, by proxy, the threat that she embodies.

The warped gender politics underlying the hardboiled detective text are forcefully spotlighted and interrogated in Abbott's first two neo-noir novels *Die a Little* (2005) and *The Song Is You* (2007), as she repositions feminine identity, agency, and subjectivity from the delimited margins to the narrative center. Focusing on Abbott's nuanced and complex reinterpretation of previously "passive" categorization of femininity—such as the femme fatale and the voiceless victim—this essay argues that Abbott actively shifts the dominant gaze of the genre while explicitly spotlighting masculinity's subjugating dependence on femininity for its own definition. As a consequence, the "house of cards" that is hardboiled masculine identity is explicitly revealed in all its violent and paranoid glory. Ultimately, this essay will suggest that Abbott's work can be read not only as an active engagement with and response to the traditions of the hardboiled novel, but also as a response to her own literary criticism.

This awareness of the patriarchal determinations of the hardboiled novel is by no means a new strand in the study and writing of crime fiction. Indeed, in their book *Detective Agency: Women Rewriting the Hard-Boiled Tradition* (1999), Priscilla Walton and Manina Jones identify a number of female writers—such as Sarah Paretsky, Marcia Muller and Sue Grafton—who have "strategically redirected the masculinist trajectory of the American hard-boiled detective novel of the 1930s and 1940s to feminist ends" (4). In these texts, the investigative process does not just involve uncovering a particular crime, but also the broader and more systemic "offenses in which the patriarchal power structure of contemporary society itself is potentially incriminated" (4). For Walton and Jones, the feminist impetus of such writing derives from the ambivalent relationship it strikes with the "literary tradition" of the hardboiled novel. While drawing on the tropes of such narratives, these texts simultaneously endeavour to "establish the distinctive voice of an empowered female subject," a move that is both a "formal" and "political gesture" (4). In most cases, this entails deviating from conventional representations of female characters, a process that is frequently enacted by situating the female protagonist as detective rather than threatening femme fatale. Heather Humann points to Sue Grafton's private eye Kinsey Millhone as an example of such self-conscious disruption, deliberately challenging "the traditional narrative that hard-boiled private investigators must be male" (64). By actively subverting a "hitherto male dominated genre" through active, tough-talking, and politicized female detectives, the works of writers like Paretsky and Grafton are positioned to examine "a range of themes and ideas that are frequently marginalised in conventional crime fiction and patriarchal society more broadly" (Beyer 228).

While this "second wave" of feminist crime writing—a term used by Walton and Jones to differentiate between women's crime writing that emerged out of the feminist politics of the 1960s and 1970s and that written during the "Golden Age" of detective fiction—has been widely discussed in critical discourse, Abbott's work, by contrast, has received very little critical attention (Walton and Jones 27). This is perhaps surprising considering Abbott's comparable preoccupation with articulations of feminine identity (even if the historical, neo-noir dimensions of her work do distinguish her from many of these writers). In a 2011 interview, Abbott describes how her early works were born out of an acute awareness that hardboiled detective novels "were heavily a world of men," a disparity that offered the potential to construct a series of narratives with "female characters who were not femme fatales (or not viewed as femme fatales and defined solely by their ability to entrap men)" (Palmer). Yet, rather than repositioning the female as detective, Abbott's work instead revisits the "destructively sexual world" of post-war Los Angeles, offering a re-examination and reframing of noir's entrenched and hierarchical gender politics from a uniquely "female purview" (Powell 179). Within this,

Lee Horsley argues that Abbott's work centers around different representations of female identity "under pressure," not solely from "male treachery and violence but from their own ambition, vanity and destructive impulses" (38). In other words, Abbott's work provides a broader, more diverse spectrum of female identity and female agency, one that not only challenges the rigid binaries of "victim" and "seductress" that epitomizes the gendered logic of hardboiled fiction, but also simultaneously exposes the extreme fragility of masculine identity more broadly.

"All These Lost Girls": *Die a Little* (2005)

The first of Abbott's early noir novels, *Die a Little*, starkly spotlights the fraught duality of 1950s Hollywood, counterbalancing the superficial glamour of celebrity culture with a percolating underworld of exploitation, corruption and violence. The narrative centers on the relationship between respectable schoolteacher Lora King and her brother Bill, a straight-arrow junior investigator for the district attorney's office. Orphaned in late adolescence after their parents were killed in a car crash, the brother and sister form a connection that vacillates ambivalently between the wholesome and the insalubrious. Domiciled together since the accident, there is a quasi-libidinal intensity to the relationship that often threatens to transgress the boundaries of the familial. In an early section of the text, Lora recounts cutting Bill's hair with a potency and sensuality that certainly hints at a form of illicit desire: *Hours afterward, I would find slim, beaten gold bristles on my finger, my arms, no matter how careful I was. I'd blow them off my fingertips, one by one* (2, italics in original). Diana Powell has similarly identified these "protective, incestuous" undercurrents within the text, an implicit hint of degradation that prefigures the recurrent patterns of duality and illegitimacy that will mark the text.

The equilibrium and domesticity of Lora and Bill's dynamic is violently disturbed when the latter falls for the mysterious and seductive Alice Steele, a former Hollywood costume seamstress with an indistinct past. As her name and appearance suggest, Alice epitomizes the dialectic of soft exterior and hard center that John Scaggs identifies as symptomatic of the femme fatale. This opposition is starkly projected when Lora spies, late at night, on the unknowing Alice as she flips through a King family photo album:

> I slide my robe on and make my way to the door. Opening it delicately, and walking down the hall, I see one of the living room lights on. As I move closer, I realize it is only Alice after all. Her legs tucked beneath her on a wing chair, she is paging through one of our thick old family photo albums.
>
> I am about to turn around and head back, not wanting to disturb her, but as I do, my eyes play a funny trick.
>
> I stop suddenly at the archway and find myself stifling a tight gasp. Under the harsh lamp, in sharp contrast to the dark room, her eyes look strangely eaten through. The eyes of a death mask, rotting behind the gleaming facade. A trick of light somehow— (Abbott 17)

The "dialectic of opposites" that characterizes both the femme fatale — and the aesthetics of noir more generally — is vividly actualized here through counterbalancing images of light and dark (Brook 105). Spotlighted by the "harsh lamp," the boundaries of Alice's corporeality are disturbed and unfixed by an uncanny merging of surface and depth. The haunting "death mask," an aberration usually concealed beneath "a pretty Alice-smile," haemorrhages to the surface, distorting Alice's face into a kind of gothic palimpsest. This blurred separation between "gleaming façade" and "rotting" foundation typifies the oscillating paradigms of seduction and death that underscore the traditions of the femme fatale paradigm, as well as the "more general divisions" between the superficial surface reality and the threatening underworld of Los Angeles, a theme that Scaggs argues is central to the "hardboiled world" (77).

While foreshadowing her threat, the extent to which Alice Steele represents a transgressive incarnation of female identity, one that challenges the traditional gender hierarchies of the genre, is perhaps questionable here. Indeed, although conceding that the "strength and dynamism" of such flawed neo-noir "anti-heroes" continue to endure and fascinate, Lee Horsley argues that Abbott's somewhat customary re-articulation of the femme fatale paradigm actually risks "fuelling the most negative stereotypes" (38). Yet, as Diana Powell suggests, as much as Alice "awakens Bill sexually" and "fulfils his fantasy of rescuing her," the typical power dynamics of the femme fatale narrative are simultaneously subverted via the equally rousing impact that Alice has upon Lora (167). This is indicative of Abbott's conscious repositioning of female identity from the margins of the hardboiled text to the narrative center as Bill's relationship with Alice becomes peripheral to Lora's own wavering attraction to and distrust of her sister-in-law. Nauseated by the lewdness and immorality she perceives bubbling underneath Alice's poised surface, Lora cannot help being equally magnetized by her enigmatic sexuality: "There was a glamour to her, in her unconventional beauty, in her faintly red-rimmed eyes and the bristly, inky lashes sparking out of them...She had no curves. She was barely a woman at all, and yet she seemed so hopelessly feminine" (10).

Lora's ambivalence towards Alice magnifies as the latter becomes progressively entrenched in her personal and professional life. After Alice takes a job teaching home economics at the same school as Lora, her poised, orchestrated persona begins to slip. Despite seeming "very present" in her classes, Alice's animation and enthusiasm are belied by an absent "faraway look in her eyes," a "slick, silver" nothingness "just hanging there, unfixed" (40). Lora's suspicion is further compounded by the sudden and then regular presence of Alice's "old friend" Lois Slattery, "a professional extra and sometimes dancer," who Alice claims to have met while she worked as a costume seamstress. With her "eternally blood shot eye" and general "dishevelled beauty," Lois emanates a sense of desecration and loss that further punctures Alice's veneer of respectability and domesticity. Yet, as Lora becomes increasingly obsessed with uncovering Alice's sordid past, the inviolability of her previously "unpolluted" life slowly begins to rupture. Lora's overpowering attraction to Alice's darkness, and indeed, the corrupt, violent underbelly of post-war Los Angeles is further intensified by her relationship with Hollywood fixer Mike Standish. A precursor to Abbott's protagonist Gil "Hop" Hopkins in *The Song Is You*, Standish is employed by Hollywood studios to bury and distort details of celebrities' salacious private lives. An embodiment of the stark duality of Hollywood, Standish further exposes Lora to the seedy underworld of the Los Angeles dream factory. Yet, rather than being seduced, exploited and corrupted by Standish—as Alice intended—Lora remains emotionally disconnected from their sexual dalliances, even when faced with signs of Mike's philandering. On discovering lipstick stains on his soiled sheets, she queries:

> Is that the usual routine?" I say, walking toward the centre of the room, then turning and facing him again.
>
> "Not always, but with you...." He smiles suddenly and, head still tilted against the wall, he twists around to catch my gaze. "Aren't I a bastard? Or maybe I'm a powder puff. You see, Lora King, turns out I'm surprising myself this time. Turns out I'm disappointed how little you care."
>
> I find myself offering a sharp giggle of shock.
>
> "Hard-boiled." He winces.
>
> Covering my mouth, I concede, "You're rotten,"

> before letting my smile spread, blowing smoke.
> I run the tip of my thumb along my lower lip,
> brushing away a stray wisp of tobacco. (Abbott
> 2005, 99)

Having previously pegged her as a "finger pointer, or a hysteric," Standish is discombobulated by Lora's seeming indifference to the discovery of his promiscuity (98). She transgresses the role of vulnerable victim while discovering her own sexual power. Diana Powell suggests Lora's "curiosity leads to her own self-discovery: her 'giggle of shock' brings an awareness of her own dark pleasure" (168). Such "hardboiled femininity" operates to subvert noir fiction's typical positioning of women as "sexual objects, domestic nurturers and vulnerable figures in need of a chivalrous male rescuer" (Smith 2010, 153). This marks a key moment in Lora's transition into amateur investigator and pseudo-fixer. Indeed, it is her active "detachment" from Standish's duplicity that, Powell argues, "accompanies her birth into this dark underworld through which she can save her brother by understanding the darkness and using it to her own advantage" (168).

Lora's desire to protect her brother from the tendrillic clutches of Alice and the underworld escalates exponentially after the mutilated body of Lois Slattery is discovered dumped in Bronson Canyon. Deliberately disfigured in an attempt to preclude identification, Lois's body nonetheless becomes the catalyst for Lora's unravelling of a dark network of corruption, prostitution, and murder. With the help of Standish, Lora discovers that Alice had previously worked for a pimp called Joe Avalon by both servicing clients and using her reputation as "the girl with tape" to recruit disaffected or struggling actresses, anyone she "thought would sell" (182). One client of Avalon's is Hollywood producer Walter Schor, a powerful sexual deviant with a penchant for violence. Schor's predilection for the extreme has been experienced first-hand by Alice, who was once hospitalized after a night of severe sexual savagery. It is therefore unsurprising when

Schor is revealed to be the murderer of Lois Slattery, whom he beat and brutalized before eventually leaving her to drown in his pool. Alice's role in the murder and cover up is more ambiguous. Although marrying Bill emancipates her from a life of enforced prostitution, she continues to act as an adjunct pimp to Joe Avalon, selling and profiting from Lois's services. Although she does not directly participate in Lois's death, she helps Avalon dispose of the body and cover up the murder.

The powerful and sadistic Schor prefigures a pattern of Hollywood exploitation that continues into *The Song Is You* in the form of celebrity dance duo, Marv Sutton and Gene Merrel. In both cases, the stark duplicity of these public figures forcefully spotlights the power of cultural spectacle to obscure and hypnotize as the "superficial fantasy world" of Los Angeles is juxtaposed against "its gloomier, dissolute counterpart — the underworld" (Ashman 19). Through these and other counterfeit figures such as Standish, Abbott exposes the corrupt and fabricated history of Los Angeles, one built upon the brutal effacement and systematic disposal of female bodies. The underlying and destructive misogyny of various institutions of power ensures the maintenance of these public personas at the cost of innumerable "lost girls" (228). Although Lois conforms to this pattern of delimitation, Lora's perception of Alice as a similarly tragic victim of circumstance is altered as the narrative reaches the denouement. Driving to confront Alice, Lora admits: "*Once I thought she was trying to escape the darkness, and she found rescue in Bill. Now I know that she wanted both. She liked the double life. It kept her alive*" (219, italics in original). Although Alice is given the opportunity to "escape" the darkness through her marriage to Bill, Lora recognizes that a conventional suburban life would not be enough to satisfy her sister-in-law's murkier cravings. Abbott knowingly positions Alice on the indeterminate boundary between traditional feminine binaries, exposing the "fine line between contaminating femme fatale" and "the good girl" (Abbott 2002, 54). This is symptomatic of Alice's ability to "volley" competing signifiers throughout the narrative, continually oscillating between oppositions such as seductress/wife, friend/enemy, light/dark.

Yet this blurring, and thus deconstruction, of binaries of femininity similarly applies to Lora. Indeed, in a farewell letter near the finale of the text, Alice recognizes this same sense of paradox and an equivalent penchant for darkness percolating beneath Lora's projected piety:

> I guess I can tell you now: I started working you right away. I knew what I was up against. I was careful how dark my lipstick was, how low I'd wear my neckline, how I hung the drapes, made the dinner, danced with him at parties, and looked at him across rooms...
>
> But then I saw that you liked my dark edges. Here was the surprise long after anyone could surprise me. You liked it.
>
> You liked the voile nightgown you saw in my closet, touched it with your milky fingers and asked me where I'd gotten it. When I bought you one of your own, your face steamed baby pink, but you wore it. I knew you'd wear it. (236-37)

The dynamic between Lora and Alice as depicted here is permeated with images of seduction and corruption. Expecting to have to indulge her sister-in-law's expectations of propriety, Alice is surprised to discover that it is her "darker edges" that captivate and intrigue Lora. Alice's predatory manipulation is juxtaposed against Lora's "baby pink" face and "milky fingers," images of virtue that vividly emphasize Lora's spectacular shift towards the underworld over the course of the text. Indeed, ultimately it is Lora's recognition and embrace of her darker potentialities that allow her to reclaim Bill not only from Alice's destructive clutches, but also from potential ruin. Knowing that Alice intends to flee Los Angeles with Bill — only after he helps her frame Joe Avalon for murder and bribe a potential witness — Lora gambles on the belief that their sibling love is stronger than Bill's commitment to Alice. After a phone call to Bill during which she elliptically implies that she is being threatened and abused by Mike Standish, Lora throws herself down her apartment stairwell, only to drag herself back upstairs to maintain the impression of a brutal, domestic attack. Bill does indeed return to rescue Lora, ultimately leaving Alice to face the violent retributions of Joe Avalon.

As Powell suggests, Lora's devious actions towards the end of the narrative reveal the "extent to which she has become hardboiled" (168). Disposing of Alice Steele and framing Mike Standish in the process, Lora must ironically channel her own "steel" to purge the corrupted facets of her and Bill's life. Lora ultimately finds empowerment and agency through touching the darkness, even if the other female characters are left faceless and lost. After being released from hospital, Lora searches for news of the missing Alice at the Los Angeles public library. Whilst trawling through newspapers articles, she is confronted with endless "stories of mutilated starlets, scorched bodies, pregnant suicides, lost girls leaping, falling, and being pushed, strangled, shot stabbed, and set in flames" (239). Buried in the archives of the library, the forgotten narratives of these "lost girls" potently illustrate the perverse cycle of sensationalism and disregard that characterize the brutalization and disposal of female bodies. Found dead in a ravine, Alice becomes just another of these unidentified women, her face "faded away, erased by water" (239). Indeed, although Abbott's female protagonists ultimately resist the "conventions of gender, genre and the vengeful propensities of the past," they are still victim to the misogynistic imperatives of post-war Los Angeles. This ambivalence is symptomatic of Abbott's work more broadly and is further compounded by the uncertainty that surrounds the end of the narrative. Although Lora is able to prevent her brother's downfall, the means via which this is achieved represent what Powell describes as an "unsettling, false and fragile compromise" (169). This is validated by the sense of haunting that permeates the final pages of the narrative, as Lora recalls an exchange with Alice "months before, before everything..." (240). Leading Lora to a back alley, she asserts:

> "It's okay. You don't have to pretend with me"
>
> "Pretend what?"
>
> "That you don't like it. All of it and more still. Darker still.
>
> [...]
>
> "You don't have to talk about it, but it's something we both have, Lora. It's something we've both got." (241)

Rather than being diametrically opposed, Lora is faced with the stark parity between herself and Alice. Whilst Abbott initially sets up the narrative as a contest between two fixed and contradictory binaries of female identity (angel/whore), over the course of the text such determinations are revealed as unhinged and violable. Ultimately, dualities such as good/evil and victim/seductress become difficult to distinguish, as Lora embraces the darkness to restore the equilibrium of her relationship with Bill. The final page of the text reveals Lora's inability to accept her own iniquity, asserting multiple times: "*I don't have it in me, I don't have it in me*" (italics in original). Defeating Alice is ultimately scant victory, as the awakened Lora must live with the psychic consequences of her immoral actions.

"She Had Whole Other Stories to Tell": *The Song Is You* (2007)

The Song Is You offers a fictionalization of the real life 1949 disappearance of movie "starlet" Jean Spangler, a case that is often compared to the similarly high-profile murder of aspiring actress Elizabeth Short (aka "The Black Dahlia"). Indeed, Diana Powell argues that this marks a conscious striving by Abbott to create a tie not only "directly to noir," but to "the Black Dahlia's chronicler James Ellroy" (169). Abbott herself has regularly cited Ellroy as a "tremendous influence" on her early work and this can certainly be seen in her comparable examination of a dark and destructive underworld percolating beneath the superficial glitz of post-war Los Angeles's phantasmagoric and sycophantic celebrity culture (Godfrey). Our conduit to this world in *The Song Is You* is reporter turned Hollywood fixer Gil "Hop" Hopkins, a slick-talking "fireman" paid by movie execs to disguise, fabricate and repress details of stars' salacious private lives to maintain their public image (Abbott 29). Yet Hop's ascent within the Hollywood studios is built upon the rotten foundations of the Jean Spangler case, a suspected murder he helped bury by ensuring "that a few names never found their way into the papers or to the police" (39). Hop's complicity in the disappearance resurfaces when, two years after the event, he is confronted and extorted by an actress named Iolene, who accuses Hop of concealing evidence related to the case to protect the reputation of certain implicated celebrities. It is subsequently revealed that Hop was in attendance on the evening of Spangler's disappearance, having accompanied the actress and friend Iolene on a booze-fuelled night out at the "Eight Ball, a sweat-on-the-walls roadhouse in a dark stretch of nowhere just east of civilization" (32). After Hop later disappears with a "burlesque blonde" in tow, the two women are left alone with "Hollywood's premier song and dance duo" Marv Sutton and Gene Merrel, celebrity superstars rumoured to have a disturbing predilection for sexual violence (33). As the night becomes increasingly debauched, Iolene reveals that Jean eventually disappeared with Sutton and Merrel, never to be seen again. Despite Hop's insistence that neither he or Iolene should feel complicit in or guilty about Jean's suspected death, Iolene blames him not only for leaving them in the clutches of the warped movie stars, but also for subsequently ensuring that neither of the men is named as a suspect in the ensuing inquiry.

Hop ultimately undertakes his own private investigation, one driven less by the desire to attain justice for Jean and more by the fear of professional and criminal reprisals should the true details of the case be revealed. This pressure to tie up any loose ends is escalated by the presence of reporter Frannie Adair, who, piqued by Hop's sudden interest in a seemingly dead-end case, resumes her own search into the events surrounding Spangler's disappearance. Through his investigation, Hop is gradually exposed to the profound ambivalence that marks hardboiled masculinity, a revolving door of desire and revulsion that becomes markedly expressed in instances of violence and sexual rage. At the most extreme end of this scale are movie stars Gene Merrel and Marv Sutton, whose wholesome on-screen image conceals a warped history of psychopathy and sadistic sexual violence. The vicious duality of both men becomes connected to the "schizophrenic nature" of Abbott's Los Angeles more broadly, a "double rendering of hallucinatory commodity spectacles counterbalanced by an underworld of death and exploitation driven by urban power" (Ashman 19). The falsity of Los Angeles's cinematic reality is vividly projected when Hop tries to conjure an image of Gene Merrel's beatific "on-screen face" in his mind, only for the "flickering movie image" to blur, darken and transmute into "something else," something "he didn't want to think about" (128).

While Hop is revolted and disturbed by the sexual deviancy of Merrel and Sutton, he is nonetheless forced to confront his own complicity, not only in the concealment of such brutality, but also in the sustainment and normalization of misogynist violence more broadly. Indeed, Diana Powell recognizes this desire to destroy and physically mark women as a recurrent pattern that punctuates Abbott's narrative. Specifically, she points to the media's handling of the Spangler case, arguing that they "lose interest in her once she is labelled a mistress to one of Mickey Cohen's hoodlums" (171). The implication here is that Spangler's disappearance is less commercially viable for the tabloids when the "sex angle" is disregarded, particularly as there is "no body, and thus no signs of torture to titillate" (171). And, despite Hop's attempt to differentiate himself from Merrel and Sutton — to reaffirm his assertion that he is "not that guy" — his own paranoid and panic-stricken masculine rage is incrementally revealed over the course of the text (Abbott 137). This escalation is foregrounded in one of the early sections of the narrative as Hop attempts to frame his relentless desire for women via a logic that flirts dangerously and disturbingly with notions of culpability and blame:

> Really, if they're going to wear those darted sweaters tucked tight into those long fitted skirts cradling heart-shaped asses, skirts so tight they swivelled when they walked in them, clack-clack-clacking away down the hall, full aware — *with full intention* — that he was watching, even as his face betrayed nothing, not a rough twitch or a faint hint of saliva on his decidedly not-trembling lip. It wasn't he who was *unusual*, so lust-filled or insatiable. It was they who packaged themselves up so pertly for utmost oomph, for him alone, really, even if they hadn't met him yet when they slid on their treacherous gossamer stockings that morning, even if they hadn't known why they had straightened the seams on their blouses so they'd hang in perfectly sharp arrows down their waiting, waiting breasts. (Abbott 70, italics in original)

Here Abbott depicts the devastatingly destructive operation of the male gaze, where "woman as icon" is displayed for the pleasure and enjoyment of men, "the active controllers of the look" (Mulvey 13). Perceived by Hop in atomized parts, the female body is fragmented, dislocated and disarticulated by the fetishistic directives of the subjugating gaze, one that renders it both passive and silent. As Lilly Pâquet suggests, these notions of "dismemberment" and "silence" connect "the theory of the gaze to crime fiction" in specific and disturbing ways, as "women are often more than just symbolically dismembered and silenced" (133). The association between the gaze and violence is significant here, as implicitly layered into Hop's appraisal of his helpless (and blameless) masculine desire is an oscillating paradigm of attraction and revulsion towards such ungoverned female sexuality. While ostensibly an appreciation of the female form, the passage is saturated with hostile and aggressive language — "sharp arrows," "rough twitch," "treacherous," "trembling" — that lend it an underlying sense of contradiction. For Abbott, such ambivalence is symptomatic of the hardboiled hero more broadly, constantly caught between shifting desires of "fascination" and "fear" (Abbott and Adams 399). Imbedded and perceptible in Hop's language is the implication that men cannot be blamed for their actions — sexual or violent — in the face of this dangerously alluring and knowing femininity.

Indeed, as Hop uncovers more about the sordid circumstances surrounding Spangler's disappearance, his identification with the sexual violence of Merrel and Sutton becomes progressively and alarmingly pronounced. This is evidenced after a chance meeting with Sutton, when, despite being once again revulsed and disturbed by the starlet's behaviour towards a young waitress (telling Hop that he intends to "fuck her blind"), Hop proceeds to engage in a violently energized sexual assignation of his own with the waitress's companion. Initially intending to slide his hand "around the back of her neck," Hop describes how — as if out of his control — he "saw his hand cover her face, the heel of his hand on her bright red mouth." Half wondering "why he was doing it" before "for[getting] to care," Hop proceeds to knock the girl's head "hard against the wall," eliciting a "sharp, excited little noise" (126). Hop's sexual aggression here is strikingly imitative of the language used to describe his encounter with Jean Spangler near the beginning of the text. Hop recalls how "it was her voice that purred and snapped and stuck in his head most ferociously, making him sick with random desire, making him want to do something foul, unmentionable, unarticulated, ugly. How he'd like to fuck her into oblivion. But someone beat him to it" (3). Notwithstanding the sadistic mutilations of Sutton and Merrel, it is via these expressions of Hop's misogynistic rage that Abbott's engagement with a broader "masculine urge to destroy the feminine" becomes most apparent (Powell 171). Rather than something immutable and controlled, Abbott exposes masculinity as a pointedly paranoid and "hysterical structure," one that displaces "its own anxieties onto an undefined, empty femininity" (Abbott 2002, 30).

Yet, while Abbott's depiction of Hop reaffirms the shaky, parasitic structure of hardboiled masculinity, her representation of female identity is far from a one-note emulation of the seductive, dangerous femme fatale. Indeed, the female characters that pose the most threat to Hop's subjectivity are those that fall outside of the traditional "seductress" paradigm. Both reporter Frannie Adair and ex-wife Midge, in particular, are able to see through the fragile veneer that Hop projects, while exhibiting an autonomy and agency that threaten to destroy the career and identity he has forged. The menace posed by femininity thus derives not from "beauty and eroticism" but from "the way that [it] establishes rule over men by utilizing the apparently 'masculine' qualities of power and authority" (Sully 57). This proves to be the case with Spangler, who, although ostensibly cast in the role of victim and "whore," becomes representative of the immense pressure exerted upon female identity by the misogynistic, patriarchal structures of Los Angeles and Hollywood film. As the narrative proceeds, Hop's conflicted attempts to both solve and quash the Spangler case lead him to uncover a festering underworld of racketeering, corruption, and death.

After implicitly revealing his connection to the Spangler case to reporter Frannie Adair during a booze-fuelled breakdown, Hop grows increasingly anxious that she will uncover his direct involvement in the suppression of evidence. He subsequently begins tailing Adair, only to be led to the familiar apartment of "Miss Hotcha," the burlesque blonde he spent the night with on the evening Spangler disappeared. Hop quickly realizes that the blonde is actually Jean's cousin, Peggy, who reveals that Jean and Iolene had been running an extortion racket surreptitiously subsidised by a Mickey Cohen "goon" called Davy Ogul. This involved Jean seducing celebrities and executives while Iolene secretly snapped compromising smut pics. Peggy later directs Hop to Iolene's secret hideaway, where he not only discovers a cryptic file tab marked "Dr Stillman," but also Iolene's decomposing corpse with a bullet wound in the temple. The Stillman clue ultimately implicates Hop's ex-wife Midge, who had once worked at Stillman's underground "celebrity" abortion clinic (with Spangler) prior to meeting Hop. While only employed for a short time, Spangler had used her friendship with Midge to swipe medical files from the cabinet to facilitate her and Iolene's extortion scheme.

Although Adair ultimately abandons the case after surmising that Iolene and Jean were whacked by Mickey Cohen for getting "greedy," Hop's trail leads him to Merry Lake, a rural, scenic getaway overlooking a "shimmering" vista of water (210). In a deliberate reversal of Chandler's *The Lady in the Lake*—where the idyllic rural landscape of "Little Fawn Lake" is corrupted by brutalized bodies—the solitude and tranquillity of "Merry Lake" is the site of Jean Spangler's resurrection. Able to flee the merciless clutches of Merrel and Sutton, Spangler reappears at the denouement of the narrative, an ending that reverses the traditional "voicelessness" of the female victim (Messent 89). Indeed, Abbott's focus on the existence of "other" narratives and "other" voices—ones that operate against the hegemonic logic of hardboiled masculinity—is foreshadowed earlier in the text when Midge tells Hop that "[y]ou think Jean was just another starlet grifting her way down. But she had whole other stories to tell. They all do" (201). The implication here is unambiguous, as Abbott underscores the importance of recognizing spectrums and nuances of female identity that operate outside of the rigid binaries of "dangerous seductress" and the "voiceless victim." Indeed, Spangler's account of her attack and subsequent escape problematizes this very opposition while vividly actualizing a ruthless world of patriarchal violence that renders such patterns of femininity less distinct and less inviolable. No longer a disembodied image onto which fantasies of male lust and rage can be projected, Jean is given the opportunity to take control of her own narrative, a narrative that counters, disrupts, and challenges Hop's masculine paradigm.

After being confronted by Hop, Jean attempts to explain her version of events, one that contests Hop's tale of seduction, manipulation and promiscuity:

> "I was a fine mother, Mr Hopkins—sure, I remember your name. I was a fine mother who got pulled into something rotten and didn't want to put my little girl into danger for it."
>
> "Pulled in, eh? Is that how you frame it? You know, when you fall into the blackmail racket, you're not falling. You're jumping. Those were some rough boys you were mixed up with. But I didn't see you kicking and screaming."
>
> "What are you talking about?"
>
> "You knew what you were doing, didn't you, doll?" Since when did he call women "doll"? He didn't like the sound of his voice, wasn't even sure what it was, but he couldn't stop. It flew out at sharp angles, shards whizzing through the air. "The biggest stars in town. And ready for a dance with you. You were seeing dollar signs all the way to the back room of the Red Lily."
>
> "That's what you think", she said, with nary a flinch.
>
> "Yes," he replied, watching her, looking.
>
> "You know all about it, huh?"

"I know enough."

"You don't know anything," she said quietly. (Abbott 217-18)

Faced with a narrative that dislocates his preconceived configuration of Jean as dangerous femme fatale turned mutilated victim, Hop begins ventriloquizing the hardboiled vernacular of the noir private eye. Yet Hop's appropriation of this language is represented as entirely out of his control, something almost spectral that inhabits and then flies out of him at "sharp angles." This seeming loss of linguistic authority is, on the contrary, demonstrative of Hop's attempts to reassert jurisdiction over the narrative. The story that Hop constructs repositions Jean as a stereotypical seductress, a fast "doll" blinded by "dollar signs" who ultimately got in too deep with "some rough boys." In the process, Hop's uncontrollable espousal of this hardboiled dialect becomes a composite part of his reassertion of a masculine identity. As Frank Krutnik suggests, the "masculinization of language" is one of the key facets of the hardboiled style, a linguistic "weapon" that is "often more a measure of the hero's prowess than the use of guns and other more tangible aids to violence" (43). Yet, having already been brutalized and physically scarred by the masculine rage of Merrel and Sutton—who quite literally carve "DEAD WHORE" onto her navel—Jean refuses to succumb to Hop's linguistic violence, to his similar attempts to inscribe her body. Through crushing Hop's protests and telling her own story, Jean is obviously neither "victim" nor "perpetrator," "angel" or "whore" (Abbott 171). These rigid determinations of identity are not applicable in a toxic, misogynistic post-war culture.

While Jean escapes being reduced to a "voiceless victim," the finale of *The Song Is You* reaffirms the cyclicality of a depraved and destructive Hollywood machine that consistently makes "women disappear" (Powell 172). The novel ends with Hop being approached for help once again by Barbara Payton, a down-on-her luck actress who had once "had it all" (237). Yet, with Payton's commercial appeal on the decline, Hop's obligation to the actress diminishes in tandem. Now that he regards her as just a "whore" whose luck "finally ran out," Hop repeats the pattern of abandonment that saw Spangler assaulted and almost killed at the hands of Merrel and Sutton. While Payton eventually persuades Hop to "make some calls," her impending and inevitable disappearance is hauntingly foreshadowed via her reference to the "shadow life":

> Hop smiled and looked surreptitiously at his watch.
>
> "Do you ever feel like none of it's real, Hop? Like"—she moved forward in her chair, eyes still, behind the skein of red, jewel-blue—"like you're not real. Like I think maybe if I reached across the desk toward you, my hand would go right through you. I know it would. Do you ever feel like that?"
>
> "No," he said, surprised at his own abruptness. Suddenly, he felt like he'd do anything to get her out of his office. What did she mean, her hand would go right through him? What did it have to do with him? "Never. But I know a lot of stars do think about that. About the persona"—
>
> "I'm not talking about that," she said. I'm talking about the shadow life. The life you're living instead. The life you're living because you can't fight yourself anymore. You're too goddamned tired to fight yourself anymore." (Abbott 240)

Hop mistakes Barbara's reference to his lack of corporality as a metaphor for the holographic reality of celebrity culture, where subjectivity becomes a mere extension of a world structured around commodity signs and cinematic simulacra. Instead,

Barbara recognizes Hop's—and her own—pervasion by the "shadow life," the seedy, corrupt underworld of the Hollywood machine that disregards, rejects, and buries. Hop's complicity in facilitating these disappearances lends him his own shadow quality, a lack of definition or spectrality that is the price of knowing "where all the bodies are buried" (238).

Whilst Abbott refuses to negate the existence of a perniciously violent and misogynistic hardboiled world in *Die a Little* and *The Song Is You,* both texts emphasize the existence and importance of "other narratives" of female identity that fall outside the rigid binaries of victim and seductress. Victimhood still prevails, but Abbott deliberately shifts the dominant gaze of the genre to those who are under pressure from the patriarchal imperatives of post-war culture. This often materializes in images of duality, ones that become connected to the schizophrenic nature of Los Angeles's social and physical topography more broadly. In the process, Abbott creatively explores her critical assumptions about the hardboiled hero, revealing masculinity as a paranoid and parasitic construction that forms a destructive reliance on the feminine for its very meaning and sustainment. Whilst drawing on the traditions of hardboiled fiction and film, Abbott's work actively interrogates and transgresses the assumptions of the form, revealing her as a new and important voice in contemporary crime fiction.

Works Cited

Abbott, Megan and Annie Adams. "A Conversation with Megan Abbott." *Sewanee Review*, vol. 126, no. 3, 2018, pp. 387-429.

Abbott, Megan. *Die a Little*. London: Simon & Schuster, 2005.

—. *The Song is You.* London: Simon & Schuster, 2007.

—. *The Street Was Mine: White Masculinity in Hardboiled Fiction and Film Noir*. Palgrave Macmillan, 2002.

Ashman, Nathan. *James Ellroy and Voyeur Fiction*. Lexington Books, 2018.

Beyer, Charlotte. "'This Really Isn't a Job for a Girl to Take on Alone': Reappraising Feminism and Genre Fiction in Sara Paretsky's Crime Novel *Indemnity Only*." *This Book Is an Action: Feminist Print Culture and Activist Aesthetics*, edited by Jaime Harker and Cecilia Konchar Farr, U of Illinois P, 2016, pp. 226-44.

Braun, Heather. *The Rise and Fall of the Femme Fatale in British Literature, 1790-1910*. Fairleigh Dickinson UP, 2012.

Brook, Vincent. *Land of Smoke and Mirrors: A Cultural History of Los Angeles*. Rutgers UP, 2013.

Godfrey, Rebecca. "Megan Abbott: An email conversation with Rebecca Godfrey." 20 July 2009. *Barnes and Noble,* www.barnesandnoble.com/review/megan-abbott.

Horsley, Lee. "From Sherlock Holmes to the Present." *A Companion to Crime Fiction*, edited by Charles Rzepka and Lee Horsley, Wiley-Blackwell, 2010, pp. 28-42.

Humann, Heather Duerre. *Gender Bending Detective Fiction: A Critical Analysis of Selected Works*. McFarland, 2017.

Krutnik, Frank. *In a Lonely Street: Film Noir, Genre, Masculinity*. Routledge, 2006.

Messent, Peter. *The Crime Fiction Handbook*. Wiley, 2013.

Mulvey, Laura. "Visual Pleasure and Narrative Cinema." *Screen* vol. 16, no. 3, 1975, pp. 6-18.

Palmer, Oscar. "An Interview with Megan Abbott." *Cultura Impopular*, 7 Mar. 2011. www.culturaimpopular.com/2011/03/an-interview-with-megan-abbott.

Pâquet, Lili. *Crime Fiction from a Professional Eye: Women Writers with Law Enforcement and Justice Experience*. McFarland, 2018.

Powell, Diana. "'A Pointed Demythologization': The Influence of James Ellroy's Novels on Megan Abbott's Revisionism of the Femme Fatale." *The Big Somewhere: Essays on James Ellroy's Noir World*, Bloomsbury, 2018, pp. 163-80.

Scaggs, John. *Crime Fiction*. Routledge, 2005.

Smith, Erin. *Hard-Boiled: Working Class Readers and Pulp Magazines*. Temple UP, 2010.

Sully, Jess. "Challenging the Stereotype: The Femme Fatale in Fin de Siècle Art and Early Cinema." *The Femme Fatale: Images, Histories, Contexts*, edited by Helen Hanson and Catherine O'Rawe, Palgrave, 2010, pp. 46-59.

Walton, Priscilla L. and Manina Jones. *Detective Agency: Women Rewriting the Hard-Boiled Tradition*. U of California P, 1999.

Janet Evanovich and the Rise of the Chick Detective

Andrea Braithwaite

Abstract

By stepping into a set of gumshoes historically and most famously worn by men, the female detective helps illuminate the gendered dynamics of crime and violence. This subversive quality is amplified by amateur female sleuths. Working unfettered — and unprotected — by any formal affiliation, amateur female sleuths establish their own networks of knowledge, surveillance, and support. Janet Evanovich's ongoing and bestselling Stephanie Plum series, launched in the mid-1990s, popularized a particular iteration of this figure: the chick detective.

> "I've been working as a bounty hunter for a while now and I'm not the world's best. I barely make enough money to cover my rent each month. I've been stalked by crazed killers, taunted by naked fat men firebombed, shot at, spat at, cussed at, chased by humping dogs, attacked by a flock of Canadian honkers, rolled in garbage, and my cars get destroyed at an alarming rate." (*Eleven* 4)

Meet Stephanie Plum. Appearing first in Janet Evanovich's 1994 novel *One for the Money*, and then in twenty-three (to date) best-selling installments, Stephanie Plum is a bounty hunter in Trenton, New Jersey, in a little neighborhood called the Burg. She is also an amateur sleuth, a former lingerie salesperson, an on-again off-again romantic partner to a local cop, an occasional sexual partner to a former colleague, and a dedicated caretaker of a hardy hamster named Rex. Stephanie Plum is a *chick detective*: a hybrid character that combines elements of detective fiction with chick lit. Rising to prominence in the early 2000s, the chick detective is easily found by scanning the spines and covers at nearly any bookstore: splashes of pink, yellow, and purple; images of shoes, cocktails, and lipstick; and tongue-in-cheek titles like *Killer Heels* (Anderson) and *Knock Off* (Pollero).

Between the pages of these seemingly frothy covers lie more sinister stories: assault and abuse; exploitation and extortion; violent and grisly deaths. The chick detective's generic hybridity creates a gendered subjectivity for investigating these kinds of crimes; informed not only by a heritage of women detectives both amateur and professional, but also by a form of pop culture femininity bound up in shifting articulations to feminism, neoliberalism, and capitalism, the chick detective formula confronts gendered experiences of crime and of passion. By examining Janet Evanovich's Stephanie Plum series as both progenitor and popularizer of this narrative form, we can see the chick detective's role in contemporary discourses about women, power, and agency—both part of this pop culture conversation, and a *partial* conversation.

This critical discourse is made possible by the way the chick detective draws upon the conventions of chick texts. Looking closely at the structure and themes of this genre clarifies how the chick detective's re-presentations navigate its tropes. In particular, this comparison highlights the work of detecting and exposure to everyday sexualized violence; the false dichotomy of the chick genre's conventional work-versus-relationship dilemma; and the role of serial storytelling in foregrounding how the chick detective engages with gendered stages of the "good life." The chick detective's debt to both crime and chick narratives results in an ambiguous, and even evasive, consideration of the cultural currency of narratives of female achievement.

"Stephanie Plum, cunning sexpot, about to embark on a dangerous mission"

As a cultural figure, the chick rose to prominence in the mass market fiction, popular film, and television of the late 1990s and into the 2000s. Appearing in texts typified by their specific set of character functions and narrative trajectories, the chick is "a young woman in her 20s or early 30s negotiating career, family, body image, and romantic relationships" (Jernigan 68). Across works like the inaugural *Bridget Jones's Diary* (Fielding; Maguire), *Sex and the City* (HBO), *Confessions of a Shopaholic* (Kinsella; Hogan), *How to Lose a Guy in 10 Days* (Petrie), and *Bergdorf Blondes* (Sykes), the chick takes shape as a cheeky, self-deprecating woman with quirky friends, a not-quite-fulfilling job, and a lonely heart. Most chick texts set out to resolve at least the latter; a meet-cute introduces the chick to an eligible man, and the story typically proceeds by bouncing back and forth between personal and professional obstacles—and shopping trips—until the hero and heroine finally recognize their feelings for each other.

The emotional impact of these events is amplified by the genre's tone. Breezy, comedic, and confessional, chick texts foreground their protagonists' private selves through a first-person address in fiction and voice-overs in film and television. This framing makes chick texts feel like a peek behind the curtain, a set of shared secrets about women's wants and needs, hopes and fears. It creates—and presumes—a set of experiences recognizable as *women's* experiences, to "reveal a shared frustration and disillusionment with many aspects of women's lives" (Guenther 95). This intimacy makes chick texts useful vehicles for a range of cultural messages and cultural work. For example, Diane Negra in "Structural Integrity" and "What A Girl Wants?" argues that Hollywood chick flicks of the early 2000s participate in a larger ideological project of ushering in a "new traditionalism" and circulating a set of conservative gender norms in which women often trade in their public and professional lives for domestic pursuits (see also Probyn).

At the same time, chick texts are credited with expanding popular representations of women's sexuality. Their confessions tone dive into sexual needs, fantasies, and desires, and many chick texts depict heroines in search of not just a romantic partner, but also a *sexual* partner. "[T]he chick heroine is portrayed as sexually active, and *experiences* rather than only *anticipates* sexual pleasure," an explicit and enthusiastic approach to sex that helps define the chick as a character (Rowntree 509; see also Kiernan). Lingering breathlessly on the promise of bulges, hardnesses, and hoohahs, chicks are active agents in their own bodily pleasure, a discursive construction of female sexuality that "provide[s] a public language to talk about me and other similar women—it may even provide women with words to talk about themselves" (Probyn 154).

The female detective, meanwhile, is "more concerned with proving her abilities as an intelligent and competent detective and 'getting her man'—in terms of catching the criminal—rather than 'getting a man'—in terms of matrimony" (Gates 6). Her travels down the means streets of crime fictions flag the ways in which crime stories often rely upon two central stereotypes: woman as victim, or woman as threat (see, e.g., Gates; Walton and Jones). Instead, female detectives claim an historically male purview in narratives that reveal the gendered nature of crime, labor, public space, and violence. Along the way, "[t]hese heroines have adventures, a commitment to justice, and a license to do what's usually done by men... And freedom—the detective earns her own pay check but isn't tied down to a desk, computer, cubicle, kitchen, or nursery" (Mizejewski, *Hardboiled* 4).

This language of freedom suggests synchronicities with the chick character. Both are recognizable by their agency and independence; both chronicle everyday experiences working in urban environments; both reflect on interpersonal relationships as dynamics of vulnerability and security. These tropes also define a formula that firmly straddles both worlds: that of the chick detective. In chick detective stories, a typical chick heroine finds herself unexpectedly and unintentionally at the center of a crime. Frustrated and feeling trapped—by the lukewarm response she receives from police, by the villain's machinations, by circumstances that make her, her friends, or her family look increasingly culpable—she decides to solve the crime herself. An amateur sleuth, the chick detective stumbles her way through a series of clues, often relying on her friends for advice and support as she tries to balance work with her slapdash investigations and with her growing interest in a hunky man (who is usually part of the official network of police and legal systems). These relationships and investigations change and are changed by the chick detective heroine. As Stephanie Plum reflects:

> I considered my own life and the choices I'd made. Until recently these choices had been relatively safe and predictable. College, marriage, divorce, work. Then, through no fault of my own, I didn't have a job. Next thing, I was a bounty hunter, and I'd killed a man. It had been self defense, but it was still a regrettable act that came creeping back to me late at night. I knew things about myself now, and about human nature, that nice girls from the burg weren't supposed to know. (*Three* 288-89)

With their intimate tone and ostensibly endearing insecurities, chick detectives offer a pop culture feminine subjectivity shaped by misogyny, sexualized abuse, and public exposure, and that suggests that young women's lives can often be read *as* crime stories.

Frequently, the characteristics associated most strongly with being a "chick"—shopping savvy, gossip mongering, women's intuition—become key to solving the crime. Just as often, the narratives' core crimes are right out of the pages of more hardboiled detective fiction: embezzling, assault, organized crime, high-stakes theft, murders. The chick detective's capabilities can be seen as critical commentaries on the plot and character devices of both crime stories and chick texts: the perceived legitimacy of women's labor *as* detectives in detective fictions; the trajectories of monogamy and marriage that dominate chick texts; and the complicating role of seriality in concepts of progress and resolution in both genres. The chick detective re-articulates how "[f]rom her first appearance in nineteenth-century fiction to the contemporary criminalist film, the female detective has struggled to be both a successful detective and a successful woman" (Gates 4). Janet Evanovich's best-selling novels concretize crime and chick fictions' contemporary gendered power dynamics of work, sex, and success in the character of Stephanie Plum, the foundational chick detective.

"You're in the middle of some crazy whodunit shit that you didn't even go looking for"

> "When I was a little girl I used to dress Barbie up without underpants. On the outside, she'd look like the perfect lady. Tasteful plastic heels, tailored suit. But underneath, she was naked. I'm a bail enforcement agent now.... And being a bail enforcement agent is sort of like being bare-bottom Barbie. It's about having a secret. And it's about wearing a lot of bravado on the outside when you're really operating without underpants." (*Five* 1)

After being downsized out of her job as a buyer for an underperforming lingerie outlet, Steph is in dire need of work, otherwise she risks losing her apartment and moving back in with her parents. She blackmails her way into a position at her cousin Vinnie's bail bonds office by threatening to tell Vinnie's wife about his extramarital sexual activities. As a bail enforcement agent, or bounty hunter, Steph's job seems simple: she tracks down people out on bail who have missed their court date (failure-to-appears, or FTAs, in bounty hunter lingo), and brings them in to the courthouse to reschedule. In each book, however, there is always a larger mystery that Steph is determined to solve—sometimes on her own, but often with the help of her colleague and occasional sex partner Ranger, or her on-again off-again boyfriend and local cop Joe Morelli.

Yet while Steph may have come to detecting in financial desperation, her decision to stick with it is bolstered by wanting to intervene in the seemingly endless instances of violence against women that she now encounters and which form the bulk of her amateur investigations: "I hate the bad people, and the ugly crimes, and the human suffering they cause" (*Four* 105). This pattern is established in the very first novel, *One for the Money*, in which her hunt for an FTA brings her to the attention of local boxing champ Benito Ramirez. Sadistic and surrounded by toadies, Ramirez enjoys abusing women. Once he sets his sights on Steph he jerks off on her door and leaves threatening messages on her answering machine, including one of a woman being raped:

> I heard laboured breathing, scuffling noises, and then someone moaned. A woman's voice carried from a distance. 'No,' she begged. 'Oh God, no.' A terrible scream split the air.... She sounded young. Her words were barely audible, thick with tears and trembling with the effort of speech. 'It was g-g-good,' she said. Her voice broke. 'Oh God help me, I'm hurt. I'm hurt something awful.' (165-66)

Ramirez's actions escalate until one night Steph returns to her apartment to find a woman beaten, raped, penetrated with a broken bottle, and left for dead on her fire escape: Lula, a sex worker Steph had met while canvassing Ramirez's neighborhood for information. Lula survives and switches professions to be a file clerk at Vinnie's office (and self-appointed partner on many of Steph's FTA apprehensions).

As Steph quickly learns, the justice system is not structured to help women like Lula. While Ramirez ends up behind bars, he is out on parole a few books later. Morelli tells her Ramirez has not changed much: "'He picked up a hooker on Stark Street last night and almost killed her. Brutalized her and left her for dead in a Dumpster. Somehow she managed to climb out, and two kids found her this morning'" (*Five* 219). Lurking outside her apartment, Ramirez gets shot by an angry FTA who has shown up to harass Steph, yet Steph remains responsible for his death in the eyes of Ramirez's admirers. Ramirez's skill in the ring made a lot of local men very wealthy and his violent misogyny emboldens others; his death marks Steph as a problem for the Burg's small-time gangs and they later put out a contract on her because "'it's not good to get collected by snatch. It's not got a high prestige factor'" (*Ten* 281).

Steph's job thus exposes her to the interlocking dynamics of community culture, family dynasties, and a lopsided legal system that make women vulnerable—some women more than others. Evanovich's books illustrate the ordinariness of violence against racialized and marginalized women. *Three to Get Deadly* turns on the secret life of seemingly perfect candy store owner Moses Bedemier, who has been working with local drug dealers to coerce young women into performing in his homemade—and vicious—pornography, including Lula's friend Jackie. In *Four to Score*, Steph meets Maxine Nowicki, who vows revenge on her abusive boyfriend Eddie Kuntz: "'I mean like breaking my nose. I mean like all the times he got drunk and smacked me around. All the times he cheated on me. All the times he took my paycheck. And the lies about getting married'" (109). *Hard Eight* features Evelyn Soder and her daughter Annie, who have been hiding from their landlord Eddie Abruzzi ever since Evelyn's abusive husband used them as collateral for his gambling debts. These women rarely fit the dominant vision of an "ideal" victim that would justify actions against them as crimes, and such legitimation is "contingent on the victim's social status: victims must be judged as innocent, virtuous, and honourable" (Dowler et al. 841). Instead, they are often people who are most likely to *be* victims and are easily characterized as such: racialized, lower class, lower education, engaged in sex work, seniors. Even when Steph decides (only temporarily) to abandon the bounty hunting business in *Takedown Twenty*, she's unable to step away from the case; the spectre of multiple elderly women killed and left in Dumpsters drives her to find the culprit because "'[i]t's bad enough that these women are murdered... but I hate that the killer throws them away'" (57).

Steph's shift from lingerie retailer to the investigative work of bounty hunter — from chick to chick detective — exposes her to casual, everyday violence against women, for in crime fictions "violence is the central trope of relationships between the sexes" (Mizejewski, *Dressed to Kill* 125). Alongside the larger mystery, most books include a handful of routine FTA captures that paint a picture of the ordinary cases that form the backbone of Vinnie's business. These are often repeat domestic violence offenders, as office manager Connie Rosolli explains to Steph: "'Got a long history. A real asshole. Every time he gets a couple beers in him he knocks Kitty around. Sometimes he goes too far and puts her in the hospital. Sometimes she files charges, but eventually she always backs off. Scared, I guess....He's out on two thousand dollars'" (*Two* 115). When Steph dispiritedly comments on the paltry bond, Connie replies, "'Domestic violence doesn't count for much of a threat'" (*Two* 115). Steph starts to derive a sense of accomplishment from this work. While her skills are still suspect and her approach doesn't always inspire confidence, she increasingly feels capable—and desirous of—making a material difference in the lives of women in her community: "My shoes were soaked through, my nose was running and I couldn't stop thinking about Jackie. Finding her car seemed totally inadequate. I wanted to improve her life. I wanted to get her off drugs, and I wanted to change her profession. Hell, she wasn't so dumb. She could probably be a brain surgeon if she just had a decent haircut" (*Three* 56).

Often unspoken but difficult to ignore is Steph's privileged position in the Burg. The "chick" figure typically benefits from socioeconomic and racial privilege, as the "heroines of this new genre [are] white and generally middle class" (Guerrero 88). Steph's agency, her ability to do good and feel good about it, is made possible by the stability of her social status. While often scrambling for money—in the very first book she trades her kitchen appliances in for a run-down used car after hers is repossessed—she has her family as a safety net. They offer a place to stay, food to eat, and a car to borrow whenever Steph needs it, a security the Burg's marginalized women do not have. She also has back-up: Ranger's skills from his time in the military and his reputation as capable of substantial violence help her out of dangerous situations; when he later launches his own private security company, Steph can then boast an entire team of burly men as back-up. She also has the informal support of the Trenton police force, thanks to her long-running relationship with Joe Morelli. His insider knowledge, together with his colleagues' willingness to help another officer's girlfriend, means that while she may be investigating crimes in an unofficial capacity—as she says, "I always feel like an illegitimate stepchild when I work with Morelli. He's a Trenton cop and I'm someone with a badge I bought on the internet" (*Nineteen* 267)—she is never far from police support. Familiar elements from chick texts, like a tense mother/daughter relationship, a sexy bad-boy, and a will-they-won't-they boyfriend, here ensure that the chick detective's material conditions are far removed from those of the women she looks out for. Her work may take her to Stark Street, the Burg's most economically depressed and crime-ridden neighborhood, but unlike Maxine or Jackie or Evelyn and Annie, Steph has the mobility and resources to leave.

"Most women try to avoid murderers and rapists. I have a girlfriend who goes out trying to find them."

No matter how much the chick detective may enjoy her amateur investigations, they become a point of contention in some of her closest relationships—perceived by others as an impediment to what she should *truly* want. Characteristic of the chick genre, this pattern presents "professional women [as] misguided at best and troubled at worst" (Negra, "Structural Integrity" 53). Negra describes this as "miswanting": when "the heroine comes to realizes that her professional aspirations are misplaced" (*What A Girl Wants?* 95). A narrative resolution as well as a character revelation, miswanting relies upon a specific and ideological construction of women's work that subordinates career to family. As Negra suggests, this character "development" works not by removing women's work from the equation, but rather by reorganizing its place in women's lives, creating "narratives of adjusted ambition" (95).

In Evanovich's novels, this perspective is articulated most insistently by Steph's mother. A lifelong homemaker, she continually bemoans Steph's investigative activities and tries to steer her toward more suitable workplaces. For Steph's mother, the problem with Steph being a bounty hunter is not really the danger, but rather the unpredictable hours that leave little room for a romantic relationship and eventual family. A different job may just be the key to Steph finally settling down. Determined to "fix" her daughter's marital status, she regularly sets Steph up with local single men regardless of suitability. In *Takedown Twenty*, for instance, she sees a chance to fix Steph's job *and* her love life by hooking her up with local butcher Randy Berger: "'He's not the butcher anymore. He owns the deli now. And he's still looking for someone to take over the meat counter. It could be a good job for you. You could get a regular paycheck, and no one would shoot at you or drop you off a bridge. And Randy is single. Who knows what could happen? He could turn out to be *the one*'" (143-44). Steph's mother's shortlist of qualities for her daughter's next husband are superficial, reflecting an unquestioned belief in more conservative credentials. In *Smokin' Seventeen* she invites Dave, one of Steph's high-school acquaintances, for dinner: "'He comes from a good family, and he was captain of the football team *and* an honour student'" (26). He also pursues Steph relentlessly, despite her lack of interest. He sends unwanted gifts, breaks into her apartment, and keeps returning—even after she breaks his nose and stun-guns him. Her instincts tell her that Dave is dangerous; by the end of the novel we discover he's behind the dead bodies turning up all over Trenton. Steph's mother, meanwhile, struggles to reconcile this behavior: "My mother's eyes were glazed, her face registering complete disbelief, her arm mechanically moving the iron over the sleeve of my father's dress shirt. 'He seemed like such a nice young man,' she said. 'I was sure he was the one. He came from such a good family'" (321).

Unlike her mother, Steph is less confident that marriage is the key to personal happiness. Some of this suspicion is based on her short-lived marriage to the philandering Dickie Orr: "Guess I was stupid. Swayed by Dickie's good looks and education. My head turned by the fact that he was a lawyer. I didn't see the flaws. The low opinion Dickie has of women" (*Eight* 28). Her mother's firmly-held belief that marriage is the superior state falters in the face of Steph's first-hand experience—and even her second-hand experience. Steph's older sister Valerie is by all accounts a paragon of perfect femininity, "'happily married with two beautiful children. She doesn't go around chasing after killers, finding dead bodies'" (*Seven* 24). Yet even Valerie finds out that marriage is not quite what conventional wisdom would have women believe. After a few years and a few children, her husband leaves her for another woman, and Valerie struggles to understand why: "'I thought we had a good marriage. I made nice meals. And I kept the house nice. I went to the gym so I'd be attractive. I even got my hair cut like Meg Ryan. I don't understand what went wrong'" (*Seven* 81).

Committed relationships are problems rather than solutions in chick detective stories. These narratives challenge "the system convincing women that marriage and romance are our only stories. The romance story in all its forms works hard to gloss over the bumps and pitfalls of heterosexuality. But the female-detective genre actually *depends* on these tensions to sustain the story" (Mizejewski, *Hardboiled* 12). Steph routinely runs down FTAs booked on violent charges, like Morris Munson, who "'ran over the victim, who just happened to be his ex-wife, he beat her with a tire iron, raped her, and tried to set her on fire. He was charged with vehicular manslaughter because according to the M.E. she was already dead when he took the tire iron to her. He had her soaked in gasoline and was trying to get his Bic to work when a blue-and-white happened to drive by'" (*Six* 9).

These FTAs are notable only for getting caught. Abusive husbands are common in the Burg, as are mean drunks: "the Mancusos and Morellis were notorious for their violent, alcohol-fueled tempers and for their ability to sweet-talk a woman into an abusive relationship" (*Two* 241). Steph may "love and sleep with men, but [she] also face[s] stubborn sexism in [her] field, abusive men in the world at large, and patterns of violence that are often directed at women" (Mizejewski, *Hardboiled* 13). In this context, Steph feels *lucky* that Joe Morelli, her on-again off-again boyfriend and local cop, does not follow in his family's footsteps. Yet even that relief is not enough to convince her to give marriage another try. Part of her reluctance stems from Morelli's attitude toward her job. Especially in the series' early novels, Steph and Morelli's relationship stalls when he insists Steph give up her job as one condition of staying together: "'For starters, you'd have to get a new job. Or even better, no job at all'" (*Ten* 262). Often presented as a solution to Steph's ongoing financial woes, Morelli's vision of Steph as a wife, mother, and homemaker illustrates the common chick flick resolution of what Negra calls "retreatism," which "showcases the rewards of an adult woman's return to a hometown space and decision to downshift her career" (*What A Girl Wants?* 88). This is often the conclusion in chick lit as well: "[I]t would seem that within this genre women are only allowed to be successful at work if this is achieved with the support and endorsement of a loving man" (Gill and Herdieckerhoff 496). Steph, on the other hand, continually rejects any version of her relationship with Morelli that relies upon her retreating from the workforce: "'Maybe it's just not the right time for us to be married. I don't want to be a bounty hunter for the rest of my life, but I certainly don't want to be a house-wife right now. And I really don't want to be married to someone who gives me ultimatums. And maybe Joe needs to examine what he wants from a wife'" (*Seven* 304).

Even their preliminary attempts at arrangements resembling marriage fail. Occasionally, Steph and Morelli try living together at his place (usually while Steph's is repaired after yet another firebombing). However, their expectations—of each other, of themselves—end up driving them apart: Morelli assumes that Steph will take over more traditional homemaking activities such as staying stocked on kitchen staples. Steph, who rarely even does this for herself, resents Morelli's assumptions at the same time as she feels she *should* be meeting them: "Okay, in all honesty, I thought this was a pretty stupid thing to break up over. And in all honesty, I should have remembered to buy bread. That didn't alter the fact that I was mad. . . . And the truth was, I wasn't entirely sure if I was mad at Morelli or mad at myself" (*Sixteen* 21). Cohabitation strains rather than supports their relationship; when they return to their previous pattern of meeting up for dinner and sex, their resentment of each other decreases dramatically.

Steph and Morelli try to redirect the chick text trajectory that culminates in commitment. Yet what they want is frequently in conflict with what they are *supposed* to want. As a result, they have been engaged-to-be-engaged a few times, a stop-gap measure to stave off further family scrutiny, and, as Steph confesses, an idea that seems more enticing in the throes of passion than it does upon somber reflection:

> Truth is, my engagement was kind of casual, being that the proposal was made at a time when it was difficult to distinguish between the desire to spend the rest of our lives together and the desire to get sex on a regular basis. . . . I suppose it would be most accurate to say we were engaged to be engaged. And that's a comfortable place for us to live because it's vague enough to absolve Morelli and me of serious marital discussion. (*Seven* 76-77)

Steph's stance on monogamy is another impediment to conventional settling down. Her sexual interludes with Ranger make it difficult for her to have a serious marital discussion with Morelli. It also complicates the chick genre's characterization of Mr. Right as an identifiable, self-evident figure. Both Ranger and Morelli are the "right" guy, and both are the "wrong" guy, making any sort of choice between them nearly impossible: "It was like choosing between birthday cake and a big-boy margarita. How could I possibly decide?" (*Eleven* 9). Morelli, to whom she lost her virginity in high-school, seems like a great match now that they've both grown up: "He'd done some time in the Navy, joined the Trenton police, set a record for barroom brawls and one-night stands, and miraculously emerged from the devastation as a disease-free, mostly mature and responsible adult" (*Twenty-One* 242). Ranger seems pretty perfect, too: gorgeous, quietly funny, and accomplished, he cares deeply for her. At the same time, he is clear about his intentions to keep their connection strictly sexual. While this stops Steph from ever fully investing in her relationship with Ranger, it also keeps her returning to him — their sexual encounters are mutually desired and momentarily convenient. Steph's unrepentant non-monogamy further distances her from the chick genre's "re-virginization" epiphany in which the sex between hero and heroine is so fulfilling that it "wipes away previous 'sullying' experiences by making them enjoy sex fully for the very first time" (Gill and Herdieckerhoff 494). Steph, in comparison, enjoys sex fully every time—with the near-hero Morelli as well as with Ranger: "Ranger is an alpha male. Leader of the pack. Always. In the bedroom he sets the pace. There's never an awkward moment because he's focused on the prize, the pleasure, the human experience. He knows where to touch. He knows when to ask the question. He's strong and hard where it counts. He's smart. He's patient. He's magic" (*Twenty-Three* 300). The chick text's contention that "sexual liberation (here represented by the notion of pursing sexual pleasure through more than one partner) is not what women really want" is upended in Evanovich's novels, as Steph repeatedly seeks out sex with multiple men and gets off on it (Gill and Herdieckerhoff 494).

Steph's sexual attitude and appetite, along with her antipathy toward a romantic commitment, problematize the chick genre's denouement of miswanting. Between the felt importance of her work and lived experience of monogamy and marriage, Steph is reluctant to rank either her work or her relationships above the other. Instead, the narratives wrap up with reminders of what she values about both of her sexual partners and of what she is willing to give to either of them. In *Turbo Twenty-Three*, after spending the night with Ranger, she concludes: "Truth is, my relationship with Morelli was probably okay. It didn't really matter that we weren't engaged to be engaged right now. We cared about each other. We enjoyed being together. And maybe sometime in the future we'd move forward with the marriage and family thing. End of discussion" (307). While this is an unsatisfying resolution for a genre in which heroines "invariably settle down in a heterosexual monogamous partnership that looks remarkably conventional," it offers another vision of how the personal satisfactions promised by romantic and sexual relationships can exist alongside rather than in competition with the professional satisfactions of a career (Rowntree 509).

"I make lots of mistakes. I try hard not to make the same mistake more than three or four times."

This irresolution serves another important function in Evanovich's chick detective novels: it helps propel the stories' seriality. While common in detective fiction—Sara Paretsky's V.I. Warshawski series is up to nineteen, and Sue Grafton's Kinsey Millhone to twenty-five—most chick texts are, with few exceptions, stand-alone works. Evanovich's books are instead organized around crime (and, by extension, the issue of Steph's shaky finances); her ambivalence toward monogamy and marriage prove almost as intractable as the kinds of crimes—and the kinds of victims — pervasive in the Burg. For example, in *Hard Eight* Steph is looking for Andy Bender, whom she has tracked down and turned in previously: "This is the guy who came after me with a chain saw" (52). He is equally displeased to see her again, and is the same aggressive, recalcitrant FTA he was before: "'I'm gonna gut [Steph] like a fish....I'm gonna filet her like a trout. No bitch just walks in and ruins *my* lunch'" (56). And in each book in the series Steph has a stack of other FTAs booked on similar charges. As Lula notes, "'Just 'cause a man looks like SpongeBob doesn't mean he can't turn violent'" (*Ten* 153). Abusive men are omnipresent and violence against women is resistant to Steph's dogged determination to solve crimes. This weighs heavily on her sometimes; in *Four to Score*, she admits, "I hate the fear. In the beginning, I was too stupid to be afraid. Now it seems like I'm always afraid" (105). Seriality here works to underscore how violence against women is an everyday act: it recurs in each novel, absorbed into Evanovich's formula.

Seriality also highlights Steph's resistance to how "'adjusted ambition' narratives work to discredit the meaning and value of work in the heroine's life or at least to insist that it be made secondary to romance" (Negra, *What A Girl Wants?* 88). Just as each novel features at least one FTA wanted for acts of violence against women, each also follows Steph through her romantic entanglements with two men. These two storylines vying for our attention, as well as Steph's attention—"There was a contract on my head, and I was weirdly involved with two men. I didn't know which was more frightening" (*Ten* 185)—suggests an equivalence between, and anxiety about, these concerns. Most often, we find Steph thinking through the status of her relationship with Morelli, an ongoing recognition of how much they care for each other as well as their mutual indifference about a permanent commitment: "Truth is, Morelli and I are pretty sure we love each other. We're just not sure we can stand to live together for the rest of our lives. I don't especially want to marry a cop. Morelli doesn't want to marry a bounty hunter. And then there's Ranger" (*Seven* 26). Her continual fantasies about Ranger, and their occasional sexual encounters, are—at least to her—indications that she is not yet ready for monogamy.

In this way, Evanovich's series resembles the narrative rhythm of television soap operas with their propensity for continually deferred answers to the question of their female characters' domestic happiness. As Tania Modleski describes, "Tune in tomorrow, not in order to find out the answers, but to see what complications will defer the resolutions and introduce new questions" (12). This leads—in soap operas and in Evanovich's work—to a narrative structure that continually evades closure to ask "Why would the detective heroine, besieged by sexist institutions and violent men, trust any man enough for a long-term commitment?" (Mizejewski, "Dressed to Kill" 13). Modleski argues that this expansive structure habituates women to anticipation and endlessly deferred pleasure; Evanovich contends that the lack of change is what makes her stories pleasurable: "I write the happy book, the book you know is going to have a good ending.... I write books about family and community and law and order" (qtd. in Dunne). In Evanovich's novels, crimes are solved and interpersonal situations do not change: Steph will always be in her thirties, her hamster Rex will remain alive, she never needs to choose between Morelli and Ranger and settle down.

These serial novels with static situations script Steph in a particular relationship to what Negra identifies as the time panic of chick texts. The chick genre establishes a feminine "good life" dependent on a gendered trajectory through "life stages [which] centre upon the discovery of personal destiny, the security of a romantic partner and motherhood, and the negotiation of the problem of paid work (seldom its rewards)" (Negra, *What A Girl Wants?* 47). Steph knows this firsthand: "There are certain expectations of girls from the Burg. You grow up, you get married, you have children, you spread out some in the beam, and you learn how to set a buffet for forty. My *dream* was that I would get irradiated like Spiderman and be able to fly like Superman. My *expectation* had been that I'd marry" (*Eight* 28). The prospect of veering off the path that leads to this promised good life animates many chick texts; protagonists often agonize over hitting one of these stages without the appropriate achievements in place. As Negra explains, "the single woman stands as the most conspicuously time-beset example of contemporary femininity, her singlehood encoded as a particularly temporal failure and a drifting off course from the normative stages of the female life cycle" (61).

Frozen in between these achievements of appropriate femininity, Steph's stories instead return again and again to the insecurities they incur. Steph frequently feels stuck: "[S]omewhere in my twenties I feel like I got stalled in the process and now I'm drifting, marking time without any great passion to move forward. It could be that I'm just liking where I'm at and want to stay there a while longer. Still, it would be helpful if I could get motivated enough to buy a toaster" (*Twenty-One* 242). Her inertia shows how "the lives of women without these experiences are temporally unmapped" (Negra, *What A Girl Wants?* 50). Keeping Steph in this same indeterminate space indefinitely, the novels offer opportunities to map these "sticky" points in more detail. For instance, in *Eleven on Top*, Steph is so frustrated with being a bounty hunter that she quits and looks for other work. Yet she finds that some of what has made bounty hunting feel so untenable, like the lecherous FTAs and the dangerous situations, reappear elsewhere: her new boss chastises her for not wearing more revealing clothing, and her car explodes from a bomb planted it in while she's at her new, supposedly safe job. As she notes, at least being a bounty hunter equips her with the skills and resources to face these difficulties: "Truth is, it was getting pretty obvious that being a bounty hunter wasn't the problem. In fact, maybe being a bounty hunter was the solution. At least I'd acquired a few survival skills. When trouble followed me home I was able to cope" (252). Meanwhile, Steph's holding pattern with Morelli aggravates her mother more than her: when her mother moans, "'I don't know why everyone else's daughter gets married but mine!'" Steph is quick to remind her: "'I *was* married. . . I didn't like it'" (*Seventeen* 20).

Meeting these expectations would only make Steph feel differently stuck, as her Grandma Mazur explains: "'It was so much easier when I was young. You got a boyfriend, and you married him. You had some kids, you got older, one of you died, and that was it'" (*Eighteen* 177-78). Married young and a housewife to Steph's now-deceased maternal grandfather, Grandma Mazur has moved in with Steph's parents and seems to be revisiting stages she never quite got to experience:

> When I was a little girl I'd never thought of my grandmother as the sort of person to eat her pie first.... My grandfather wouldn't have had it any other way. He'd worked in a steel mill all his life. He had strong opinions, and he dwarfed the rooms of their row house.... Lately I've been wondering who my grandmother would have been if she hadn't married my grandfather. I wonder if she would have eaten her dessert first a lot sooner. (117-18)

Grandma Mazur's glee at her freedom—no longer a wife, no longer running a household—manifests in adventures that rival Steph's own: she has burned down a funeral home, catfished men online, ordered pay-per-view porn, and been a back-up singer for a local rock band fronted by the Burg's only drag queen Sally Sweet.

Yet Grandma Mazur's break from the timeline of the feminine good life comes at a cost: she is frequently—and sometimes even literally—bound up in Steph's investigations; she has been stabbed, shot at, kidnapped, tied up, drugged, dragged down multiple dark alleys, and nearly killed and left in a Dumpster by an aging mob boss after he is unable to perform sexually. Her determination to be out in the world—to be eating her pie first—makes her vulnerable, and her age and gender make her a target. Tellingly, the only woman in Steph's family to remain safe throughout the entire series so far is Steph's mother—a dedicated homemaker who doses her stress and regret with shots from liquor bottles hidden around her kitchen. Even perfect sister Valerie ends up abducted in *Hard Eight*, after returning to the Burg and having a child out of wedlock. Fending off any significant character development, Evanovich's books pin the Plum women to divergent understandings of what constitutes the feminine good life, and replay these perspectives in each installment. Steph remains more committed to her career than her relationship, Grandma Mazur continues to create the life she wished she had led earlier, and Steph's mother quietly nurses her disappointment. This constancy within a serial narrative offers a critical rejoinder to the "positive resolutions inherent to the genre" (Ferriss 190). By continually avoiding this kind of conclusion, the Stephanie Plum series refocuses our attention on the conditions in which the series' women find themselves: continually choosing work and multiple men, challenging the perception that older women fade into the background, cracking the façade of the happy homemaker.

"She tracks down dirty rotten fugitives just like on television. She's got a gun and everything"

Elements of Evanovich's best-selling formula can be found in the chick detective stories appearing in her wake. For instance, Sarah Strohmeyer introduces us to Bubbles Yablonsky, a hairdresser and aspiring newspaper reporter caught between a persistent ex-husband, a sexy news photographer; Tori Carrington's Sofie Metropolis, a waitress-turned-sleuth, is popularly regarded as a Greek Stephanie Plum; Sheryl J. Anderson's Molly Forrester is trying to parlay her sex advice column into a hard news beat thanks to the dead bodies she keeps finding; and Rhona Pollero's Finley Anderson Tanner is a paralegal whose skill at tracking down discount designer goods comes in handy when she starts solving crimes.

The chick detective can now also be found on television: series like *Veronica Mars* (UPN; The CW), *Pretty Little Liars* (ABC Family/Freeform), and *Riverdale* (The CW) chronicle the lives of young women crime-solvers, and adapt the apparent mystery of young women's safety and autonomy for serial television programming (Braithwaite). Like Evanovich's work, these other chick detective texts bring together the humorous and the horrifying, a "mixed bag of ambition, disappointments, successes, and carefully chosen accessories" as an effective storytelling strategy within crime fiction (Mizejewski, *Hardboiled* 5).

Chick detective narratives incorporate the conventions of female detective fiction into the chick genre to focus on issues of sexualized violence and violence against women. These discourses of power, autonomy, and vulnerability are "effective [sic] precisely because they lodge in the real; they are attached to other ideological frameworks" of responsibility and choice that follow female protagonists throughout contemporary popular culture (Probyn 158). As a revision of the chick trajectory, this alternative feminine subjectivity foregrounds without filling in the gaps in the genre's construction of the "good life," leaving the chick detective to figure it out on her own. By continually returning to the effects of the sexism and misogyny deeply embedded in systems of crime and justice, Steph's work as a chick detective complicates popular pictures of romantic relationships and fulfilling careers. Or, as Joe Morelli puts it: "'Cupcake, your middle name is trouble'" (*Four*, 250).

Acknowledgements

The author wishes to thank Jeannette Sloniowski for making *One for the Money* required reading.

Works Cited

Anderson, Sheryl J. *Killer Heels*. St. Martin's Press, 2005.

Braithwaite, Andrea. "'That girl of yours, she's pretty hardboiled, huh?': Detecting Feminism in *Veronica Mars*." *Teen Television: Essays on Programming and Fandom*, edited by Sharon Ross and Louisa Stein, McFarland, 2008, pp. 132-149.

Bridget Jones's Diary. Directed by Sharon Maguire, Miramax, Universal Pictures, and StudioCanal, 2001.

Confessions of a Shopaholic. Directed by P.J. Hogan, Touchstone Pictures and Jerry Bruckheimer Films, 2009.

Dowler, Ken, et al. "Constructing Crime: Media, Crime, and Popular Culture." *Canadian Journal of Criminology and*

Criminal Justice, vol. 48, no. 6, 2006, pp. 837-50. DOI: 10.3138/cjccj.48.6.837.

Dunne, Susan. 2016. "Hartford-bound Author Janet Evanovich Tells Us Why We Love Stephanie Plum (and Whether Rex Will Live Forever)." *Hartford Courant*, 6 November 2018, www.courant.com/ctnow/arts-theater/hc-fea-janet-evanovich-hartford-1111-story.html. Accessed 4 January 2019.

Evanovich, Janet. *Eleven on Top*. St. Martin's Press, 2005.

---. *Explosive Eighteen*. Bantam Books, 2011.

---. *Four to Score*. St. Martin's Press, 1998.

---. *Hard Eight*. St. Martin's Press, 2002.

---. *High Five*. St. Martin's Press, 1999.

---. *Hot Six*. St. Martin's Press, 2000.

---. *Notorious Nineteen*. Bantam Books, 2012.

---. *One for the Money*. Harper Collins Publishers, 1994.

---. *Seven Up*. St. Martin's Press, 2001.

---. *Sizzling Sixteen*. St. Martin's Press, 2010.

---. *Smokin' Seventeen*. Bantam Books, 2011.

---. *Takedown Twenty*. Bantam Books, 2013.

---. *Ten Big Ones*. St. Martin's Press, 2004.

---. *Three to Get Deadly*. St. Martin's Press, 1997.

---. *Top Secret Twenty-One*. Bantam Books, 2014.

---. *Turbo Twenty-Three*. Bantam Books, 2016.

---. *Two for the Dough*. Pocket Books, 1996.

Ferriss, Suzanne. "Working Girls: The Precariat of Chick Lit." *Cupcakes, Pinterest, and Ladyporn: Feminized Popular Culture in the Early Twenty-First Century*, edited by Elana Levine, U of Illinois P, 2015, pp. 177-195.

Fielding, Helen. *Bridget Jones's Diary*. Picador, 1996.

Gates, Philippa. *Detecting Women: Gender and the Hollywood Detective Film*. SUNY Press, 2011.

Gill, Rosalind and Elena Herdieckherhoff. "Rewriting the Romance: New Femininities in Chick Lit?" *Feminist Media Studies*, vol. 6, no. 4, 2006, pp. 487-504. DOI: 10.1080/14680770600989947.

Guenther, Leah. "*Bridget Jones's Diary*: Confessing Post-Feminism." *Modern Confessional Writing: New Critical Essays*, edited by Jo Gill, Routledge, 2005, pp. 84-99.

Guerrero, Lisa A. "'Sistahs Are Doin' It For Themselves': Chick Lit in Black and White." *Chick Lit: The New Woman's Fiction*, edited by Suzanne Ferriss and Mallory Young, Routledge, 2006, pp. 87-101.

How to Lose a Guy in 10 Days. Directed by Donald Petrie, Paramount Pictures, 2003.

Jernigan, Jessica. "Slingbacks and Arrows: Chick Lit Comes of Age." *Bitch*, vol. 25, Summer 2004, pp. 68-75.

Kiernan, Anna. "No Satisfaction: *Sex and the City, Run Catch

Kiss, and the Conflict of Desires in Chick Lit's New Heroines." *Chick Lit: The New Woman's Fiction*, edited by Suzanne Ferriss and Mallory Young, Routledge, 2006, pp. 207-18.

Kinsella, Sophie. *Confessions of a Shopaholic*. Random House, 2001.

Mizejewski, Linda. "Dressed to Kill: Postfeminist Noir." *Cinema Journal*, vol. 44, no. 2, 2005, pp. 121-27. DOI: 10.1353/cj.2005.0010.

---. *Hardboiled and High Heeled: The Woman Detective in Popular Culture*. New York: Routledge, 2004.

Modleski, Tania. "The Search for Tomorrow in Today's Soap Operas: Notes on a Feminine Narrative Form." *Film Quarterly*, vol. 33, no. 1, 1979, pp. 12-21.

Negra, Diane. "Structural Integrity, Historical Reversion, and the Post-9/11 Chick Flick." *Feminist Media Studies*, vol. 8, no. 1, 2008, pp. 51-68. DOI: 10.1080/14680770701824902.

---. *What A Girl Wants? Fantasizing the Reclamation of the Self in Postfeminism*. Routledge, 2009.

Pollero, Rhonda. *Knock Off*. New York: Kensington Books, 2007.

Pretty Little Liars. Created by I. Marlene King, ABC Family/Freeform, 2010-2017.

Probyn, Elspeth. "New Traditionalism and Post-Feminism: TV Does the Home." *Screen*, vol. 31, no. 2, 1990, pp. 147-59.

Riverdale. Created by Roberto Aguirre-Sacasa, The CW, 2017-present.

Rowntree, Margaret R. "Feminine Sexualities in the Chick

Genre." *Feminist Media Studies*, vol. 15, no. 3, 2015, pp. 508-21. DOI: 10.1080/14680777.2014.952759.

Sex and the City. Created by Darren Star, HBO, 1998-2004.

Sykes, Plum. *Bergdorf Blondes*. Miramax Books/Hyperion, 2004.

Veronica Mars. Created by Rob Thomas, UPN and The CW, 2004-2007.

Walton, Priscilla L. and Manina Jones. *Detective Agency: Women Rewriting the Hard-Boiled Tradition*. U of California P, 1999.

Cruel and Usual: The Criminal Quotidian of Shirley Jackson

Het Phillips

"It could be said that there is danger everywhere."
—Shirley Jackson, *We Have Always Lived in the Castle*

Abstract

Focusing on Shirley Jackson's short stories "Nightmare," "The Missing Girl" and "Journey With a Lady" and her novels *Hangsaman* and *The Road Through the Wall*, this article will demonstrate how Jackson adapts and subverts crime writing genre elements in order to question how society categorizes harm and violence. Stripping crime narratives of both an explanatory dénouement and any meaningful form of justice, her writing radically disperses the criminal, rendering it nebulous and obscure, unable to be contained within individual actions or agents, thereby forcing us to consider its hegemonic collective and social underpinnings.

In so-doing, she centers the surreal excess of the experience of trauma and its disorienting lack of fit with the public face of how the world supposedly works, creating a world in which the normal, the criminal, and the supernatural mutually coexist.

Her disorientating quasi-realism vividly defamiliarizes and dramatizes the injustices and oppressions of life under mid-twentieth-century American capitalism, standing as a rebuke to power and unthinking tradition and highlighting the overlooked omnipresence of everyday violence and subjugation in the lives of those who live within this system. By re-presenting and subverting the logic of crime and detection, cause and effect, motive and investigation, and so breaking with the conventions of realism, Jackson is able to convey more closely the impossible horror inflicted on those who experience oppression, a horror that society prevents them from naming, much less avenging. In Jackson's work the everyday is the real crime, and convention and capitalism the real culprits.

Although frequently identified as belonging to the horror genre, Shirley Jackson's works are profoundly concerned with crime, depicting numerous criminal events and frequently borrowing from crime genres. Her work creates a universe saturated with crime, mystery, and investigation, yet no straightforward solutions are offered. Instead, guilt and the chain of cause and effect, the path between evidence and criminal, action and outcome, are obscure, detached, misaligned: a reality underpinned by the harmful, unsettling, and intrusive. Crime in its broadest sense—by which I mean actions and experiences that encompass transgression, violence, violation, non-consent, disruption, harm—is the substance of her writing.

These harms are often redirected from being recognized as crimes in two sets of ways, often to jarring effect. Firstly, they are presented as disconcertingly ordinary and, as such, impossible to unpick from apparently benign ways of living. They are misrecognized within the world of the story, with other characters often responding indifferently, callously, or otherwise inappropriately. This creates a gulf between the felt experience of the character in question and the way that it is perceived by others, and, in turn, the way that they are able to express it, even to themselves. Secondly, the insult is often displaced onto an apparently otherworldly source and so rendered outside a social explanatory framework. The lack of meaningful distinction between the experience of haunting and earthly harms in Jackson's work operates on a textual, plot, and character level as well as on the level of authorial practice: the ease with which she replays the same events with either explanation encapsulates this porousness. By blending elements of crime fiction (and non-fiction) with the paranormal, realism, dystopia, and kitchen sink level social minutiae, Jackson makes a radical ontological statement about what harms we consider crimes and the inadequacy of legal and criminal-justice models to apprehend our experiences.

Her works contain numerous allusions to and echoes of real crimes, the most obviously direct reference being the short story entitled "Jack The Ripper," the name given to a globally famous hypothetical serial killer responsible for a series of unsolved gruesome murders of sex workers in 1888 London. Her two versions of "The Honeymoon of Mrs. Smith" seem to be directly referencing the "Brides in the Bath" murders in the 1910s, in which the English bigamist George Joseph Smith killed three women, whom he had married, by bathtub drownings. *We Have Always Lived in the Castle* more subtly references the famous Lizzie Borden case in which the young Massachusetts woman was tried and acquitted for the still unsolved 1892 axe murder of her parents. As I shall discuss in more depth in this article, "The Missing Girl," "Louisa Come Home," and *Hangsaman* all reimagine the disappearance of Paula Welden, a local student whose unsolved vanishing in 1946 Jackson was familiar with. Jackson takes elements of mood and detail of true crime writing's establishment of place and atmosphere, but removes the fig leaf of specificity, forcing an expansion of the frame to encompass the collective; it is not that *these people* are cruel, brutal, and awful, but that the conditions of being alive itself, and the American mid-century world she depicts, is. That diffuse threat, that miasma of crime, is her point; any individual act of crime merely crystalizes for a moment its generally diffuse expression as it pervades everything. Reality under these conditions is the true crime: "No live organism can continue for long to exist sanely under conditions of absolute reality" (*The Haunting of Hill House* 3). Yet "reality" in Jackson's work is not merely a general vague state of being, but a specifically historicized moment: her stories dramatize occasions when the conditions of existence under capitalism in mid-twentieth-century America are thrown into monstrous relief. Ultimately, Jackson blends the supernatural with realism to expose an existent reality in which capitalism is as culpable as the criminal, and as uncannily threatening as any spectre. The theme of diffuse crime, which I identify as central to Jackson's work, is the pivot linking her supernatural horror elements with an exposé of capitalism's hidden hand.

Capitalism, Genre, and Space

It is appropriate that this article should appear in *Mean Streets* when cruelty and public space are central to Jackson, her works taking as their setting for Gothic dread the shared terrain—the accommodation, commerce, and transportation—of mid-century American life. Tennessee Williams locates the Southern Gothic outside castles and antiquity in "a sense, an intuition, of an underlying dreadfulness in modern experience" (cited Flora and MacKethan 315); Jackson's Gothicism is likewise that of suppressed panic and alienation saturating the landscape and interactions of apparently ordinary, up-to-date modern life.

Christine Wilson identifies Jackson's "sentient, animated, malign house" in *The Haunting of Hill House* as her defining contribution, which reshaped the haunted house genre and set its parameters "for the next 50 years" and provided a means of exploring "how the subject relates, and should relate, to space, particularly space that does not conform to the subject's desires and expectations" (200-01). Yet this delineation of the malignity of place need not be confined to sites of potentially supernatural horrors. In fact, Jackson's oeuvre is suffused with spaces in which everything, living, dead, or inanimate, potentially possesses malign agency and animate malice. Darryl Hattenhauer identifies an external locus of agency in Jackson's characters, arguing they are "victims of those empowered with too much agency, or of a Foucauldian system in which agency is unidentifiably diffuse," only able to "experience agency as something from without" (3). This diffuse agency from without is a defining feature of the world Jackson depicts. Yet whether announcing itself as supernatural forces, or the spectre of criminal violence (and male violence in particular), the "diffuse" agency that is a defining feature of Jackson's narratives ultimately points to the distant invisible hand of capitalism pressing down hard on the players in her drama and at times sweeping them off the board without emotion or even, necessarily, intention. Jackson's 1948 debut novel *The Road Through the Wall*, for example, portrays the seething underlying tensions of a claustrophobic suburban Californian community as they are brought to a head by the destruction of a boundary wall between it and a wealthy estate and the unsolved disappearance and murder of a young child swiftly followed by the suicide of a scapegoated child suspect. The crimes and torments of the text are mapped onto a physical, geographical trauma in the form of the wall being breached. The novel offers in its opening lines a paradigmatic summary of privilege and the unfair terrain of society: "The weather falls more gently on some places than on others, the world looks down more paternally on some people. Some spots are proverbially warm, and keep, through falling snow, their untarnished reputation as summer resorts; some people are automatically above suspicion" (1). This pithily illustrates, by projecting such inequality onto the landscape, the weather and the apparently innate characteristics of people in general, the socially constructed illusion of inequality's inevitability and naturalness.

 The unexplained, the supernatural, the criminal: all of these genre elements conspire to maintain the illusion, so central to capitalist society, that "individual passions, drives, and greed, and the social order itself—bourgeois society—have to be accepted"—treated as natural and inevitable—"regardless of shortcomings and injustices" (Mandel 47). David Schmid develops Mandel's point, arguing crime fiction is a cultural form, which is particularly dependent "upon reductively individualistic understandings of the causes of and solutions to crime." Schmid adds that "it is difficult for most crime fiction to acknowledge the complex and contradictory ways in which hegemony saturates the consciousness of a society because of its individualistic emphasis. The protagonist may be more or less aware of the power structures that are arrayed against him, but that awareness remains pre-political" (Schmid 6), a form of what Slavoj Žižek calls "objective violence," "a normally invisible type of violence that represents the smooth everyday functioning of the capitalist system" (Schmid 10). Jackson's hybrid of crime, horror, psychodrama, and the weird is thus not only formally experimental, but also highlights and turns in on itself the logic of individualism within the everyday flow of power in capitalism. She foregrounds individualism as inadequate to the task of compensating for, or combating, injustice, instead promoting only alienation. Her characters' typical experience (whether of crime, the supernatural, or simply a threatened or actual harm) is of all power and agency located outside of themselves, and of this as the moral and existential fabric cohering the universe. Lacking a collective identity and a framework with which to understand the nature of their oppression, they flounder in a hectic, cruel, destabilizing world, suffering intensely felt but incomprehensibly inflicted pain. Transportation, the street, the store: these are our shared spaces under capitalism, and Jackson's Gothic forces the return of the material and economic in her treatment of them, reinforcing Hattenhauer's point that Gothic is realism for marginalized groups and for the experience of capitalist modernity: "Their lives were quietly governed for them by a mysterious faraway force" (*Road Through the Wall* 178). Jackson re-inscribes labor and power and capital onto the (modern, sub/urban) landscape itself: "Its very paving had been laid down by men now far away, planned by someone in an office building" (178). Jackson identifies the "unseen governors" of the lives of Pepper Street's inhabitants as:

> the prices in a distant town, regulated by minds and hungers in a town even farther away, all the

> possessions which depended on someone in another place, someone who controlled words and paper and ink, who could by the changing of a word on paper influence *the very texture of the ground*.... The very chair on which Mr. Desmond sat... belonged to him only on sufferance; it had belonged first to someone who made it, in turn governed by someone who planned it, and Mr. Desmond, although he did not know it, had chosen it because it had been presented to him as completely choosable. (178; my italics)

Hattenhaur rightly emphasizes Jackson's focus on language: "she explicitly textualized power" (92). Yet Jackson also *materializes* it. Like a spell or like the way the supernatural and the operations of earthly and unearthly power saturate her works, so commerce and government are shown to have the power to unmake the ground beneath your feet—as does the mind, as does a haunting. It is power that haunts. In the passage from *The Road Through The Wall* quoted above, the spatial element of (capitalist) power's ability to haunt, to operate invisibly, mysteriously, and beyond geographical confines, is insistent. The scene moves inward from the macro to the micro through types of space. From far distant city, to the flow of goods and workers along transit routes, to the small-town suburb, to the house, to the very chair you—reader and character—sit on to read, each is, in spite of its overlooked familiarity, the medium through which you are locked into systems of power and placed in a position relative to agencies, forces, and people alike. Richard Pascal argues the sudden announcement in the final paragraph of the death of the "the old lady who had owned the wall"—previously mentioned only passingly once in the text—has the effect of personifying "the depersonalizing ethos" of what he calls "newer ways of communal life." Significantly, he does not choose to identify capitalism as the culprit of this teleological happenstance, but he does characterize this dénouement as signalling that in fact she "has been all along, the one 'major character' in the novel" embodying and enacting "socioeconomic agency, the power of the marketplace" over "events and people" in a way that "is unobtrusive, impersonal and uncaring. Her covert centrality is not eerie or evil" "but simply a prosaic fact of contemporary society. She is no witch, but her well-hidden, callous power is, in its modern way, very spooky" (95). This coheres with Mark Fisher's identification of a key feature of eeriness as "the suspicion that an entity to which we do not normally ascribe it possesses a deliberative agency" (65). The lack of "normal" ascription of agency to the workings of capitalist kyriarchy, and the return of that agency to it —as well as the removal/revoking of it from her characters—constitutes a radical defamiliarizing and reassertion of the nature and experience of power in the lives of mid-century Americans and indeed all our lives. It is a maneuver that reveals how the harm wrought by an obfuscated capitalist network of power can appear not only criminal, but also supernatural—precisely because its agency is at once unexpectedly, insistently present and eerily hidden.

The Street Harassment Thriller

In "Nightmare," an office worker, Miss Morgan, attempts to deliver a package for her boss only to become embroiled in a thriller-like chase where she is pursued by an apparent ad campaign that is out to get her. The story is dominated by an escalating fear of one's own visibility and of being exposed and vulnerable in public space—and thus may be drawing on Jackson's own agoraphobia. Yet, mental illness is socially constituted, shaped by the cultural terrain for its means and methods of expression, and this is also reflected in "Nightmare." Just as ideology can be defined as emerging from the imagined realm of social relations connecting the subject to material and social conditions of existence, likewise mental ill-health also arises from internal responses to traumas inflicted by and within real social and material conditions. A member of a minority is genuinely at risk in the street, and the fear of being harassed, stalked, attacked, or apprehended by law-enforcement is not an idle or a foolish one. Miss Morgan is concerned about being apprehended by the police—as if she herself is the criminal for being outside in the street and will have to account for herself—and the reality of "Nightmare" justifies this affect. The entire public is in fact being invited to apprehend her: she is quite literally fair game: "'All you have to do is find Miss X folks, just find *the one girl who is walking around the city alone*'" (49; my italics). Jackson, as a fat woman, experienced both intimate and diffuse societal oppression that was visually and physically hyper-constituted (indeed, all oppressed groups are, in differing ways, so constituted: the locus of their otherness is projected bodily and spatially). In the case of a fat person the very space taken up is weaponized against the subject while at the same time presented as evidence of their supposedly constituting a threat against, an impingement on, and an outrage to, the aesthetic and moral sensibilities of those of the acceptable norm, and as such, of society itself. The panoptic surveillance gaze focused upon Miss Morgan, and the fact that the announcer cannot be spoken to or interceded with even as he changes the announcement to match her attempts to disguise herself, simultaneously places the narrative on the scale of state and corporate power yet also puts the menace beyond simple harassment and at the edge of the natural, everyday threat, instead protruding into some realm beyond, a realm of either delusion or psychic persecution. True crime and crime fiction alike live also in this borderland, between the unpleasant, awful, unimaginable, but everyday, cruelty that we can broadly assimilate into our understanding of the world — and some chasm of madness and horror that threatens to undo everything we thought we knew. The distancing and insulating of power from those it impacts, the attenuating effects of capitalist atomizing of labor, is emblematized in the unseen announcer in the truck who follows her, the obscurity of the motive or perpetrator of the chase, and the way in which the driver merely drives the speaker, with no power to intercede (47).

The term "rape culture" describes the way in which the Western US-dominated anglosphere is a "culture in which rape is pervasive, prevalent, and normalized through societal attitudes about gender, sex and sexuality," and the everyday experience of women in both public and private space is one of needing to take conscious steps "in their day-to-day lives to protect themselves from being sexually violated." "Every action of women within a rape culture is tainted by that culture. Going to get their mail, driving to work, going out with friends—none of these actions are 'free'" (Olfman 9). In addition to direct allusions to sexual assault (particularly in *Hangsaman*), Jackson's work is full of ambiguous threats encountered in public space, particularly while walking. Among these, "Nightmare" and "Lovers Meeting" perhaps most fully capture the danger and uncertainty—and self-doubt in one's own fear—involved in living as a woman in a culture that will not only harm you but also disavows that fact, alienating you from your own knowledge of its true nature. A story rife with echoes of *The Haunting of Hill House*, "Lovers Meeting" depicts a woman experiencing some combination of mental breakdown, supernatural manifestation, or stalking by a man. She leaves and returns to her apartment under pressure of an unknown chaser, is followed through the street, in a taxi, the theatre, and a bus, ambiguously aided by a series of strangers who appear to be "in on" some secret script; the effect is one of a coherent shared whole, of which everyone else is part but she is not, not even within herself. Behaving as if they can all see her invisible assailant, it is unclear if they are trying to aid or thwart him, but their remarks of apparent sympathy seem hollow and they exhibit a keenness to disassociate themselves from her. Whatever horror pursues her is part of the workaday world to them, of fines and reprimands and inconvenience. She cannot tell if she is being led away from a danger or herded towards it; others' motives are opaque and she exhibits, throughout, an emotional tension between defying the wishes of some external force and following unknown compulsions, never able to trust her own instincts.

The intensity and centrality of the ambiguous threat in Jackson's work at least in part derive from the way women's suffering at the hands of men is so often diminished, derided, and dismissed—rendered not-crime. Its moral universe is one in which everything and nothing can truly be considered a crime and in which there is no criminal exceptionality. We might think of her experience of marital rape as a literal biographical example of experiencing harm in such a way. Ruth Franklin's biography reports the mistreatment Jackson endured by parents and husband alike, a litany of infidelities, public and private mockery, fatphobia, gaslighting, belittling and abuse, as well as at least one instance, referred to in her diary, of rape. Repeatedly and consistently "shamed" over "legitimate and rational desires" and forced into "choking back words she so dearly wished to say" (120), Jackson considered leaving numerous times but was unable to do so. In this light, the repeated theme of lost women desperate for escape and starved of the inner resources with which to accomplish it takes on a yet more poignant air. Being unable to rely on her own judgment or either express or act upon her knowledge of the reality of the situation, Jackson seems to have developed a subtle and dexterous craft of creating this sensation in her writing. As Heather Havrilesky argues in her review of Franklin's biography, "Jackson's works conjure a slow, simmering resentment that becomes almost hallucinatory, as if years of muting emotional reactions naturally warp perception, fuelling a state of delirium"—a theme which, as Havrilesky identifies, Franklin emphasizes "throughout her biography, tracing the lineage of belittlement from Jackson's mother to her husband." The true cruelty of the universe of Jackson's fiction is its false promise of beneficence—a feature Jackson creates at a formal level as well, going "out of her way to conceal the climax by a narrative tone that at the outset is placid, benign, and innocuous almost to excess," as S.T. Joshi observes (33). This twist of fortunes is key to the emotional impact of her work—as Havrilesky comments, Jackson "knew that horror requires an emotional seduction that is revealed to be a malevolent ruse: The ingenue experiences herself as radiant and powerful right before all her power is stripped from her. Clever young girls imagine they were born to be cherished, when instead they're created merely to be destroyed." In an undated letter to her husband in which she states her reasons for wanting a divorce, Jackson says

"'You once wrote me a letter. . . telling me that I would never be lonely again. I think that was the first, the most dreadful, lie you ever told me'"—a statement that, Franklin points out, "echoes the confession by one of Glanvill's witches of her relationship with the devil: '"He promised her, when she made her Contract with him, that she should want nothing, but ever since she has wanted all things"' (257).

"Nightmare" depicts a weaponized spatiality in which the landscape itself seems alive and malevolently focussed towards Miss Morgan, with posters apparently multiplying to cover every surface and leaflets that "*glared* up at her from the ground under her foot" (50; my italics). Like that of *The Road Through the Wall*, its apparently solid, permanent ground has been malignly altered by words, by commerce: "The street ahead was roped off and policemen were guarding the ropes" (54). This is a literal policing of space, in which the coercive power of law enforcement is brought to bear on non-criminal matters in the interests, apparently, of a private company—and, in so doing, abetting the villains of this story. The parade and all its forced bullying jollity—its compulsory fun, its occupation of space—employs the military pomp of an occupying force to take up room and create a spectacle, demanding to be celebrated, to be rejoiced, for seizing public space and barring people's way—a dramatic counterpoint to Miss Morgan's growing terror at being visible in public. The advertising campaign throughout the story is representative of a creeping and horrifying capitulation of public space to capitalism, to the interests of companies and power. The crowd is atomized, each member alone and "helpless" (51), re/constituted as subjects only in relation to the demands of capital (sell this, buy this, drive that, deliver this, attend to this, watch this), reconstituted as a mass backdrop of consumers and spectators, a herd to be managed, with even labor effaced as entertainment. Underlying this is the suspicion and criminalization of all who resist, even internally, its spectacle and scrutiny: Miss Morgan literally finds herself on the run. The golden mannequins eating dollar bills on the parade float (55), could hardly be a clearer symbol of capitalism, exaggerated to a ridiculous level, and this sense of trickery, of everything as rigged, a con, is voiced by a woman Miss Morgan meets in the crowd, who rather than recognizing or apprehending her as Miss X, reflects that "'someone in the company of the people putting it on always wins these things anyway'" (53). Yet, in failing to identify her and hand her in, the woman only continues and intensifies Miss Morgan's anxiety; in captivity she could assert herself and defend her right to exist, but on the run she cannot. The heroine being stalked harassed and chased by some mysterious criminal capitalist enterprise with enormous reach and clout is reminiscent of Agatha Christie's thrillers (for instance, *The Man In The Brown Suit, The Secret Adversary, Passenger to Frankfurt, The Big Four*) or Graham Greene's *The Ministry of Fear*, which features a fortune teller, a sinister cake at a fete, and an escape from a séance through a bathroom window. Yet by distorting crime genre features and distancing her work from a reading straightforwardly comprehensible through the conventions of the crime fiction genre—and most importantly withholding the resolution—we are led by both culture and text to see the heroine's peril as more her mental unravelling than the work of some clandestine criminal cartel. Without the suspension of disbelief demanded by the crime fiction genre, the reader looks a little too closely and considers a different set of explanatory possibilities. Indeed, it is a necessary feature of the thriller, noir, conspiracy fiction, etc., that the ordinary *should* suddenly be shown by a bizarre and disorientating rupture to be organized by a hitherto unrecognized external agency (in both senses)—a hidden hegemony if you will. Character and reader alike in Jackson's work are denied the explanatory relief of a culminating "big reveal" that explains everything; rather, there is a stacking up, an accruing, of an alarming number of tiny discordant notes. The solution to the mystery is. . . more mystery: the revelation the impossibility of explanation.

Jackson uses the thriller as a conduit or a tool, a jumping-off point. Rather than an enemy government, a cabal of criminals or a terrorist cell, the powerful forces massed against her protagonists are those of ordinary life and its landscape of inequality and coercion. In this sense, her use of the criminous mirrors her use of the supernatural. Both are devices through which her tales reveal the workings of the hidden hand of capitalism within American society, but they also reveal, crucially and paradoxically, the very *hiddenness* of capitalism even as its influence suffuses all things. In this sense, capitalism resembles the criminal investigation that reveals only further mystery, or the numinous and unknowable forces of the supernatural. Her villains aren't outside the normal, even as they appear to be so. They are that which is normal itself, characterized as a nebulous, impersonal, diffuse, reified agency operating through discourses and practices of cultural, social, and interpersonal power and the apparent collective cruelties and contradictions that seize public and private life and cannot be apprehended or even conceptualized with any directly concrete clarity or certainty. It is not just that capitalism is the "real culprit" as it were, but rather that these are all subtypes of invisible power and ordering logics. Her bending of crime in these directions is a subversion, or repurposing, of the genre; she warps it away from the individual criminal towards, in one direction, our collective responsibility, and, in the other, towards preternatural forces beyond human comprehension. It is this unknowability that is key in each case: a single answer cannot be given and a single intelligible culprit identified. Jackson takes the de-familiarizing effect of the mystery or thriller—which posits that a secret system has infiltrated the quotidian world—and doubly de-familiarizes by rendering even the generic shape of the texts—the reading equivalent of the ground beneath one's feet—strange and disorientating. By using a hybrid blend of horror and crime, Jackson makes the affective experience of being locked into such systems arrestingly vivid, and the ready cultural availability of crime entertainment and reportage itself, its ubiquity and familiarity, allow her to add to the sense of shock for the reader as we, like Jackson's characters, are confronted with the awful through and in the everyday.

  The "Find Miss X" advertising campaign of newspapers, announcements, posters, etc., in "Nightmare" plays into the crime genre's generic features and its tendency to self-depiction, mutually showing and taking part in the selling of crime and intrigue themselves as a commercial enterprise. It acts as a reminder of newspapers' reliance on genuine crimes being inflicted on real people for one of their sources of copy. Jackson's use of crime genre features is self-aware and foregrounds them *as* text: for example, in "Paranoia," the protagonist, on the run from an unknown pursuer, at first half-unbelievingly finds himself "now racking his brains for detective tricks, for mystery-story dodges" (39). Like "Nightmare," "Journey With a Lady" also concerns surveillance, a fugitive, travel, public space, and the consumption of commercial and media artefacts. In it a female criminal on a train needs to acquire an outward signifier of being the proper, "right" sort of woman—of "womaning" correctly as it were—by convincing a young boy to pretend to be her son and thus provide cover so the police do not apprehend her. Yet the frisson of fear throughout is not (just?) that she may be caught but that she may be a wholly different kind of criminal—and improper woman—altogether. The double meaning of the term "lady" in the title implies both a childish politeness for "adult woman," the sort of mannered politeness habitually imposed by other adults—e.g. "say thank you to the lady"—but also connotes such "ladylike" behavior of propriety, respectability, etc. It is this latter quality which she is having to employ her decoy son to counterfeit and present an outward sign of. Yet, he also is in a similar predicament, constrained by adult society's surveillance of public space and his subordinate power position into enforced politeness towards adults and strangers, to be impinged upon at their behest not his. But the story also presents this unlikely pair of co-conspirators indulging together in crime-as-entertainment. The consumer pleasure of crime representations and the textual are foregrounded by the exciting, much-anticipated mystery comics she interrupts him from reading, their later reading of them together—presented with much relish and detail—and his asking her about her reading of it out loud while calling her "Ma" in front of the police in a deceptive performance of filial concern. As a result, in "Journey With a Lady," there are two crime fictions going on at once.

As I will discuss in the final section of this article, this overlayered coexistence of fictions—about ourselves as people and as community or family members, about the kind of society we live in, about how the universe works — becomes increasingly key to Jackson, particularly in relation to her fictionalization of the case of Paula Welden.

The Paula Welden Multiverse

On the afternoon of December 1, 1946, Paula Welden, a student at Bennington, a liberal arts university where Jackson's husband Stanley worked, went missing after setting off for a hike on Vermont's Long Trail. No trace of her was ever found and the criticism surrounding local police handling of the case led directly to the creation of the Vermont State Police. Jackson fictionalized the mystery in her short stories "The Missing Girl" and "Louisa Please Come Home," and her novel *Hangsaman*, while hints and echoes of it pepper her oeuvre. The case was also, more famously, a close inspiration for Donna Tartt's *The Secret History*. Bernice M. Murphy asserts that at this time the "student body[...] was only about 300" and Jackson's "husband was on the faculty" thus "it seems likely that Jackson would have been more than familiar with the case" (125). I would add that this likelihood is increased by Bennington having been, like its fictionalized analogue in *Hangsaman*, a campus university in a rural area and so doubly isolated, thrown in upon itself.

In her biography of Jackson, Franklin notes that Jackson's "file on Paula Welden shows that the Bennington Banner published updates on the case every day for the majority of December," "dominat[ing] the local paper for weeks" (542), creating numerous theories. "The most likely," apparently,

> was that she had suffered a hiking accident, but rumors spread that she had been seen in a car with a man. A waitress in Western Massachusetts claimed she had served a man accompanied by a girl fitting Welden's description; when he went

up to pay the bill, the girl asked the waitress where she was and how far to Bennington. A psychic said that Welden has walked through a covered bridge and along the banks of a river, where she would be found alive inside an old shack. Others suggested that she might have 'run away to start a new life.' Search parties combed the area for days but Paula Welden was never found.(254)

This uncited claim about starting a new life suggests a certain wish fulfilment, both for the missing Welden and for the speakers themselves. Ultimately the proliferation of unproven claims seem to cancel each other out, leaving a gap where an explanation or solution should lie.

Franklin adds that "Jackson became preoccupied" with this "real-life case of a woman's disappearance" immediately prior to beginning work on the James Harris stories of *The Lottery*. These stories present a recurring enigmatic "daemon lover" figure, Harris, who appears under a variety of guises and "brings women to the point of disintegration," which Franklin considers "the true theme of the collection" (254). Harris's mutable, translatable face and attributes, and the many half-recognized versions of him, create an atmosphere that blurs attribution and agency, rendering it diffuse and hard to trace. Rather than one criminal, one crime, that can be apprehended and moved on from, Jackson creates a world made up of an ambiguous haze of men like him, threats like this. Franklin asks if, rather than Hell, "What would happen if James Harris walked the streets," highlighting the presence of evil, cruelty, that which takes women apart, in an ordinary place where you might be right now. But the essence of Harris is not just his potential for destroying women, but also the simultaneous glimmer of possibility he offers of *escape*—a theme Jackson returns to repeatedly. For example, in the two versions of "The Honeymoon of Mrs. Smith," Mrs. Smith was willing to risk death in the avoidance of loneliness, both paths being unified in the ambiguous figure of Mr. Smith—who, in one version at least, may be another of Harris's aliases. In the version subtitled "The Mystery of the Murdered Bride" such is the overlap of the two types of men that Mrs. Smith apparently welcomes her own murder and attempts to plan for it without drawing attention to what she is doing, heading off attempts by those around her to intervene. The intensifying bracketing effect of ordinariness in these two "Mrs. Smith" stories, whereby the horror of her situation is both undermined and amplified by the mundanity of the terrain of space and interaction in which it takes place, is directly mirrored in "Home." These are near-identical stories, depicting middle-class snobbish women seeking to find belonging in a new locale while shopping in local stores but failing to heed to warnings of working-class people. In "Home" the warning is about ghosts, while in the other stories it is that the woman's new husband is a wanted murderer with a penchant for wife-killing. Yet each is equivalent in their textual function; crime and the haunting are rendered as aliases of the same thing. Other such parallels are provided by the incomplete and multiple explanatory palette in "Nightmare," "Lovers Meeting," "Jack The Ripper," "Paranoia," "Pillar of Salt," and many more throughout her oeuvre. She creates a criminality that slips the bonds of crime—a diffuse crime—wherein the connotational sense versus the affective sense of what is and isn't a crime in texts, what its boundaries are, and how it should be felt and understood, become central questions.

In "Louisa Please Come Home" the missing girl is shown to have run away of her own volition in order to escape her family. Persuaded into returning by a chance meeting with the story's unprepossessing would-be Harris-style "daemon lover," Paul, Louisa is rejected by them as an yet another imposter (apparently one of several Paul has provided in an attempt to secure the reward money) and so returns to her new life, realizing her family are happier with the spectral imaginary of her that her status as a missing person allows them, and their image of themselves searching, than they were with the realities of her as their flesh and blood daughter. Murphy states that Paula Welden's "father made a series of anxious radio broadcasts requesting information" (125), and this is directly referenced in the plot and title of "Louisa Please Come Home," and indeed the story's first and last lines are Louisa's mother reading a plea on the radio for her return and the broadcast recurs like a refrain (12; 29). We may also see echoes of it in *The Haunting of Hill House*'s chalked message "HELP ELEANOR COME HOME" (146), a concrete manifestation of a haunting, which echoes parent's requests. Like Jackson for Welden, like Uncle Julian in *We Have Always Lived in the Castle,* and Mrs. Smith's neighbor, Louisa collects clippings about her case. Something in Paula's story apparently niggled at Jackson, the possibility that she, unlike Jackson herself, could have, like Louisa, been "free" and be "getting along fine, with never a thought [...] about ever going back" (24). Perhaps Paula was the one who, one way or another, had got away, though by what means and whether to freedom or death or something in between it remained impossible to say. The real disappearance, a crime *in potentia*, became like the grit in the oyster around which the many different potential backstories and outcomes could cluster, with each layer becoming a different reading of the case. In her circling retellings of Welden's disappearance, Jackson creates indeterminacy and frustrates neat explanatory categories. In *Hangsaman* and "Louisa Please Come Home" she removes criminal possibilities and in "The Missing Girl" suggests them, revealing in so-doing an oft-overlooked truth: every unsolved crime is, until its solution, potentially at least not a crime at all, and that, sometimes, it represents the righting rather than the committing of a wrong.

In *Hangsaman,* college itself performs the role of mingled threat and longed-for escape for Natalie from her claustrophobic demanding family life and threat of annihilation produced by institutional anonymity and social constraints. James Dobson asserts,

> A major plot element of Jackson's novel, Natalie's or possibly even Tony's departure from college for the woods, closely resembles the real-life disappearance of. . . Bennington student, Paula

> Jean Welden.... Welden was never found and her sudden disappearance haunted Jackson's imagination. A later story ["The Missing Girl"...] evidences the long-term impact of Welden's disappearance on Jackson [and] continues her exploration of the logic which allows a figure within an institution to disappear without a trace. (127)

He notes "how much easier and more acceptable it is" to all concerned including her own family "to erase Martha [the "missing girl"] from existence than to acknowledge the social failures of the camp to look after its own campers" (127). Likewise, in society at large, it is easier to accept things as they are, to doubt one's own instincts and fears, even as those instincts are right to point to the status quo as doing real damage (both mental and physical) to oneself, individually and collectively. Franco Moretti argues in his influential essay, "Clues," the purpose of crime fiction's very existence is "to expel the doubt that guilt might be impersonal, and therefore collective and social" (135). Moretti uses not to "dispel" but "expel," suggesting something more visceral and concrete than mere avoidance but rather a casting out, from society and from ourselves, of knowledge of our connection to one another and our exploitation by forces of authority from the realm of the apparently natural and the thinkable. Jackson instead disrupts the neat and orderly pattern of the crime narrative—of cause and effect, of personal guilt—with a miasma of generalized guilt and incomprehensible happenstance that forces this return of that which has been cast out.

Mandel argues that the conventions of crime fiction reinforce the idea that law-enforcement agencies serve the interests of the citizenry, obscuring "the class nature of the state, property, law and justice" (47). In Jackson's world the police are a vestigial force in no way connected up with justice or resolution, and her detectives range from inept, absent, and harmful to phantasmal. The rural policeman in "The Missing Girl" is hopelessly out of his depth with seemingly little interest in solving the case and even less aptitude for the task: it was "the first time that Chief Hook had ever been required to determine facts" (376), and "No one doubted Chief Hook's complete inability to cope with the disappearance of a girl" (376). He makes a few vague, tentative inquiries with a voice that was "almost quavering," "visibly afraid that his questions would sound foolish" (376), and diffidently searches the vanished girl's room "with some embarrassment" (378), "rubb[ing] his forehead nervously" (380), but quickly deflates under the personalities of the women he encounters and his own haplessness. His behavior alternates between a kind of naïve honesty and play-acting fictiveness, in the latter instance demanding of a camp counsellor, who only reported a vague shadowy figure of a person or creature ducking behind a tree, "'Can you face the girl's parents and honestly tell them you never lifted a finger to save her? .... That innocent girl?'" (381). In playing detective he seems embarrassed at the unreality of his performance, but he is ultimately required to do little beyond the most cursory gesture, dissuaded by the girl's family who evidently find their allotted role as fellow victims, grieving relatives, demanders of justice, etc., as difficult to pull off and empty of authentic meaning and agency as the passive cop has found his. He finally puts a stop to all efforts, summarizing the lacklustre ramshackle mood of the case throughout, "'we might as well give up. The boy scouts quit a week ago and today the girl scouts went'" (383), closing his conversation with the girl's uncle, and the investigation itself, with "'Never mind. . . . Nearly suppertime'" (383). Like the hazing mock-interrogation of freshmen in *Hangsaman*, for Jackson the justice system is a "ritual gone to seed" (60).

Hangsaman's detective is not real but rather a "secret voice which followed her. It was the police detective" (5). A crime genre bricolage, this spectral detective is part projection, part escapist fantasy, part intrusive psychological threat; this demi-character constitutes another partially-real masculine proxy of both threat and escape, just like the recurring figure of James Harris. Interrogating Natalie on a series of imagined crimes while, in spite of her "terror," she maintains a calm demeanor and never wavers in her alibi, the detections function as a trial to be overcome. This is a way of imagining the central figure of importance in a life thus far dominated by her parents' own psychodramas, and of representing herself as powerful, a figure as cool and collected and as in control of her emotions and as unassailable as an unrepentant murderer easily evading the aggressive questioning of the police: "A lovely little shiver went down Natalie's back. 'I may be in danger every moment of my life,' she told the detective, 'but I am strong within myself'" (8). Her later experience of sexual assault, traumatically collapsing her sense of wholeness and invulnerability, is all the more upsetting because firstly, it begins concomitantly with her inner dialogue with the detective, with her soon-to-be attacker's questions and actions threaded through her continuing daydream or delusion. Secondly, it echoes and inverts this fantasy of pleasurable interrogation and triumphant agency; her attacker isolates her and draws her away from safety through increasingly aggressive questions, to which she is forced to respond evasively as she has with the imaginary detective, repeatedly rephrasing the same question, twisting her words, and then he begins his assault proper by saying, "'Tell me what you thought was so wonderful about yourself'" (43). In doing so he moves from the present tense "what she thinks *is* so wonderful" to the past tense (41; my italics): he knows very well the time for feeling at home in her own self is over now. Echoing her earlier assertion that danger may be everywhere but her strength is within her, suddenly she realizes as he approaches her that "The danger is here, in *here*" (42): the miasma of Jackson's universe of fear coalesces, only for a moment, into the locatable singularity of a crime.

 On the one hand Jackson's rejection of the textual and judicial authority of the police follows an established crime thriller pattern of destabilizing authority, but on the other she rejects the replacement of this structuring agency with that of the criminal's subjectivity. Instead, she is carrying out in practice what the theories of Mandel and others suggest is lacking in the form—a recentering of social and narrative power, an establishing of a lens of collective rather than individual responsibility. Jackson rarely dedicates time to the killers, their mental state or backstory, and the solving of anything is always both impossible and beside the point. In *The Road Through the Wall*, for example, as Hattenhauer contends, Jackson "has written a detective story that exposes the detective story" (90), and no resolution is given either to narrative or the crime depicted therein by Jackson. In this text it is not just the police investigation that lacks the information to apportion blame—even the text itself refuses to do so: even the third person narrator, whose utterances create and describe the whole world of the novel, refuses to pronounce on this matter.

Her consistent lack of resolution in her crime narratives allows no closure for the reader and the characters but rather enacts a sort of uneasy, compulsive circling of the issue at hand, a porousness of meaning that suggests such indeterminacy and uncertainty extends beyond the page, into the reader's own world. Jackson's repeated return to certain motifs, for example the disappearance of Paula Welden, is another example of this circling which re-enacts the case with each time a different framework, different genre, different explanation, but always the same hollow outcome. As emblematically seen in "Louisa Please Come Home," it is not simply the search which is futile; the truth is unwanted: when their missing daughter appears and wishes to return to them her family rejects her, claiming she is a stranger. The story opens up the apparently happy possibility not only of disappearances but of reappearances, only to frustrate the power of these to provide any kind of solution or resolution.

We might remember that *Hangsaman*'s title refers both to a children's game and a method of judicial execution, and that Natalie's rapist never experiences any kind of judicial intervention. Depressingly, her encounter with him before she goes to university might be seen, in light of the prevalence of sexual violence both in higher education and the world at large, as a tragically fitting and timely introduction to her future life as a student and as a woman. Havrilesky argues her coming of age is the unravelling of faith in her own meaningfulness as a subjective being in the face of a world that cares nothing for that. We also see this un-signifying, this un-making of characters' meaning, experience, and agency in the suffocating dread of not being able to address the matter of their specific predicament, the crimes and harms threatening them, directly (for example in "Trial By Combat" and "A Cauliflower in Her Hair" among many others). In these and other works by Jackson, the specificity of the action is unimportant in and of itself compared to the emotional payoff dramatizing the question of what is and is not considered a crime, and how contingent and how arbitrary such a distinction is, the product of a bureaucratic exercise not a philosophical or experiential one. Both crime and haunting are transgressions of an order, a capitalist, patriarchal order that has been naturalized and made to seem unquestionable, and both are ideological, constructed by the exclusion of various things. Jackson's overlaying of crime templates onto a radically expanded moral and explanatory universe forces the return of that which, in a capitalist society whose workings are hidden in plain sight, have always already been expunged from the frame.

Works Cited

Dobson, James. "Knowing and Narration: Shirley Jackson and the Campus Novel." *Shirley Jackson, Influences and Confluences*, edited by Melanie R. Anderson and Lisa Kröger, Routledge, 2016, pp.123-141.

Fisher, Mark. *The Weird and the Eerie*. Repeater, 2016.

Franklin, Ruth. *Shirley Jackson: A Rather Haunted Life*. Norton, 2016.

Hattenhauer, Daryl. *Shirley Jackson's American Gothic*. State University of New York P, 2003.

Havrilesky, Heather. "Haunted Womanhood." *The Atlantic*, 26 Oct. 2016, www.theatlantic.com/magazine/archive/2016/10/the-possessed/497513.

Jackson, Shirley. *Hangsaman*. 1951. Penguin, 2013.

---. *The Haunting of Hill House*. 1959. Penguin, 2009.

---. "A Journey with a Lady." *Just an Ordinary Day*. Penguin, 2017.

---. "Louisa Please Come Home." *Dark Tales*. Penguin, 2016.

---. "Nightmare." *Just an Ordinary Day*. Penguin, 2017.

---. "Paranoia." *Just an Ordinary Day*. Penguin, 2017.

---. *The Road Through the Wall*. 1948. Penguin, 2013.

---. *We Have Always Lived in the Castle*. 1962. Penguin, 2009.

Joshi, S.T. *The Modern Weird Tale: A Critique of Horror Fiction*. McFarland, 2001.

Mandel, Ernest. *Delightful Murder: A Social History of the Crime Story*. Pluto, 1984.

Moretti, Franco. "Clues." *Signs Taken For Wonders*. Translated by Susan Fischer et al., Verso, 1988, pp.130-56.

Murphy, Bernice M. "'The People of the Village Have Always Hated Us': Shirley Jackson's New England Gothic." *Shirley Jackson: Essays on the Literary Legacy*, edited by Bernice M. Murphy, McFarland, 2005, pp.104-26.

Olfman, Sharna. *The Sexualization of Childhood*. Praeger, 2009.

Pascal, Richard. "*The Road Through the Wall* and Shirley Jackson's America." *Shirley Jackson, Influences and Confluences*, edited by Melanie R. Anderson, et al., Routledge, 2016, pp. 76-98.

Schmid, David. "Base and Superstructure in Crime Fiction." States of Crime: The State in Crime Fiction Conference,17-18 June 2011, Queen's University, Belfast. Conference Presentation. www.academia.edu/31811385/Base_and_ Superstructure_in_Crime_Fiction

Williams, Tennessee. Introduction. *Reflections in a Golden Eye* by Carson McCullers. 1950. *The Companion to Southern Literature: Themes, Genres, Places, People, Movements and Motifs*, edited by Joseph M. Flora and Lucinda Hardwick MacKethan, Louisiana State UP, 2002, p.315.

Wilson, Christine. "Haunted Habitability: Wilderness and the American Haunted House Narrative." *Popular Ghosts: The Haunted Spaces of Everyday Culture*, edited by Esther Peeren and Maria del Pilar Blanco, Continuum, 2010, pp. 200-12.

Žižek, Slavoj. *Violence: Six Sideways Reflections*. Profile, 2008.

APPRECIATIONS

Violent Justice: The Real Hero in C.S. Harris's St. Cyr Series

Mary C. Rawlinson

Detective fiction often has been cast as a masculine genre, where the anatomy and destiny of masculinity are at stake. In his classic analysis of the detective genre, Raymond Chandler clearly identifies its protagonist as male, a "man" who can walk the "mean streets" without himself being "made mean." The narrative tests masculine virtues of honor and physical bravery. Violence does not dismay these heroes. Neither "tarnished nor afraid," these men resist the forces of power and wealth that produce structural injustice and profit by the suffering of the weak.

In this milieu, women are relegated often to one of two categories. As exemplified in Chandler's paradigm for the genre *The Maltese Falcon*, she is either a "girl Friday" like Effie, who supports the detective in his quest, or, more often, she is a *femme fatale* like Miss Wonderley, who tests the hero's honor. As Julie Grossman argues, "an overemphasis on the 'femme fatale' has not only resulted in a misreading of... noir..., but [also] has fed into cultural and critical obsessions with the bad, sexy woman, which inevitably become prescriptive and influence cultural discourse about female agency in counterproductive ways" (5). Such readings miss entirely the long history in crime fiction of trenchant critiques of the law of property as the source both of gender inequity and of the unequal concentrations of wealth and power. The first detective novel in English, Wilkie Collins's *The Woman in White*, exposes the evils of nineteenth-century English laws governing marriage and property, which created inequities of class and gender and rendered women themselves little better than property. Collins, foreshadowing Chandler, describes a world in which "the Law is the servant of the long purse" (33). Collins explores how this economic milieu perverts and constrains both male and female agency. The moral agents of the text, Walter Hartwright and Marion Holcombe, complicate the norms of gender under the law of property. Walter, the artist, exhibits feminine characteristics of passivity and feeling, while Marion displays not only a somewhat masculinized countenance, but also a masculine intellect and fortitude. Neither alone is capable of achieving justice. Only Walter's collaboration with Marion succeeds in obtaining a measure of justice in this world of structural injustice: her intellect, patience, and courage prove essential to his male agency.

Contemporary detectives like Sara Paretsky's V.I. Warshawski and Sue Grafton's Kinsey Millhone exhibit the same combination of honor and courage that defined Spade, Marlowe, and other male *noir* detectives. These women display the same fearlessness in the face of lethal violence and the same commitment to resisting forces of structural injustice and to defending the vulnerable.

C. S. Harris's St. Cyr series, though set in Regency England, continues to develop the figure of the *noir* detective. Harris effectively evokes the landscapes and infrastructures of the period to achieve a palpable sense of place. P.D. James remarked that once she had chosen the place of a crime—a publishing house, a religious cloister, a country house—her plot and characters appeared. Harris's characters and conflicts do seem to arise out of the teeming streets of a London just embarking on its imperial destiny, a surging metropolis where the most extravagant wealth joined the most hopeless poverty. Her description of the construction of Regent Street effectively invokes the violence of government town planning focused on maximizing wealth and power, while the evocation of the grassy fields beyond Sloan Square reminds the reader just how recent the development of the megalopolis is, and just how near are the ghosts of the ways of life that were erased by it.

Harris creates the sort of characters that Chandler requires of the genre: ones you can believe in and ones that you will care about. A first read moves too fast because the reader cannot stop turning pages. Unlike the Warshawski or Millhone series, which are largely episodic, Harris's series unfolds major narrative lines that carry forward from book to book. Through the series, fundamental changes take place in the lead characters, and each book ends with several important points of character or plot unresolved. This trans-book temporality lends the series great depth and coherence, while yielding richer characters than can appear in episodes that largely repeat a formula.[1]

Sebastian St. Cyr, Lord Devlin, is, as Chandler remarks, the "best man in his world and a good enough man for any world." Though a wealthy viscount, Devlin has endured the brutalities of war and witnessed the indifference of wealth and power to ordinary human suffering and want. His dearest friend Gibson is an Irish surgeon from those campaigns, and Sebastian often relies on Gibson's autopsies in solving murders. Contrary to the image of the detective as a lone agent, Devlin collaborates with a team including Gibson, the magistrate Sir Henry Lovejoy, and his "tiger" or groom, the young urchin Tom. The mutual loyalty, camaraderie, and compassion create a collaborative agency on which Devlin relies.

Devlin frequently risks lethal violence to solve a murder because he feels he must avenge the life that has been stolen from the victim. Harris several times repeats the scene of Devlin staring at the body of a young murder victim—Emma Chase, Gabrielle Tennyson, Dominic Stanton—as he imagines a future that will no longer be. This moral imagination on behalf of others impels him to act. Devlin proves both fearless and hard to tarnish as he tangles with forces of wealth and power in seeking justice for victims and the vulnerable. Like Spade or Marlowe, Devlin operates liminally at the edge of the law, and he regularly comes into conflict with the ruling powers of politics and wealth.

Devlin, however, deviates further from the *noir* script by taking on a female partner.[2] Indeed, Miss Hero Jarvis arguably displaces Devlin from the position of hero. Like Devlin, she is dedicated to addressing structural injustice, but she is no more pious or utopian in her thinking than he is. She has a clear-eyed view of social inequity and the position of women, and she means to maintain her independence and not to be subjugated, while using her position and talent to advocate for the vulnerable. Her critical perspective on the pomposities and inequities of her class is no less acute than Devlin's, and she is no less determined than he to exert her agency on behalf of the victims of injustice and poverty.

Like Devlin and the other *noir* detectives, Hero is capable of lethal violence. When the carriage in which she and her mother are riding is waylaid by hired assassins, she calmly uses the carriage pistol to shoot one in the face and to gravely wound the other. She has the presence of mind to try to keep the wounded one alive so that he can reveal who hired him. When she is abducted along with her maid or "Abigail" by three other hired assassins, they brutally butcher the maid in front of her, but, through wit and physical courage, she manages to kill all three. Sebastian arrives on the scene too late to be of any help, and not only this time.[3] Most chillingly, when she and a friend are walking in Berkeley Square and they are approached by the Dutch diplomat van der Pals who intends to kill them, Hero calmly shifts her muff and fires the little muff pistol hidden in it. Afterward, her concern is all for her muff which has caught on fire. Indeed, later that evening she is still tending her muff, apparently unruffled, even content, that she has just killed a man. Devlin says sadly that "most people's capacity for evil is infinitely greater than we'd like to believe." Neither Devlin nor Hero seem morally ambivalent about the violence they deploy against this evil. After the kidnapping episode, Devlin offers to claim that he killed the abductors in order to spare her the social embarrassment that would inevitably ensue when her actions became public knowledge. She refuses.

Hero's very appearance transgresses the idea of the ladylike, as she is very tall, almost as tall as Sebastian, who is a very tall man. She is not conventionally pretty, but she acquires a striking glow after she, at her own initiative, engages Sebastian in an intense sexual passion. She is constantly going where ladies do not go and talking to people that ladies do not talk to—costermongers and prostitutes, sweepers and sewage men. She constantly disconcerts her powerful father by failing to engage in lady-like pursuits—shopping, social visits, perhaps a little needlework—rather than in her research into the lives of the poor and her public advocacy for the vulnerable and dispossessed.

In their own relationship, Sebastian and Hero transgress the infrastructures of property and power that sustain both their own wealth and privilege and the structural injustice against which they struggle. A woman sold herself one way or the other. Either she became a prostitute, or a servant, or she was exchanged in a marriage contract between her father and her husband. The contract stipulated both her subservience to her husband and her financial dependence on him. Hero had vowed never to marry, until circumstances led her to accept the viscount's proposal. She had already come to think of him as having an uncommon respect for women as thinkers and agents, but even she is shocked by the marriage contract that her father brings home. Devlin has insisted that she retain control of her property and wealth and that she not be subject to his judgment in any matter. Hero's father Jarvis thinks the contract is mad, but he goes along with it because of his confidence in *her* judgment.

Devlin also respects the sovereignty of Hero's body, rather than exerting his property rights in it. He stands at his window the night of their marriage, fully prepared to take up a life of celibacy if she does not come to him rather than betray his vow or force himself on her. Later, during her pregnancy, delivery, and early maternity, Devlin shows an abject respect for her fortitude, suffering, and courage. No man takes charge during her labor, as Hero is attended by Alexi Sauvage, a French doctor and intimate of Gibson. Though her father disapproves, thinking it beneath her class, Hero nurses the baby herself and Devlin defers to her in the matter. After the birth of the baby, Hero and Sebastian grow as partners in solving crimes. They continue to negotiate a relationship entirely outside the marriage rules of the time, so that Hero claims and Sebastian respects an integrity and freedom of person and property that the law would deny her.

Transgressive in themselves and in their relationship, Devlin and Hero also transgress the ruling forces of wealth and power each time they seek justice for a victim deemed too inconvenient or too insignificant to deserve the law's attention. Devlin constantly comes up against Hero's father, the Machiavellian Charles, Lord Jarvis, the most powerful man in the kingdom, who often wants to hide the crime rather than expose the truth and see justice done. The aim of maintaining power, not the claims of justice, determines Jarvis's actions, and sets him inevitably into conflict with Sebastian. That conflict—along with the question of Hero's loyalties to her father and her husband—hangs over the series as a looming cataclysm.

Hero regularly finds herself at cross-purposes with her father, not only over her work on behalf of the poor and vulnerable, but also over his cruel disdain for her mother. So far circumstances have not required a rupture, but her deepening bond with Sebastian and the consonance between their views on inequity and in their sense of justice, as opposed to Jarvis's politics of expediency, only heightens the sense of an impending collision.

Chandler remarks that "in everything that can be called art, there is a quality of redemption," and the theme of redemption courses throughout this series. Devlin feels himself beyond redemption for some of the actions he committed as a soldier. Harris ties his compulsion to seek justice for murder victims to his sense of having participated in and failed to prevent terrible injustice during the war. Hero also carries a sense of guilt, not because of particular actions or events, but because of the advantages of her birth, the wealth and privilege that she enjoys. Far from sentimental, she does not spend her days in charitable acts but in researching social policies and conditions to support legislation aimed at ameliorating the inequities of gender and class. Both Devlin and Hero are ambiguous agents, for they enjoy wealth and privilege while taking aim at the very powers and structures that sustain that wealth and privilege.

Far from being a genre focused only or even primarily on masculinity and its fate, detective fiction repeatedly creates masculine characters like Viscount Devlin who are at ease in their masculinity and who understand themselves in relation to equally independent and capable women. It includes many female detectives like Kinsey Millhone and V.I. Warshawski, who, like Sam Spade, act by a code of courage and honor toward the aim of securing justice for the vulnerable.

Moreover, Devlin and Hero, like most *noir* heroes, raise the troubling question of the necessity of violence to justice in a world of structural injustice. If the law is "the servant of the long person," then will not an extralegal agent of justice be required?

Like most detectives in the genre, Millhone, Warshawski, and Spade act as individual agents whose intimate relationships are either transitory or somewhat static friendships. Harris's St. Cyr series explores the possibility of a collaborative agency in the possibility of marriage as a partnership of equals, a collaboration that may be, like the collaboration between Walter Hartwright and Marian Holcombe at the beginning of the genre, just the kind of transgressive infrastructure needed to address structural injustice and inequity.

Notes

1. This is one reason it is difficult to recommend particular titles: best to start at the beginning and read through. My own favorites are volumes 4, 5, and 6, where Hero and Sebastian are working out the terms of their relationship while solving several brutal murders. Harris, C. S., vol. 4, *Where Serpents Sleep*, New York: Signet, 2008; vol., 5, *What Remains of Heaven*, New York: Signet, 2011; and vol. 6, *Where Shadows Dance*, New York: Signet, 2012.

2. The detective, especially the noir detective, rarely takes on a partner, especially a female one who becomes a genuinely equal agency. Nora, charming as she may be, is hardly Nick Charles' equal as a detective. Despite the collaboration between Walter Hartwright and Marion Holcombe at the beginning of the genre, detectives, particularly noir detectives, tend to operate alone, with a very small supporting cast or none at all.

3. For example, when the murderous Bullock threatens to shoot Gibson and Hero, Hero kills him with a poker just before Sebastian arrives. She needs no prince charming to come to the rescue.

Works Cited

Chandler, Raymond. *The Simple Art of Murder.* Vintage, 1982.

Collins, Wilkie. *The Woman in White.* 1860. Penguin, 1981.

Grossman, Julie. *Rethinking the Femme Fatale in Film Noir: Ready for Her Close-Up.* Palgrave Macmillan, 2009.

Neuro-Noir, Bipolar Detectives, and Abigail Padgett's Bo Bradley

Susan Elizabeth Sweeney

I began my study of detective fiction in reverse, writing a doctoral dissertation on "metaphysical" detective stories by Borges, Nabokov, Pynchon, and Robbe-Grillet that pose self-reflexive questions about reading. The dissertation led to a co-edited book, *Detecting Texts: The Metaphysical Detective Story from Poe to Postmodernism*, and further work on Poe, Nabokov, experimental narrative, and detective fiction. Recently, I've gotten interested in another stage of the genre's development, which I call "neuro-noir" (Sweeney 231-32). Ever since Poe invented detective fiction, the genre has emphasized the mind of the detective. In neuro-noir, however, the eccentric sleuth epitomized by Dupin, Holmes, and Poirot becomes an investigator whose neurological disorder both hinders and helps her crime-solving. This isn't surprising, since neuroscience has replaced psychoanalysis—which illuminated detectives' thinking in works such as Hitchcock's *Vertigo* and Robbe-Grillet's *The Erasers*—as a grand narrative that seemingly explains all human behavior. There are now more and more protagonists like Abigail Padgett's groundbreaking Bo Bradley, an investigator for Child Protective Services with a mood disorder.

Neuro-noir emerged as a new subgenre in the early twenty-first century, thanks to three particularly influential works:

Christopher Nolan's film *Memento* (2001), Mark Haddon's *The Curious Incident of the Dog in the Nighttime* (2003), and Jonathan Lethem's *Motherless Brooklyn* (1999). The notion of an amnesiac detective, already a resonant trope in novels like William Hjortsberg's *Falling Angel* (1978), expanded considerably in Nolan's tale of an insurance investigator who seeks his wife's murderer despite suffering from anterior retrograde amnesia and being unable to make new memories. Since *Memento*, other detectives have surfaced with memory disorders ranging from Alzheimer's to hyperthymnesia, or total recall. The traits associated with Asperger's syndrome, meanwhile, may suggest an archetypal detective—as in the BBC's *Sherlock*—but Haddon refused to assign this label to his young hero. Nevertheless, *Curious Incident* led to other detectives who have been hailed as individuals with Asperger's, from strong female characters, such as Lisbeth Salander (in *The Girl With the Dragon Tattoo*) or Saga Norén (in the Danish and Swedish TV series *The Bridge*), to Alexei Maxim Russell's *Trueman Bradley, Aspie Detective*. The protagonist of *Motherless Brooklyn* has a condition that seems unrelated to detection, yet his Tourette's syndrome fosters rapid flights of association that help him solve a murder. Subsequent detectives have been characterized by various other diagnoses: post-traumatic stress disorder, phobias, Cotard's syndrome, synesthesia, *alexia sine agraphia*, obsessive-compulsive disorder, narcolepsy, and more. Meanwhile, the detective story's influence on science fiction, cyberpunk, new weird, and other genres has yielded protagonists with *fictional* neurological disorders.

A detective with manic-depressive disorder is another instance of this phenomenon, although perhaps not entirely new: the narrator of "The Murders in the Rue Morgue," observing Dupin's behavior, fancies that he has a "Bi-Part Soul" with two aspects, "the creative and the resolvent" (Poe 533). The most famous bipolar investigator is probably Carrie Mathison, the protagonist of Showtime's series *Homeland*. However, Abigail Padgett's Bo Bradley was the first sleuth explicitly identified as bipolar. Padgett had a background in education and counseling before becoming a court investigator for Child Protective Services in San Diego; that experience, along with sympathy for a family member's struggles and a desire to advocate for the mentally ill, inspired her to develop this character (Lindsay 196). Padgett's protagonist always addresses herself as "Bradley"—for example, "This is crazy, Bradley. Take a pill!"—so that's how I refer to her (*Stork Boy* ch. 14). She appeared in five critically acclaimed novels nearly a decade before Haddon's, Lethem's, and Nolan's influential works: *Child of Silence* (1993), *Strawgirl* (1994), *Turtle Baby* (1995), *Moonbird Boy* (1996), and *The Dollmaker's Daughters* (1997).

Padgett's novels, while less formally innovative than Haddon's and Lethem's, are remarkably thoughtful. As their titles suggest, they focus on traumatized children: a four-year-old Anglo boy, tied to a mattress on a Paiute reservation, who turns out to be deaf; an eight-year-old girl whose younger sister was raped and murdered, supposedly by Satanists; an eight-month-old Mayan baby from Guatemala, found poisoned on the American side of the Mexican border; an orphaned boy with Attention Deficit Hyperactivity Disorder; an abused girl in foster care. After two decades, during which she produced other detective novels and story collections, Padgett returned to the Bo Bradley series with *Stork Boy* (2019), a novel currently available only as an e-book, which features a brilliant outsider artist—a French teenager with bipolar disorder who runs away after witnessing a murder. Padgett's detective responds to each child's plight with determination, ingenuity, empathy, and respect for individual experience. The mysteries are original and complex; Padgett develops entirely believable characters while integrating research on various cultures, belief systems, neurological conditions, and modes of creativity into her plots. Indeed, her series has been recognized for its use of the Southern California desert (Barrasso 71-73), its awareness of other cultures (Macdonald and Macdonald 76-78), and its revision of hard-boiled tropes that stigmatize female characters in order to produce a defiant, resourceful feminist heroine (McRae 41-42).

Bradley's bipolar disorder is essential to her detective process; she feels "grateful for the peculiar neural wiring that allowed her to sense things she could never grasp" (*Stork Boy* ch. 19). She identifies the exuberant sense of meaningfulness and increased ability to discern patterns, which can accompany the onset of a manic episode, with the second sight her Irish grandmother boasted of having. Although she takes her prescribed medications, adjusting them as needed, Bradley still experiences "metaphoric feelings," "nervy energy," and a heightened perceptiveness that help her in recognizing and connecting clues (*Stork Boy* ch. 7, ch. 14). At the same time, comprehending her own condition makes her aware that others may have unusual abilities, sensitivities, strengths, and understandings. Even before she locates Marc Guerin, runaway artist in *Stork Boy*, Bradley sympathizes with him as "the captive of a mind prone to illusive fantasies no one else could ever see, hear, or understand" (ch. 17). Bradley not only identifies with children like the Stork Boy, protects them, and advocates for them, but she also finds that attending to their unique insights helps her to solve each crime. In keeping with the history of detective fiction and the recent emergence of neuro-noir, Abigail Padgett's pioneering novels enable her readers to learn to think "differently" (*Stork Boy* ch. 11) about thinking itself.

Works Cited

Barrasso, Sibylle. "Murder in Rural Southern California: Drowning in the Desert." *Crime Fiction and Film in the Southwest: Bad Boys and Bad Girls in the Badlands*, edited by Steve Glassman and Maurice J. O'Sullivan, Bowling Green State University Popular Press, 2001, pp. 58-73.

Lindsay, Elizabeth Blakesley. *Great Women Mystery Writers*. 2nd. ed., Greenwood, 2017, pp. 196-98.

Macdonald, Gina and Andrew Macdonald. "Ethnic Detectives in Popular Fiction: New Directions for an American Genre." *Diversity and Detection*, edited by Kathleen Gregory Klein, Bowling Green State University Popular Press, 1999, pp. 60-113.

McRae, Tim. "The Revenge of Carmen Sternwood: How Abigail Padgett's Bo Bradley Series Speaks to and Changes the Hard-Boiled Form." *Clues*, vol. 22, no. 1, 2001, pp. 41–51.

Padgett, Abigail. *Child of Silence*. Mysterious Press, 1993.

---. *The Dollmaker's Daughters*. Mysterious Press, 1997.

---. *Moonbird Boy*. Mysterious Press, 1996.

---. *Stork Boy*. Kindle, 2019.

---. *Strawgirl*. Mysterious Press, 1994.

---. *Turtle Baby*. Mysterious Press, 1995.

Poe, Edgar Allan. "The Murders in the Rue Morgue." *The Collected Works of Edgar Allan Poe*, edited by Thomas Ollive Mabbott, vol. 2, Belknap Press of Harvard UP, 1978, pp. 521-74.

Sweeney, Susan Elizabeth. "Unusual Suspects: American Crimes, Metaphysical Detectives, Postmodernist Genres." *A History of American Crime Fiction*, edited by Chris Raczkowski, Cambridge UP, 2017, pp. 221-35.

REVIEWS

Female Corpses in Crime Fiction:
A Transatlantic Perspective

Glen S. Close
Palgrave Macmillan, 2018 (261 pp.)

Crime fiction typically requires a trio of characters: the victim, the criminal or perpetrator, and the detective who investigates, identifies, and captures the criminal. In *Female Corpses in Crime Fiction: A Transatlantic Perspective,* Glen S. Close chooses to focus on the victim, specifically on the female victims of male murderers. To do so, he introduces a Kristevan perspective of cadavers as examples of the abject, and links male identity to the process of separation from the maternal body. According to Julia Kristeva, "the male subject finds itself ever threatened not only by corpses and other forms of bodily waste, but also by signs of female sexual differences such as menstrual blood, the object of innumerable taboos in patriarchal cultures" (17). The torture and killing of female victims is an exercise of male power over the mystery of the female, from whose body each male has come.

In "Necropornography in Modern Crime Fiction," Close — a noted Hispanist— discusses the *nota roja* or yellow journalism of Spanish America to demonstrate the morbid connection between sexual desire and the torture and death of scantily clad, beautiful women, comparing the front page of such publications with similar imagery on the covers of crime fiction by Mickey Spillane and Erle Stanley Gardner, among many others. He briefly traces the close relationship of Eros and Thanatos from as early as the fifteenth century and the debt of crime fiction to the gothic. He locates the origin of crime fiction in the early stories of Edgar Allan Poe and the lurid murders in "The Mystery of Marie Rogêt" and the aptly titled "The Murders in the Rue Morgue." Both stories probably arose from actual events. Marie Rogêt was clearly based on the unsolved murder of the beautiful Mary Rogers of New Jersey, whose murder triggered sensationalist newspaper articles as well as a kind of death tourism. The Rue Morgue story shares certain characteristics with the ax murder of Helen Jewett, a stylish prostitute in New York City. Both the press and the stories themselves depend on the beauty of the women murdered and the depravity of the treatment of their bodies to engage and excite their audience. Close then discusses a Hispanic precursor, *La hella del crimen* [The Trace of the Crime] by Luis V. Varela, considered the first detective novel published in Spanish, published serially in the newspaper *La Tribuna* over two months in 1877. Once again, a beautiful woman is found dead, her physical beauty noted by the detectives who find the body, which is later exhibited in the Paris morgue, where spectators can examine corpses through a glass partition.

"Hard-Boiled Misogyny" is the next section of "Necropornography," and it makes a case for what the critic John G. Cawelti states is the "embodiment of the fear, hostility, and ambiguity [...] toward women that are built into the hard-boiled detective formula" (72, 187). Using cover images of novels by Mickey Spillane, Carter Brown, Jonathan Latimer, and Ed McBain, among others, he notes once again that the beautiful, nude and abused female body is the object of the male detective's gaze, the "female cadavers staged as spectacles for scopic consumption by desiring male subjects [...] female bodies reduced to a state of perfect submission and passivity" (86-87).

Chapter 3, "The Hispanic Hard-Boiled," traces the arrival and development of hard-boiled crime fiction in Spain and Spanish America. Cover art of dead women with breasts at least partially exposed while the detective stands over and observes the body again confirms that "the sexualization and glamorization of dead female bodies are constant, as are the compositional assertions of male visual and spatial mastery" (90-91). Perhaps ironically, many of these cadavers are blonde or redheaded women, despite the rarity of such hair color in Hispanic cultures generally. He analyzes the novels of the Spanish writer Llaugé Dausá as evidence of the influence of the "sociosexual policies of the Franco dictatorship" (102), which view women as either mothers (good) or prostitutes (sinful), and of course prostitutes are punished for their wanton lifestyle by being brutally murdered, their cadavers serving the necropornographic pleasures of men.

In Chapter 4, "Femicide and Snuff," Close contrasts the hard-boiled analysis of previous chapters with the Chilean writer Roberto Bolanño's *2666*. A famously complex novel of over nine hundred pages, the fourth section, "The Part About the Crimes," is a compilation of femicides in the fictional town of Santa Teresa, Mexico. Close sees the novel as a "reworking of *novela negra* conventions" (138) in that most of the more than one hundred murders Bolaño details no perpetrator is identified (the criminal remains at large), and no detective is able to decipher clues well enough to arrive at a solution, or even an explanation. The murders themselves bear striking resemblance to the infamous and unsolved murders of hundreds of women in Ciudad Juárez, Mexico, on the border of Texas. Bolaño rejects the necropornographic norm of the *novela negra*, substituting forensic medical realism in its place, forcing the reader to "resist voyeurism" (152). Bolaño's references to snuff photography and film, says Close, are his way of raising the consciousness, and perhaps the conscience, of readers.

Close then contrasts *2666* with the works of snuff fantasists, stating that snuff themes no longer exist in the dark underground but "pervade mainstream television fare" (155-56) and have been present in the works of writers in the United States such as Elmore Leonard and James Ellroy. After examining a series of works with disturbing snuff scenes, Close returns to Kristeva's theory of the abject and the male's attack on the female as an attack of the source of life upon which he is dependent and from which he seeks his autonomy.

Chapter 5, "Conclusion," traces the development and changing representations of women and female cadavers in Patricia Cornwell's Scarpetta series based on a woman forensic medical examiner and television dramas such as *Bones* and *CSI* in its various iterations. Though the corpse remains an erotic subject, on occasion these shows demonstrate some empathy for the victim.

The author closes by claiming that "artists who spectacularize and sensationalize death and violence while suppressing awareness of the resulting grief and pain are artists who deserve our scorn," though he has spent over two hundred pages analyzing them. Much of his analysis is quite explicit and therefore nearly as disturbing as the original texts themselves. Close's *Female Corpses in Crime Fiction* is a well-researched scholarly work with a feminist bent, intended for a scholarly reader with a rather strong stomach.

—Linda Ledford-Miller
Professor Emerita of Spanish, Portuguese,
and Literature of American Minorities
Department of World Languages and Cultures
University of Scranton

Domestic Noir: The New Face of 21st Century Crime Fiction

Laura Joyce and Henry Sutton, editors
Palgrave Macmillan, 2018 (292 pp.)

With a preface by Julia Crouch, fourteen essays by fourteen authors and an afterword by Megan Abbott, *Domestic Noir* focuses on the female experience, whether as victim or perpetrator. After an Introduction by Laura Joyce, general categories include "The Origins of Domestic Noir," "The Influences of Gillian Flynn´s *Gone Girl*," "Gendered, Sexual, and Intimate Violence in Domestic Noir," "Home as a Site of Violence," and "Geographies of Domestic Noir." In her opening remarks, crime writer Julia Crouch shares her invention in 2003 of the term "domestic noir," and notes that women's experience is at the center of this subgenre and that the "home as sanctuary" is often subverted, with that supposed sanctuary "a cage, a place of torment, of psychological tyranny, of violence" (vii). But she also observes that women may be perpetrators as well as victims.

In "The Origins of Domestic Noir," Fiona Peters argues that the works of Patricia Highsmith serve as a strong influence on domestic noir. Peters defines contemporary domestic noir as "a literary and cinematic phenomenon foregrounding the home and/or workplace which, by exposing those seemingly 'safe' spaces, highlights and reflects women's experience" (12). She focuses in particular on *Deep Water* (1974), set in a small New England suburb, and the domestic dysfunction of its protagonists. Though Highsmith's work precedes the domestic noir label, Peters asserts that her "forensic examination" of the fraught relationships of the domestic sphere is a clear precursor. Stefania Ciocia also examines a "trailblazer of domestic noir" in her discussion of Vera Caspary's novel, *Laura (1943)*, better known for the successful film by Otto Preminger (1944). With its latent violence and psychological undercurrents, Ciocia sees the novel as a predecessor to such contemporary works as Gillian Flynn's *Gone Girl*.

The essays in "The Influences of Gillian Flynn's *Gone Girl*" focus on "the archetypal domestic noir" of Flynn's enormously successful novel in which the victim isn't dead after all. In fact, she herself perpetrates a horrific crime, and in so doing manages to exonerate the (cheating) husband she had labored to make guilty of her disappearance and perhaps murder. In his essay, "Gone Genre: How the Academy Came Running and Discovered Nothing Was As It Seemed," Harry Sutton provides an overview of the history of crime fiction criticism and the complex relationship between successful, popular literature and formal literary criticism. Eva Burke's essay investigates "the allure of female victimhood" and repositions the question of whether *Gone Girl* is a feminist novel as a means of critiquing "the social obligation of female likeability" (81).

Section III, "Gendered, Sexual, and Intimate Violence in Domestic Noir," contains three essays. Emma V. Miller focuses first on the female corpse as the passive role expected of women, countered by women "on the move" like Amy of *Gone Girl* and Rachel of Paula Hawkins' *The Girl on the Train*. Leigh Redhead examines Gillian Flynn's *Sharp Objects* and Megan Abbott's *Dare Me* to argue that the contrast between adult females and teenage femme fatales in these novels constitutes a feminist critique of the double standards and sexism ingrained in contemporary Western society. Nicoletta Di Ciolla and Anna Pasolini investigate the "violent mother" with an "intersectional analysis" of women versus mothers; the "multiplicity of female identity," which suggests that though women may be victims of violence, they also may be survivors or even victimizers; and questions of power, not exclusive to gender relations (141). They observe that the social expectations of mothers are enormous, at the same time as social dysfunction may prevent mothers from meeting such expectations, leaving women to struggle to negotiate the tension between motherhood, victimhood, and a hoped-for female agency.

"Home as a Site of Violence" is comprised of three essays that examine the home, not as sanctuary, but as an alien, dangerous, or even deadly space. Shelley Ingram and Willow G. Mullins examine Tana French's gothic "psychodrama," *Broken Harbour*. The middle class dream of the Spain family becomes the nightmare of the haunted house—haunted by the economic collapse of the Celtic Tiger and the family's inability to perform the social and economic functions of their class. Ela Avanzas Álvarez discusses Liane Moriarty's *Little Lies*, in which fine homes and membership in the privileged upper classes cannot save a wife from an abusive husband. In both the novel and the Emmy award winning HBO series, home is a façade, not a sanctuary but rather a theatrical setting to satisfy public expectations. Diane Waters and Heather Worthington analyze the relationship between American cozy and domestic noir, which often share domestic and community spaces as settings. Domestic noir, however, tends to explore the psychology of its characters and focus on alienation as a result of modern society, in marked contrast to the community engagement of the cozy.

Section V, "Geographies of Domestic Noir," deals with works from beyond the United States and the United Kingdom. Rosemary Erickson Johnsen examines the Dublin Murder Squad novels of Tana French in the context of the Irish gothic, and the house as the site of gothic plots and characters, and even hallucinations by those characters. Andrea Hynynen investigates the French thrillers by Pierre Lemaitre in translation, noting that despite the lack of a domestic noir tradition in France, or in thrillers in general, Lemaitre's novels contain many traits common to the genre. The final essay, by Patricia Catoira, examines the translation of *Our Lady of Solitude*, by the Chilean writer Marcela Serrano, seeing it as an unconventional detective novel about a protagonist that is unable to write one herself.

Megan Abbott's afterword closes the volume, commenting that popular crime fiction continues to be considered simply, and only escapist literature, despite its discernment.

Domestic Noir is a refreshing addition to serious crime fiction criticism—to literary criticism, in fact. Well written and well researched, the essays engage the academic as well as a general audience. Highly recommended for scholars of crime fiction and for undergraduate and graduate libraries.

—Linda Ledford-Miller
Professor Emerita of Spanish, Portuguese,
and Literature of American Minorities
Department of World Languages and Cultures
University of Scranton

The Detective and the Artist: Painters, Poets and Writers in Crime Fiction, 1840s-1970s

J.K. Van Dover
McFarland & Company, 2019 (197 pp.)

    J.K. Van Dover's book contains a summary of the role of the artist in works of detective fiction. He examines the artist as detective, suspect, bystander, victim, villain, and, occasionally, love interest for the detective. The dual role of detective and artist is found in early works of detective fiction and in the Golden Age, which he primarily dates as beginning in the 1920s (with A.E.W. Mason's *Murder at the Villa Rosa* in 1910 and E.C. Bentley's *Trent's Last Case* in 1913 as notable exceptions). He transitions to the American hard-boiled genre with a focus on Erle Stanley Gardner, Dashiell Hammett, and Mickey Spillane, among others. His approach is to concentrate on each writer and examine artistic characters as they appear in various works of detective fiction, noting any recurrences and highlighting the role of the artist in the plot.
    Van Dover begins by tracing early discussions about murder: Thomas De Quincey's 1827, 1839, and 1854 trilogy discussing the Ratcliffe Highway Murders of 1811 and Oscar Wilde's 1889 "Pen, Pencil, and Poison" examination of the poisoning murders committed by artist, poet, and critic Thomas Griffiths Wainwright. Van Dover suggests that De Quincey's romanticizing of the emotions of the survivors and those nearest to the crime, in addition to Wilde's focus on the aesthetics of the crime and the criminal, helps to develop the genre of crime fiction.

Van Dover tracks the role of the artist/poet and suggests their fanciful nature evolves from Edgar Allan Poe's Dupin who, by the third work featuring him, relies heavily on his poetic nature to solve the puzzle. Van Dover suggests that Dupin,

> like the brilliant criminal, succeeds in solving (and in committing) the greatest crimes by exercising the supplemental virtues of the poet. But having thus in the third Dupin tale arrived at the figure of the mathematician-poet as the ideal protagonist for a series of popular and profitable tales of crime detection, Edgar Allan Poe abandoned the series. Revived by Conan Doyle fifty years later, Poe's half poet-half detective would become a one-twelfth musician-detective. The deluge of claimants to Sherlock Holmes's estate would, with rare exceptions, be thoroughly prosaic detectives. (14)

Holmes's claim of "art in the blood" with his familial link to the painter Claude-Joseph Vernet is juxtaposed with his emphasis on rational thought in solving his cases.

Van Dover briefly discusses the connection between Oscar Wilde and Arthur Conan Doyle. Wilde met Joseph Stoddart, editor of *Lippincott's Monthly Magazine*, at an 1889 dinner at the Langham Hotel during which Wilde was recruited to provide a story and wrote *The Picture of Dorian Gray*. Also present at that dinner to have work commissioned was Conan Doyle, and *The Sign of Four* was the result (23, 26). Van Dover links the two with their "artful commission of murder and their artful detection of the murderer's choice of time, place, and tools" (26). Van Dover explores the seeming contradictions between the ratiocinative-based form of the detective story with the creative temperament shown by artistic characters in their respective works.

The author provides an excellent study of the role of the artist in the Father Brown mysteries, highlighting the character of Valentin in his journey from renowned policeman in "The Blue Cross" to murderer and artist of crime in "The Secret Garden." In tracing that path, Van Dover emphasizes how the artistic temperament and ego become damaged and warped when a superior mind triumphs.

Van Dover comments upon the tendency of female writers during the Golden Age to give their male detectives a detecting companion with an artistic bent: writer Ariadne Oliver joins Agatha Christie's Hercule Poirot in detecting, and both Dorothy L. Sayers's Lord Peter Wimsey and Ngaio Marsh's Roderick Alleyn find partners in detection and romance in, respectively, writer Harriet Vane and painter Agatha Troy.

Van Dover thoroughly details the role of artists in English and American writers of classic detective fiction, emphasizing how this popular art form can include a serious consideration of art as part of its subject mattter. He studies the role of the artist/writer/actor in works produced by popular writers from the Golden Age onward. It is a thorough detailing, though Van Dover occasionally gets lost in explaining plot details to the detriment of the analysis of the role of the artist.

In his chapter studying the connections between hard-boiled detectives and artists, Van Dover demonstrates how the category eschewed any detectives who were also of artistic temperament. As Ogden Nash would comment on the artistic prattle of S.S. Van Dine's Philo Vance, "Philo Vance/Needs a kick in the Pance," an attitude presumably shared by hard-boiled authors. As the American writers cultivated a more hard-boiled, pragmatic, and occasionally violent detective in the genre—though artists were plentiful as suspects, criminals, and victims—there were no detectives who were also artists.

This work allows for a wide audience to engage in and understand more about favorite detective characters. As the book's structure follows a chronology of the development of detective fiction, a casual reader can easily pick out a chapter or two that focuses on a favorite character or time period in the genre. A desultory fan of detective fiction can easily learn more about the role of the artist in a story or novel, but a scholar in detective fiction will find mostly surface analysis about the role of an artist in a work, and should instead use this as a reference to jump into further research.

—Monica Lott
Composition Instructor
Kent State University-Geauga

CONTRIBUTORS

Nathan Ashman is a Lecturer in Crime Writing at the University of East Anglia. He has previously held teaching posts at both the University of Surrey and the University of Gloucestershire. He is the author of *James Ellroy and Voyeur Fiction* (2018) and has published articles on writers such as Ross Macdonald, E.C Bentley and Don DeLillo. His research spans the fields of crime fiction, contemporary American fiction, and ecocriticism, with a particular specialism in the works of James Ellroy. He is currently in the early stages of a new research project examining the relationship between crime fiction and ecocriticism.

Cathrine Avery is a lecturer at Oaklands College, where she teaches Film Studies. Her academic research focuses on gender and crime fiction, in particular, the hard-boiled genre with its capacity to contribute to socially desirable gender constructions and to change in response to contemporaneous gender anxieties. Her current research examines novels that illustrate the representation of a feminist embodiment, challenge the objectification of the female victim and unapologetically incorporate the generic violence, as an expression of female agency. Her Ph.D. (2017) is on the female detective - *Talking Back to Chandler and Spillane: Gender and Agency in Women's Hard-Boiled Detective Fiction*, Birkbeck, London University. Her paper "Subjects of Violence: Sarah Dunant's Hard-Boiled Detective Fiction" has recently been published in *Contemporary Women's Writing* (2019, OUP). She contributed to the **Queens of Crime Conference (2014) Institute of English Studies, Senate House, University of London with a paper titled:** "Violence as an Expression of Female Identity in the Hard-Boiled Detective Novel."

Andrea Braithwaite, Ph.D. is an Associate Professor (Teaching) at the University of Ontario Institute of Technology, in Communication and Digital Media Studies. She holds a Ph.D. in

Communication Studies from McGill University. Her research examines gendered discourses of sociability and belonging in pop culture, with an emphasis on what is often referred to or described as "women's culture." She looks at gender, crime, and detection stories across media, especially Canadian media. Her work focuses specifically on the figure of the amateur female sleuth in fiction, television, film, and video games. She also discusses representations of and responses to feminist activism in online and gaming communities, as well as "marginal" and gendered games and gaming practices like independent games, casual gaming, and interactive stories.

Peter Bush is teaching elder at Westwood Presbyterian Church, Winnipeg, Manitoba, Canada and an independent scholar. He fell in love with mysteries as a child reading Edin Blyton's Five Find-outters and Dog series. Prior to moving to Winnipeg he served congregations in Flin Flon, Manitoba and Mitchell, Ontario. His writing has included a history of the Canadian Presbyterian Church on the Prairies, 1885-1925, and a book about the death and rebirth of congregations. A focus of his research has been The Presbyterian Church in Canada's involvement with Indian Residential Schools in Canada, doing contract research for the Truth and Reconciliation Commission regarding Indian Residential Schools. Peter was the Moderator of The Presbyterian Church in Canada in 2017-2018. He is married to Debbie, and they have one son.

Nicole Kenley Ph.D. is a Lecturer in the English Department at Baylor University. She is currently at work on her book project, *Detecting Globalization*, which explores twenty-first-century detective fiction's entanglement with globalization to suggest that global crime's inability to be contained signals a larger crisis underscoring contemporary fiction's global turn. This book project represents her ongoing interest in the connection between contemporary crime fiction and globalization, a relationship which she has explored in her articles "Global Crime, Forensic Detective Fiction, and the Continuum of Containment" (*Canadian*

Review of Comparative Literature 46.1) and "Hackers without Borders: Global Detectives in Stieg Larsson's Millennium Trilogy" (*Clues* 32.2). Her engagement with globalization and crime fiction is also evident in her chapters for the edited collections *Crime Uncovered: Antihero* (Intellect), *Teaching Crime Fiction* (Palgrave Macmillan), and the forthcoming Routledge *Companion to Crime Fiction*, *The Cambridge Companion to World Crime Fiction*, and *Animals in Detective Fiction* (Palgrave). She is also the co-editor, with Malcah Effron of *The Journal of Popular Culture*'s forthcoming special issue on place, space, and the detective narrative, as well as a reviewer for *Crime Fiction Studies*. Her scholarship on detective fiction has also appeared in *Mississippi Quarterly* (65.3).

Linda Ledford-Miller has a Masters in Comparative Literature from the Pennsylvania State University, and in Luso-Brazilian literature and Comparative Literature from the University of Texas, Austin, specializing in Literature of the Americas. She has published widely on travel writing and women writers. An avid reader of mysteries, she has shifted focus to crime fiction, working on Robert Downey Jr.'s interpretation of Sherlock Holmes, gender roles in the In Death series by the American author J.D. Robb, the village mysteries of the Canadian writer Louise Penny, the philosophical Inspector Espinosa series by the Brazilian Luis Alfredo Garcia-Roza, the medieval mysteries of Ellis Peters' Brother Cadfael, and the importance of food for the Italian detective Guido Brunetti in Donna Leon's Venetian series and Salvo Montalbano in the series by the Sicilian Andrea Camilleri.

Monica Lott Ph.D. is the writing tutor at the Kent State University-Geauga campus and teaches composition at the Kent State-Twinsburg campus. Her doctoral dissertation focused on the works of Detection Club writers with an emphasis on the themes of war, gender, and nostalgia in the works of Dorothy L. Sayers and Agatha Christie. She has been published in *Michael Chabon's America: Magical Words, Secret Worlds*, and *Sacred Spaces; Interdisciplinary Literary Studies*; and *the Steinbeck Review*.

Rebecca Martin Ph.D. holds the title of Professor Emerita of English at Pace University in New York. She has published in the areas of the eighteenth-century Gothic novel, American detective fiction, crime writing pedagogy, French Poetic Realism and film noir, and Alfred Hitchcock's Cold War films. She has edited collections of essays on *Bonnie and Clyde* and *Crime and Detective Fiction* for Salem Press and guest edited a special issue of *The Human: Interdisciplinary Journal of Literature and Culture: Crime Writing*. She earned her Ph.D. (English) and a graduate certificate in Film Studies from City University Graduate Center in New York City and recently retired from a career teaching literature and film studies. She now resides in New Orleans.

Het Phillips Ph.D. an independent scholar currently working in the legal sector, holds a doctorate from the University of Birmingham on cultural representations of the "Moors Murders" and "Yorkshire Ripper" criminal cases in true crime, literature, television, film, and popular music. She has published on Gothic femininity as mapped onto spatial and class imaginaries in the television and music of Maxine Peake in *Social Class and Television Drama in Contemporary Britain* ed. David Forrest and Beth Johnson, and has co-edited and introduced, with Dewi Evans, a special edition of the journal *Harts and Minds* on embodied masculinities.

Walter Raubicheck is professor of English at Pace University in New York. He has published several books on Alfred Hitchcock's films, including *Hitchcock and the Cold War* (Pace University Press) and, with Walter Srebnick, *Scripting Hitchcock* (University of Illinois Press). In addition, he has published articles on such American authors as Dashiell Hammett, F. Scott Fitzgerald, Walt Whitman, and T. S. Eliot. He currently edits a philosophy journal, *Lex Naturalis*, in addition co-editing *Mean Streets* with Rebecca Martin.

Eric Sandberg Ph.D. is an Assistant Professor at City University of Hong Kong and a Docent at the University of Oulu. His research interests range from modernism to the contemporary novel, with a particular interest in the borderlands between literary and popular fiction, especially crime writing. He co-edited *Adaptation, Awards Culture, and the Value of Prestige* with Colleen Kennedy-Karpat for Palgrave in 2017, and edited *100 Greatest Literary Detectives* for Rowman & Littlefield in 2018. He is an assistant editor for Edinburgh University Press's journal *Crime Fiction Studies*, and an associate editor with *English Studies*. His work has appeared in numerous edited collections, and in journals including *Ariel*, *The Cambridge Quarterly*, *Critique*, and *Neohelicon*. He has recently published on Dorothy L. Sayers in the *Journal of Modern Literature*, and on Thomas Pynchon's use of the hardboiled form in *Partial Answers*.

Mary C. Rawlinson Ph.D. is Professor and Director of Graduate Studies, Department of Philosophy, Stony Brook University in New York. Rawlinson's publications include *Betrayal of Substance: Death, Literature, and Sexual Difference in Hegel's Phenomenology of Spirit* (Columbia University Press, 2020), *Just Life: Bioethics and the future of sexual difference* (Columbia University Press, 2016), *Engaging the World: Thinking After Irigaray* (SUNY, 2016), *The Routledge Handbook of Food Ethics* (Routledge, 2016), *Labor and Global Justice* (Lexington, 2014), *Thinking with Irigaray* (SUNY, 2011), and *Derrida and Feminism* (Routledge, 1997), as well as articles on Hegel, Proust, literature and ethics, food justice, bioethics, and contemporary French philosophy. Her next book *Liminal Ethics* investigates the idea of justice in crime fiction. Rawlinson was the founding editor of *IJFAB: International Journal of Feminist Approaches to Bioethics* (2006-2016) and Co-founder and Director of The Irigaray Circle (2007-2017). In 2018 she was appointed Senior Visiting Research Fellow at the Institute for Advanced Studies, University College London.

Susan Elizabeth Sweeney Ph.D. is the Murry Professor of Arts and Humanities at the College of the Holy Cross. Besides publishing many essays on the detective genre, she coedited the volume *Detecting Texts: The Metaphysical Detective Story from Poe to Postmodernism*. Beth has written extensively on Poe's detective fiction—most recently, "Solving Mysteries in Poe, or Trying To," in the *Oxford Handbook to Edgar Allan Poe*—and is a past president of the Poe Studies Association. Her current project, "Inside Poe's Darkroom: Early Photography and the Development of New Forms of Fiction," includes chapters on his detective and horror tales, one of which received the Gargano Award for an outstanding essay on Poe. Beth's interest in metaphysical detective stories extends to her study of Nabokov. She has published over thirty essays on his fiction and was twice elected president of the International Vladimir Nabokov Society. Her recent coedited volume, *Nabokov and the Question of Morality: Aesthetics, Metaphysics, and the Ethics of Fiction*, includes her essay on how Nabokov's novels invite readers to serve as judge, juror, or executioner in determining the fate of criminal protagonists. In 2019, Beth received the Distinguished Faculty Scholar Award from Holy Cross for an exceptional record of scholarly achievement.

Ramie Tateishi Ph.D. holds a doctorate in Literature from the University of California at San Diego, and is an Associate Professor at National University in San Diego, California. He currently serves as the Program Director of the M.A. in Film Studies program at National University, where he teaches courses on Japanese cinema, animation, and science fiction. He also teaches classes on literary theory, contemporary science fiction, and detective fiction in the M.A. in English program at National University. His work on film, television, and popular culture has appeared in journals such as *Asian Cinema*, and in collections such as *Fear Without Frontiers*, *The Language of Doctor Who: From Shakespeare to Alien Tongues*, and most recently, *Doctor Who and History: Critical Essays on Imagining the Past*. He has given presentations on a wide range of literature and film-related topics at academic conferences of the Pacific Ancient and Modern Language Association, the Popular Culture Association, the Visual Communications Conference (VISCOM), and the

International Association for the Study of Environment, Space, and Place (IASESP), among others. As a popular culture scholar, he is a frequent guest commentator on KPBS, San Diego's local public radio station, and a guest panelist at San Diego Comic Fest.

Call for Papers
Second issue of *Mean Streets: A Journal of American Crime and Detective Fiction*

Topic: New York State of Crime

Proposals: August 15, 2020
Final essays: January 15, 2021

Raymond Chandler's "mean streets" were the deceptively sun-dappled streets of Los Angeles, but the streets of New York City and its environs have a longer history of association with crime fiction. The vice-filled streets upon which Horatio Alger's ragged newsboys trudged were the gritty New York City streets of the 1860s. Detective Nick Carter made his first appearance in the *New York Weekly* in September of 1886 in a serial focused on a crime in Madison Square, the original location of Madison Square Garden.

Decades later, Rex Stout, Chester Himes, Elizabeth Daly, Ed McBain, Ellery Queen, S.S. Van Dine, Amanda Cross, George Baxt, Julia Dahl and so many others found in New York the perfect setting for crimes, genteel or gruesome. The neighborhoods, bars, waterfronts, precinct offices, theaters, subway tunnels and gleaming towers of New York have provided rich settings for sordid activities. Upstate New York--the Westchester suburbs, Hudson Valley hamlets, the political cauldron of Albany, the once-thriving Catskill resorts, the Rust Belt, and the Snow Belt—has been featured in much crime writing, too.

For the second issue of *Mean Streets*, the editors seek proposals focusing on crime literature of New York City or elsewhere in the Empire State.

Abstracts of 250 words with proposed title should be directed no later than August 15, 2020, to the editors: Rebecca Martin (doc. rmartin@gmail.com) and Walter Raubicheck (wraubicheck@pace.edu).

Final papers of 7000-8000 words will be due by January 15, 2021, with publication anticipated later in the year. Feel free to send questions to both editors.

About *Mean Streets*

The journal is published by the Pace University Press (New York City), which has been sponsoring scholarly journals since the 1980s.

While American detective writing has been associated since the twenties with the "hard-boiled" tradition established by Hammett and Chandler, many American authors have excelled in the "whodunit" mystery tradition of British writing, and numerous other sub-genres. The journal is open to discussion of all types of crime fiction. *Mean Streets* is essentially a literary journal, so while discussion of film or other media is welcome, the balance of discussion will deal with literature.

Mean Streets is a refereed journal edited by two scholars in literature and film and guided by an Editorial Board comprised of distinguished scholars from several disciplines. Submissions will be reviewed by the editors and selected Board members.

The journal's first issue appeared in spring 2020.

The first volume of *Mean Streets: A Journal of American Crime and Detective Fiction*
was published in Spring 2020
by Pace University Press

Cover and Interior Design by Francesca Leparik
The journal was typeset in Gandhi Serif
and printed by Lightning Source in La Vergne, Tennessee

Pace University Press

Director: Manuela Soares
Associate Director: Stephanie Hsu
Design Consultant: Joseph Caserto

Graduate Assistants: Delaney Anderson and Francesca Leparik
Student Aide: Shani Starinsky

www.ingramcontent.com/pod-product-compliance
Lightning Source LLC
Chambersburg PA
CBHW061439300426
44114CB00014B/1750